Loving Choices

Dr. Bruce Fisher
and
Nina Hart

Loving Choices

An Experience in Growing Relationships

Revised Second Edition

RebuildingBooks
For Divorce and Beyond

Impact Publishers
ATASCADERO, CALIFORNIA

ATTENTION ORGANIZATIONS AND CORPORATIONS:
This book is available at quantity discounts on bulk purchases for educational, business, or sales promotional use. For further information, please contact Impact Publishers, P.O. Box 6016, Atascadero, CA 93423-6016, Phone: 1-800-246-7228. E-mail: sales@impactpublishers.com

Permission to excerpt lyrics from the song "Nature Boy" by Eden Ahbez granted through the courtesy of the publisher, Golden World of Desert Hot Springs, California.

Library of Congress Cataloging-in-Publication Data

Fisher, Bruce, 1932-
    Loving choices : an experience in growing relationships / Bruce Fisher,
      Nina Hart
        p. cm.
    Includes bibliographical references and index.
    ISBN 1-886230-30-7
      1. Man-woman relationships. 2. Interpersonal communication. 3. Divorced
men--Psychology. 4. Divorced women--Psychology. 5. Intimacy (Psychology)
I. Hart, Nina. II. Title.

HQ801 .A595 2000
158.2--dc21
                                                  00-029572

Publisher's Note
This publication is designed to provide accurate and authoritative information in regard to the subject matter covered. It is sold with the understanding that the publisher is not engaged in rendering psychological, medical, or other professional services. If expert assistance or counseling is needed, the services of a competent professional should be sought.

Impact Publishers and colophon are registered trademarks of Impact Publishers

Cover design by K.A. White Design, San Luis Obispo, California.
Printed in the United States of America on recycled acid-free paper.

Published by
Impact Publishers®
POST OFFICE BOX 6016
ATASCADERO, CALIFORNIA 93423-6016
www.impactpublishers.com

A TRIBUTE TO MY HUSBAND
by Nina Hart

FOR BRUCE
MY LOVE

A moment in time
that is forever etched
on my heart and in my soul.
My life changed in that one instant
when you softly and tenderly died in my arms on
that fateful May afternoon.
My heart bursts with gratitude.
Thank you, my love, for sharing with me this very precious lifetime.
Thank you for gently loving and trusting me.
Thank you
for allowing me to cherish and nurture you in return.
Thank you for joyfully and boldly joining with me in the
Mystery and the Magic.
Thank you for your open, willing commitment
as my wise and clear Master Teacher.
Thank you for being Rob's father.
Thank you for always dancing with me to our heart's song.
Thank you, Bruce Franklin Fisher, for courageously giving me
the greatest gift of my life.
I MISS YOU.
All I know NOW in this moment is that
I will never be the same again.

♥

DEDICATION

This book is dedicated to…

Our son Robert William Hart Fisher
better known as Rob Hart-Fisher
Nina's children Kelle Hart Ashton, Kim Rothwell,
and Alex Ashton
Bruce's children Todd Fisher and Sheila Lenius
our dreams come true.

Our parents who gave us the gift of life and
the possibility and the opportunity
to be all that we can be.

Our friends and family
who so generously support and nurture us daily with their love.

The thousands of people in our Seminars and private clients.
Over the past 20 years these incredible people have been our
profound relationship teachers and mirrors.
Thanks to them we have learned
directly in our own lives about
Living Loving Choices.

And each other with honor, love, and respect.

CONTENTS

Preface: Is This Book for You?   *xiii*

Introduction   *1*
Your Loving Choices Challenge   5

Section One:
YOUR RELATIONSHIP WITH YOURSELF   7

1   An Overview of the Loving Choices Process   9
Changing Challenges into Loving Choices

2   Feelings   23
A Feeling Is Neither Right nor Wrong, It Just Is

3   The Family Inside You   39
Getting to Know Your Critics, Adaptive-Survivor Parts, Inner Children, and Wise Nurturer

Section Two:
COMMUNICATING WITH YOURSELF AND OTHERS   59

4   The Self-Encounter   61
Learning to Communicate with Yourself

5   The Repetitive Self-Encounter   77
Going Emotionally Deeper into Yourself

6 Conversations with Your Internal Family 83
   Assisting You with Inner Peace

7 The Healing Encounter 95
   Using the Self-Encounter to Communicate with Others

Section Three:
YOUR RELATIONSHIPS WITH OTHERS 109

8 Family of Origin 111
   Creating Peace with Your Parents and Your Childhood

9 Seeking Your Identity 127
   Growing from Shell to Rebel to Love with Help from Your Internal Family

10 Your Inner Children 157
   It's Never Too Late to Have a Happy Childhood

11 Power Struggles 169
   What Am I Growing Through?

12 Boundaries and Ownership 185
   What Is You and What Is Not You

13 Relationships Are Your Teachers
   Working Together as a Vehicle for Growth

14 Loving Choices 211
   Changing Challenges into Loving Choices

   Appendix A: Breathing and Centering Exercise 219
   Appendix B: Bibliography 225
   Index 239

♥

PREFACE

Is this book for you?

IF YOU'RE SATISFIED with your life and your relationships, you may not find this book of much interest. You can continue your present way of relating to yourself and others and, if you do pretty much what you've always done, you'll most likely get what you've always gotten.

On the other hand, if you'd like to make some changes for the better, you have two choices. You could end your present relationships and start new ones. The problem with this choice is that you'll probably develop new relationships similar to the ones you just ended! Your other choice — the one most folks take — is to "recycle" your present relationships, creating something new and fresh from the old and tired.

This book is intended for those who want to make such a fresh start. More specifically, it's for:

- Those who are committed to building and creating more healing and healthy relationships with themselves and with others.

- Any person who is intrigued by the concept that "relationships are your teachers," helping you learn the lessons you need to learn about yourself and life.

- Any person — whether or not in a committed relationship with another — who wants to explore and discover the richness that is within herself or himself. You can choose to find your "one and only" inside of you. Paradoxically, it is only when you discover you can live the rest of your life alone with happiness and contentment that you are really ready for a committed relationship with another.

- Those who are tired of finding fault with others. Perhaps you are motivated to understand more about your own contribution to the problems you are experiencing in your relationships with others.

- For those (the vast majority) who want a more fulfilling relationship than their parents had.

- Any person who wants to learn why we say that better communication with others begins with learning to communicate with yourself.

- People in primary love relationships who don't have the kind of relationship they envisioned and wanted when they began their journey as a couple.

- Those who have been through the painful transformation of a past relationship that ended in divorce. Perhaps you want to learn how to transform relationships without divorce.

- Any person who is so afraid of commitment that you can't say "m-m-m-m-m-marriage" and instead call it the "big M-word."

- Any two people who are beginning a primary love relationship and who want to get beyond honeymoon salad into enjoying the main course of the relationship.

- Any person who wants to choose which inner part of you is "driving your personality car," instead of allowing your *inner critic* to take the wheel most of the time.

- Any person who is challenged by the concept of doing "soul healing" in your relationship with yourself and others.

- Any couple who has read about a "Healing Separation" in Bruce's book, *Rebuilding: When Your Relationship Ends,* and wants to know more about carving out a new relationship.

Give some thought to why you picked up this book. If any of the shoes above fit, we think you'll like what you find here. And you'll be making more Loving Choices in no time!

— Bruce and Nina

ACKNOWLEDGEMENT

*A word of profound gratitude
to our editor, publisher and friend, Bob Alberti,
who once again assisted in bringing our work to the planet.*

INTRODUCTIONS

Greetings from Bruce,

Writing a book together for Nina and me is like having a baby together. She says it is only fair for me to do the labor of actually typing most of the words into the computer. After all, she did the labor when our son Rob was born. I did the coaching. Our joint effort was a natural, no medication, Lamaze birth resulting in a ten-pound baby. Nina has done the coaching for this book. We let the book rumble around inside of us during the gestation period. We did the labor pains of putting it on paper. Our result is *Loving Choices*.

We began teaching this relationships model in 1982. I thought it would be easy to write another book because writing *Rebuilding: When Your Relationship Ends* was so easy for me. We discovered it is difficult to write a sequel! Part of our Challenge is writing about concepts we haven't experienced ourselves individually or as a couple. We also learn from the participants in our educational seminars who become our teachers while we are attempting to teach them. After growing ourselves and learning from the participants, we are finally able to create a "full term baby" book instead of the six premature book babies we produced over the last thirteen years. We hope this full term baby will assist you in making more Loving Choices in your lives!

I have had two lives during this lifetime. My first is my B.D. — Before Divorce — life, and second is my A.D. — After Divorce — life. In my B.D. life I was an Iowa farmer living out my life script. I belong to the eighth generation of farmers since the first immigrant from Germany came to the William Penn colony in 1749. I became restless on the farm, did my life-course correction, and ended up being a marriage and family therapist and author in my A.D. life. I observed thousands of people making the crisis of divorce into a creative experience. Many created a new A.D. life as I did.

I have found it challenging to integrate and internalize the differences between my B.D. and A.D. life styles. For example, I was shy, bashful, and introverted in my B.D. life. Now I enjoy traveling and speaking all over the world and feeling confident and extroverted. Our son Rob has become a source of joy and happiness for me. He recently shared with me that "a dream is a thought with a mind of its own."

I started creating and teaching the ten-week Rebuilding Divorce Seminar in 1974. It is presently being offered in communities worldwide with over a quarter-of-a-million graduates. It has been challenging for me to internalize and believe emotionally that this "little ol' Iowa farm boy" wrote *Rebuilding*, which has sold nearly three-quarters of a million copies and has been translated into seven foreign languages.

Do you have a song that seems to have been written about you? The song that I always believed was written about me is titled, *Nature Boy*. It was made famous by Nat King Cole. It goes like this:

> *There was a boy,*
> *A very strange enchanted boy.*
> *They say he wondered very far,*
> *Over land and sea.*
> *And then one day,*
> *He came my way.*
> *And this he said to me,*
> *The greatest thing you'll ever learn,*
> *Is just to love,*
> *And be loved in return.*

It is my desire and vision that *Loving Choices* will assist you in learning more about how to love and be loved in return.

Lovingly,
— Bruce

(Editor's note: Bruce lost a courageous two-year battle with cancer in 1998. He wrote this introduction for the first edition of *Loving Choices* in 1994. It has been edited very slightly for this second edition of the book — published in 2000. This new edition has all of Bruce's original substance, and is updated and revised to make his important contributions even more helpful to his readers.)

Hello from Nina,

Choosing to write an Introduction letter for this book presents an enormous Challenge. I feel grateful for this opportunity.

Who I am is a Player in this game called Life. I like a "full plate" and as a Player I have chosen many roles. My roles are my Passions. It is a joy to share a few of these roles with you.

One of my most important, fulfilling, and challenging roles I play is MOTHER
- two daughters, Kelle and Kim, and a son Rob. All three are powerful Relationship Teachers for me.

Exuberantly, I play the role of LOVER
- Lover of Humanity, Lover of the Ocean and all of Nature, Lover of Beauty, Lover of Angels, Lover of Truth, Lover of Peace, Lover of Freedom, Lover of Love.

A rewarding role I play is of CREATOR
- writer, artist, cook and homemaker, photographer, dancer, singer.

I actively play the role of CHOOSING PARTICIPANT
- choosing communication, health, risking, relationships, and LIFE.

This role plays me, that of HEALER
- Therapist, Reiki Master, Teacher, Visionary, Facilitator, Seminar Leader, Friend.

Sharing some of my roles and passions is fun and easy. Out of this exercise emerges a Truth. As I play these various roles they constantly assist in showing me that I am so much more than my roles.

The Challenge is in describing the indescribable — the Player. And who is the Player? The Player is Self, Truth, Source, Essence, Potential, Freedom, Consciousness. From all of these, my passionate roles are expressed and manifested.

The most Loving Choice I can make is to keep asking from moment to moment "Who Am I?"

From this Self-inquiry comes the deepening recognition and realization of who I truly am.

I warmly invite you to come along with us on this Journey of Loving Choices.

I gently encourage you to choose to keep looking at yourself and your life.

I fully support you to commit daily to Self-Exploration.

I lovingly challenge you to be silent and to simply and honestly ask yourself, "Who Am I?"

The result will be the greatest and most rewarding gift you will ever encounter.

A very Loving Choice.

— Nina

Your Loving Choices Challenge

When you really learn that "Relationships Are Your Teachers,"
You will know that you learn the most about yourself by
being in relationships.

And you will know
that what you cannot see in yourself,
You can see from the reflection of yourself
That all your relationships mirror back to you.

And you will realize
that what is important in your relationships
Is that you are growing through
all of the leftovers
you have collected through the years.

All of this leads you to take responsibility
For all the things
that you had blamed others for.

Which leads you to be free
To make Loving Choices in your life.

— Nina and Bruce

♥

Your Relationship with Yourself

THIS BOOK IS DIVIDED into three sections: "Your Relationship With Yourself," "Communicating With Yourself and Others," and "Your Relationships With Others." This first section — your relationship with yourself — is about the foundation of all relationships. A healthy relationship with yourself provides a fertile seedbed from which healthy relationships with others can grow.

How to Read This Book

We suggest you read and integrate each chapter before going on to the next. It is especially important to learn the communication skills so you can apply them to the Challenges facing you in your relationships. We expect some readers will want to read the whole book first. If you do, we suggest you go back later and spend more time processing each chapter. We also suggest you use a highlighter to emphasize key points. If you read the book a second time, use another color highlighter. You'll find it interesting to notice your different highlights. We have also prepared a *Loving Choices*

Workbook, which will help to make the concepts in this book more real for you.

There are many paths to the truth. We have described the path that has assisted us and thousands of Loving Choice Seminars participants. The important thing is for you to create the joy and happiness you deserve. We support you to explore whatever path will assist you in your journey.

Improving Your Communication Skills

There are many ways to improve communication skills. The quickest and simplest method is to learn to use "I-messages." Most of us use lots of "you-messages" in conversation. But "you-messages" are like sharp poisoned darts. They result in poor and destructive communication.

Here's an example: "You really make me mad!" Notice the "you"- message: you did something to me. Contrast that with, "I get really mad when you do that!" This time I'm taking ownership of the "mad" feeling.

There are four different kinds of I-messages that we suggest you use. They are: "I think _____," "I feel _____," "I want or need _____," and "I will _____." These are the foundation of the communication skills described in this book. We strongly suggest you start using "I-messages" immediately. You may be surprised and pleased at how much difference they make in your communication.

An Overview of the Loving Choices Process

CHANGING CHALLENGES INTO LOVING CHOICES

*The **challenge** is to learn about the process of developing healing and healthy relationships with yourself and others.*

*The **loving choice** is to make life decisions using the three-legged stool of awareness, commitment and communication.*

Sometimes the longest foot in the world is the twelve inches from your head to your heart! One of life's greatest challenges is to have your head and your heart work together. Loving Choices are those that connect the thoughts in your head with the loving feelings from your heart.

You're probably like most people, using either your head or your heart to make decisions much of the time. We challenge you to make decisions in harmony with both your heart and your head. This book is designed to assist you in this process. It is possible to transform the pathway between your head and your heart into a well-traveled super-highway.

You'll notice that we talk a lot about the concept "Relationships Are Your Teachers." Each person you have a relationship with is your teacher. Each of these teachers assists you with the life lessons you have not finished working through, intellectually, emotionally, and spiritually.

For example, if you have an internal voice inside of you that is very critical, you may find an external person, such as your boss, to reinforce that voice. Why does the other person's criticism affect you? You may discover that the other person echoes the critical voice inside you. The other person provides a mirror to help you learn more about your internal critical voice.

You could project your feeling and become angry at him because you believe he is responsible for making you feel not okay. Or, you could play victim and decide that there is nothing you can do because life doesn't treat you fairly.

When he is critical, does this bring up old feelings you experienced as a child when your father criticized you? Do you feel not-okay? Guilty? Inadequate? Worthless? Afraid you will be abandoned if your boss fires you? Did you project, or play victim, to avoid feeling? Try this instead: let yourself feel those feelings. Stay with them until they transform and they are no longer easily triggered by the criticism from your boss.

Your longest foot is starting to be the super highway as you make the choice of looking at that relationship as your teacher. By combining the choice (head) and the feelings (heart) you begin to recognize how the relationship with your boss can be a teacher.

Allowing your head and your heart to work together may help you become able to say (at least to yourself), "Thank you, boss, for helping me become more aware of the critical voice inside me. Every time I become upset when I hear you being critical, I'm learning that you are an echo of my father's critical voice. I've decided to make a Loving Choice: not to let my father's criticism control me any more in my adult relationships."

You could make a different choice: "I have unfinished business in my relationship with my father. You remind me of my father. With your help I may be able to better understand him and eventually to make peace with him."

Your most stressful external relationships are probably your best teachers. Who is your most stressful relationship person? Is it your love partner, a former love partner, your teenage son or daughter, your elderly parent? Making the Loving Choice to look at that stressful relationship as your teacher is an important step toward healing.

Letting your head and heart work together as you make choices helps you put into practice the concept of relationships as teachers. Relationships can be a laboratory for growth, helping you reach the potential of being the person you choose to be.

The Three Legged Stool:
Communication, Awareness, Commitment

Have you ever tried to sit on a one-legged stool? Bruce, who grew up on a farm in Iowa, often sat on such a stool to milk a cow. He learned how to steady this one legged stool by using his own two legs to make a three-legged stool. We suggest you think of *communication, awareness,* and *commitment* as the three legs of your stool, assisting you in making your relationships a laboratory for growth. The Challenge is for you to use these three concepts as the primary goals of your growing and healing process. The Loving Choice is to allow this three-legged stool to give you balance and stability as you take this journey of connecting your head and your heart.

We will provide you with a "one-legged stool" — our communication model — and you will add the two legs of awareness and commitment to complete the balanced three-legged stool. Reading this book will expand your awareness, too, if you choose to allow it. Your commitment to learn the communication model and to develop greater awareness will bring it all together.

Our communication model begins with you learning to communicate with yourself first. Learning to listen to the messages inside yourself will aid your communication with others as well.

John, for example, recognizes a message within himself that says, "My love relationship is not working. I think I should end it." At the same time, however, he hears another inner message that says, "I've been in this relationship for fifteen years. We have lots of shared happy memories around our life together and our three children. I think I should give the Loving Choices concepts in this book a chance, to see if they will work for me." Both messages are valid and honest and — though they appear to be in conflict — John is learning that he can listen to both messages, recognize the difference, and seek ways to respond to each.

He may choose to share these voices with his partner. "Today my loudest inner voice says that I want to work on our relationship. I have another voice inside — not as loud — that says I should leave. For now, at least, I'm committed to stay, to work, and to learn all I can from you. You're my best relationship teacher. I will keep you informed about any changes in my feelings."

Awareness is a wake-up call. Greater consciousness in all areas of your life — your feelings, your attitudes, your beliefs — may range from simple "aha" moments to a "cosmic two-by-four." Each wake-up call offers you the opportunity to make a Loving Choice. Can you describe one of your wake-up calls?

Kathy saw no reason for coming to the Loving Choices Seminar. After all, she thought, things were okay in her marriage. Then Kathy and her husband came to the intake interview, and she discovered he was thinking about leaving and filing for divorce. Kathy's wake-up-call to awareness was of the "being-hit-over-the-head-with-a-two-by-four" variety. She decided she'd better take the seminar to help herself understand why Ken was thinking about becoming a single person. Eventually she learned she needed the seminar more than he did!

Commitment is an action word! It is measured by actions — not just words. Are you committed to learn to communicate better with yourself — and your partner — by using new tools for communication? Are you open to trying the proven communication model described in this book? Are you committed to discover ways to change Challenges into Loving Choices through greater awareness of yourself and your relationships?

Bill and Mary had been married for fifteen years. He began to feel unhappy and decided to leave the relationship because he no longer felt love for Mary. They separated, and Bill discovered to his surprise that he was still unhappy living alone. He started listening to his inner messages and began learning to communicate with himself. A friend loaned him this book. He read it, chose to see a marriage counselor, and made a commitment to take responsibility for his own unhappiness, instead of projecting the blame upon his partner. (Needless to say, Mary breathed a sigh of relief when he stopped blaming her for his unhappiness.)

Now let us introduce you to the remainder of this book and the process of learning how to live your life by making Loving Choices.

SECTION ONE:
YOUR RELATIONSHIP WITH YOURSELF

Chapter 1. An Overview of the Loving Choices Process

As you've already discovered, in this chapter we're laying the foundation for the work — and fun — to come. You're beginning to discover the process of bringing your heart and your head into balance to make loving choices. You've found that communication, awareness and commitment are the three elements of your "learning stool." And you're beginning to recognize the meaning of the concept, *relationships are your teachers*. The remainder of this chapter introduces the rest of the book, and outlines the basic concepts of making Loving Choices in your life.

Chapter 2. Feelings

The Challenge presented in this chapter is to be able to access and express both your feelings and your thoughts, so you may become more balanced in making your Loving Choices.

Whenever someone talks about something that happened years ago and it sounds as though it is in the present, you may suspect that person has difficulty accessing and sharing feelings. Unexpressed feelings are an obstacle to growing emotionally. Many people, for example, find it difficult to let go of emotional losses through the grief process and to adjust to change.

Often it is the "feeling person" in a love relationship who is most dissatisfied. She or he may often talk about needing more intimacy, wanting better communication, and wanting to know what the partner is feeling. The non-feeling person may talk about the children, sports, business successes and failures. He or she may take an active part in activities with the partner and/or family — games, gardening, chores — and do quite well until someone asks, "What are you feeling?"

How can human beings have an intimate, feeling relationship without sharing feelings? We have found in our classes that when two people can share feelings with each other, they almost always experience greater intimacy.

Louise told us that Harold thought talking about feelings was a sign of weakness, and he didn't like her to talk about her feelings with him. In fact, he told her that if she became angry one more time he would leave. His attitude denied the validity of Louise's feelings as well as his own, and left little room for intimacy in the relationship.

We are very fond of the concept of "I-messages" as a way to increase awareness, ownership, and communication of feelings. A Loving Choice might be making a commitment to concentrate on doing ten "I feel _____ " messages every day for a month in order to access and share feelings more easily.

Chapter 3. Inner Voices and Coping Strategies

We all talk to ourselves (though most of us don't share that self-talk with others!). The Challenge here is to listen to the many messages inside of you and use them to become better acquainted with yourself. You may recognize that some of the voices may be ways you have learned to cope.

Sharon, eighteen, was coming for therapy, hoping to resolve some of her family issues. She began by saying, "'Old Nagger' has been after me all week." *Are you talking about your mother?* "No, I'm talking about a voice I keep hearing inside of me." *Do you hear any other voice?* "Oh yes. I call the other voice 'Let-Her-Off.' When Old Nagger starts nagging me, Let-Her-Off comes in and urges Old Nagger to stop criticizing me, to let me off." Sharon had become aware of the mixed messages inside of her and was starting to listen to them. She had begun the process of getting to know herself better. By listening to the "voices" inside herself, she began to identify that her coping strategies are actually "survivor parts."

You will gain awareness as you take this journey into yourself and begin to hear your inner voices more clearly. Instead of having the internal parts of you in conflict, awareness of these parts encourages them to become a team and to start working together.

Your Loving Choice at this stage is to become as balanced as possible by integrating and using all of your inner voices. Can you imagine how empowered you may feel as you create an internal team working together instead of an internal conflict?

SECTION TWO: COMMUNICATING WITH YOURSELF AND OTHERS

Chapter 4. The Self-Encounter

The Challenge of this chapter is indeed challenging: to begin to communicate with yourself by identifying ten different messages inside of you. Which of your parts have you been listening to the most and which do you seldom hear?

When we started teaching the "Ten-Week Relationship Seminar" in the early 1980s, we emphasized communication between two people. Over many years teaching the class, we came to realize how important it is for you to *communicate with yourself first.* You cannot effectively communicate with another until you are clear about what's going on within yourself and what it is you are trying to communicate.

The *Self-Encounter* described in this chapter — a structured way to talk to and listen to yourself — can change your life, if you spend the time learning how to do it. We like to call it a "paper-therapist" or "self-therapist." One of our goals is to teach you skills that will empower you. If you learn to do this Self-Encounter, your need to see a therapist will be greatly diminished.

Joan came home from work and informed Dennis that she needed to talk to him as soon as she completed her Self-Encounter. Thirty minutes later, she said to him, "Never mind." She had resolved the conflict herself. When she first got home, she didn't think it would be resolved until Dennis changed his behavior. She was surprised to learn the problem was an internal conflict, not a conflict with her husband.

The Loving Choice is to do "solo time" first, before you attempt to communicate with the other person involved. The Self-Encounter communication tool is the core process we teach in this book. We invite you to make using this communication tool one of your top commitments.

Chapter 5. The Repetitive Self-Encounter

The Challenge is to learn as much about yourself as possible by doing a repetitive Self-Encounter. When you write out a Self-Encounter, you go into yourself in greater depth. Sometimes you will not feel finished with your encounter. You will often find that the issue is not what you thought it was. The repetitive encounter is a pathway into deeper and more profound awareness. The repetitive Self-Encounter presented in chapter 5 illustrates this process.

Mike's encounter began with the topic of doing his homework at the last minute on the way to class. After completing the first encounter, he decided to do another one and discovered the topic was really time management. He was not managing his time properly. He went even deeper and eventually discovered he was keeping busy in order to keep from experiencing his painful feelings of low self-worth. He found doing the repetitive Self-Encounter was worth his time and effort.

The Loving Choice for chapter 5 is to use this communication tool to create as much healing and health as you can in your relationship with yourself.

Chapter 6. Discovering Your Internal Family

The Challenge is to discover the voices inside of you that are similar to an internal family of father, mother and many children.

When you listen to your inner voices, you may discover a voice which seems to be masculine, with conditional love and mainly concerned with *action*. You may discover another voice that is more feminine, with unconditional love and concerned with *being* rather than *doing*. You may discover you have many voices representing various "Inner Children."

We want you to know that you can create a healthy internal family and learn to have them dialogue among themselves, Eventually you can even go off by yourself and have a family reunion!

Joseph learned that he could access his internal family whenever he felt hurt and sad. He would let his little boy inside experience the hurt feelings, let the adult feminine part nurture and console his little child and then the adult masculine part would suggest some positive action. "This sure beats sitting around feeling sorry for myself, as I used to do."

Joseph used to think that love and attention had to come from someone else. His Loving Choice to access his internal family allowed him to feel nurtured from within, resulting in greater inner peace.

Chapter 7. The Healing Encounter

This chapter takes the Self-Encounter to the next level, offering the Challenge of using the procedure to learn to communicate effectively with another person. This enables you to communicate in a deeper and more profound way. The Healing Encounter is basically one person doing an *initiator* Self-Encounter and the other person doing a *respondent* Self-Encounter.

Chuck, an engineer, watched two other group members share a Healing Encounter. He pointed out that Sue and Ted were each accessing ten different voices, noting that ten voices times ten voices meant there were one hundred different relationships going on between Sue and Ted. We and the other members of the group applauded him for pointing out how complicated relationships are between two people.

We can recall some unusual topics discussed by couples in their Healing Encounters. Jim initiated a Self-Encounter about the topic of "green slime." He had been upset with his wife for leaving green slime in the kitchen sink — residue left when Betty rinsed the dishes. Jim finally used the Healing Encounter to communicate his dissatisfaction with the green slime. His intention was to find a solution. He was chagrined to discover that part of the solution was for him to take his turn at washing the dishes! This was a turning point in Jim's process.

A Loving Choice is to make a commitment to use the Healing Encounter to communicate more effectively with another person.

SECTION THREE:
RELATIONSHIPS WITH OTHERS

Chapter 8. Family of Origin

As you explore your "roots," the Challenge is to discover the many influences from your family of origin and childhood upon your adult relationships. Take a minute to think of the person in your family who has most influenced how you relate to other people. Let this reflection help you understand how your background affects your present relationships. You'll find that you often relate to others now much like you did with this influential person from your childhood. Perhaps you have relationships with particular persons now to complete growing through the unfinished business from your past.

Brad wondered when he enrolled in our seminar why we were talking about family of origin. "We came here to work on our marriage. What does my family of origin have to do with solving our relationship problems?" When he completed the twelve-week seminar, he shared with his wife that their problem was that his family of origin was fighting her family of origin!

Your Loving Choice comes from discovering, integrating, and making use of the "gifts of love" and the "gifts of pain" from your family of origin.

Chapter 9. Seeking Your Identity

The Challenge of identity is to find your own, separate from the expectations of family of origin and society. A person seeking her own individual identity may makes a "life-course correction" as part of the process, which may change the form of her present relationships. With awareness, commitment, and good communication skills, however, relationships don't have to end. You can choose to transform them along with yourself.

Paul came to see us for a therapy session, confiding that he never thought in his wildest dreams that he would ever see "a shrink." The chapter on rebellion and seeking identity described him so accurately that it motivated him to talk to the authors. "How did you know what I was feeling and thinking?" Therapy expanded Paul's awareness of his life-course correction and helped him take greater responsibility for his relationships.

It is interesting to notice that people who are seeking to discover their true identity all go through a similar process. The Loving Choice is to create a working balance between all of your inner voice messages. With awareness and ownership the result will be a stronger self-identity.

Chapter 10. Getting to Know Your Inner Children

The Challenges here are to get to know your inmost self, to connect with and build healthy relationships with your many "Inner Children," and to allow each to feel listened to, accepted and loved. Without attention, the Inner Children often sabotage what you really want. They may become "little tyrants" and end up controlling and manipulating you.

You learned a basic set of beliefs about life, relationships, self-worth, and intimacy when you were growing up. You've spent the rest of your life more or less living out these beliefs. How do you react when someone gives you a compliment? If you have low self-worth, if your Inner Children believe you are unworthy, any compliments you receive may be difficult to hear, because they conflict with the beliefs of your Inner Children.

Roberta never felt loved by her parents. As a result, she never learned how to accept love. Although she looked unconsciously for a partner who would love her the way she had not experienced as a child, she didn't realize that her Inner Children believed they were not lovable. No matter how much her partner tried to love her, she couldn't receive it. The Internal Family exercise described in this chapter allowed Roberta to become aware of her Inner Children, and to recognize that they didn't feel lovable. When she acknowledged those needs, she was able to start giving herself the love she needed.

The Loving Choice is to listen to, accept and heal the wounds of all of your Inner Children. You may come to understand what we mean when we quote Claudia Black's great book title, "It's Never Too Late to Have a Happy Childhood."

Chapter 11. Power Struggles

Here's another Challenge: figure out, when you find yourself in a power struggle with someone important in your life, how much of what's going on has to do with your own *internal conflicts* that you're projecting onto your relationships with others.

Here are a few red flags that may indicate you are having a power struggle in a relationship: you argue over superficial issues, such as how to squeeze the toothpaste tube; you feel you have no power or control in your relationship; you continually argue with each other with no resolution of the issues; you start your sentences with "you" when talking to each other (example: "You make me angry."); you notice a similar pattern in your other relationships.

We have found that overcoming a power struggle can be a very difficult Challenge. You can begin to tackle it in these ways:

- learn to use "I-messages," especially "I feel" messages, in your communications;
- develop an awareness of your own internal power struggles, so you know what you may be projecting onto the relationship;
- accept that you are responsible for your own happiness and/or unhappiness.

When you discover the personal unfinished business that you may be projecting onto a relationship, you can begin to change your power struggles into growing pains. "What am I growing through?" is an important question to ask when you are experiencing a power struggle.

One memorable Healing Encounter is a good example of a power struggle over "nothing." The couple had been arguing for many months over a worn out pair of tennis shoes he wore whenever they went out for the evening. As they untangled their power struggle, Joe discovered he was rebelling against his domineering mother — represented by his wife in this case. Anne was the dominant one in the relationship — behavior modeled in her family by her own mother. Their Healing Encounter provided a way for both of them to discover what they were growing through. Joe learned that he could make a choice about making peace with his domineering mother. Anne learned that she had a choice as to how she wanted to act in this relationship.

Your Loving Choice is to use awareness, commitment and communication to take responsibility for your contribution to the disharmony in your relationships.

Chapter 12. Boundaries and Ownership

The Challenge of boundaries is to become aware of them — to recognize the internal and external *boundaries* in your relationships.

We (Bruce and Nina) laughed at ourselves because we taught the Loving Choices class for six years without discussing boundaries. We discovered that we didn't have any! We had become so enmeshed with each other that we needed to recreate our own individual identities. Have you lost your individual identity in your relationships with others because you haven't learned to identify — or create — your own internal and external boundaries?

An important parallel to your boundaries is *ownership*. In a healthy relationship, you'll own your own feelings and behavior patterns — rather than taking on the other person's patterns.

Sandra told us how she had lost her identity in her last relationship. "I kept meeting his needs at the expense of never taking care of myself. I took on and felt many of the feelings that he wasn't aware of or expressing. Pretty soon I didn't know which feelings were mine and which were his! I need to develop clearer boundaries so I can own what is mine and let my partner own what is his."

The Loving Choice regarding boundaries is to become able to separate your feelings and thoughts from those of the other person. By choosing to maintain appropriate boundaries, you are empowered to take ownership and responsibility for your life.

Chapter 13. Relationships Are Your Teachers

The Challenge of this Chapter is to *use* the communication tools and awareness you've gained from reading Loving Choices, applying them to your relationships with yourself and others. Relationships can be your most valuable laboratory for growth. You can become more balanced and healthy in relationship. You can learn to emotionally bond with yourself and others in relationships. You can heal childhood pain and trauma in relationships. In a healthy relationship, you can grow through any stages of development you haven't finished previously.

Phyllis had been divorced three times. "Each time the relationship became stressful for me, I just left. I've begun to realize that the same lesson kept happening in each relationship. The lesson became more obvious and painful each time. I'm finally at a place where I want to learn about myself and what I am doing to contribute to the disharmony in my relationships." She became committed to using the communication tools and the expanded awareness in this book to learn about herself.

Your Loving Choice is to learn your lessons from each of the relationships that you have created. This enables you to become a more loving human being.

Chapter 14. Loving Choices

Recognize and acknowledge that you are a unique individual — that's the Challenge here. You are — like all other human beings — precious. The rewards of feeling healed and healthy are tremendous. When you find freedom to be yourself you are able to make more Loving Choices.

Karen had ended several love relationships. Whenever a relationship became stressful, she chose to bail out. During the course of the Loving Choices Seminar she learned a lot about herself. It was obvious that she became involved with emotionally unavailable males (like her father). She had not found an identity separate from the expectations of family and society. She had no idea how to heal her wounded Inner Children. She frequently used "you-messages" in her relationships — resulting in frequent power struggles. She rescued others because she had not clearly identified her internal or external boundaries. She had failed to learn important lessons from her relationship teachers and thus kept repeating and repeating the same patterns.

Karen was determined to grow from the seminar. She did all the homework suggested in the twelve "lesson plans." She committed to using the Self-Encounter daily. She started doing the Internal Family Dialogues. She did Healing Encounters in many of her important relationships with others. Gradually she began to make more and more Loving Choices. She was able to make the "long foot" between her head and her heart a strong connection. She worked on building a better relationship with herself, instead of looking for another person to make her happy.

Invest in yourself and your personal growth every day for the rest of your life. That's your Loving Choice.

HOW ARE YOU DOING?

At the end of each chapter of this book, you'll find a check list which summarizes what we said in the chapter and gives you a way to check out your progress. Place a check mark beside the ideas to which you can claim ownership. Do you think you are ready to move on the next chapter? We support you to be as honest with yourself as you can.

1. *I have read the Foreword to this book and have determined which of the "this book is intended for" statements applies to me.*

2. *I am interested and motivated to learn to communicate better with myself.*

3. *After reading this chapter, I have identified the areas I choose to work on so I can improve my relationship with myself.*

4. *I am committed to practicing "I-messages" in order to improve my communication skills.*

5. *I have examined the breathing and centering exercise explained in Appendix A of this book, and have decided to give it a try.*

CHAPTER TWO

Feelings

A FEELING IS NEITHER RIGHT
NOR WRONG, IT JUST IS

*The **challenge** is to become friends with your feelings.*

*The **loving choices** are to integrate your thoughts and feelings and to learn constructive ways to express your feelings in your relationships with yourself and others.*

I t's important to find a balance between thinking and feeling, and this chapter will help you get your heart and mind working together in balance. The result can be a more meaningful, rewarding, fulfilling, freeing, healthy, intimate life with yourself and others.

We will be emphasizing the heart in this chapter. The heart — the feeling aspect of relationships — is multifaceted. Feelings are like the weather—they come and go and change, often very quickly. In fact, a rainbow is a useful image for describing feelings. Each feeling that you experience has its own vibration and uniqueness. Although a rainbow has a number of different colors that are beautiful by themselves, it is all of the colors together that create the totality of its beauty. The whole range of your feelings from anger, peace, grief, joy, fear, laughter, rejection, guilt, and love, are within you to assist in learning more about yourself.

As you read this chapter, we encourage you to think of what color each feeling represents in the rainbow of your heart. Each feeling you express assists you in communicating who you are. As you *own* your feelings — accept them and take responsibility for them — and let yourself *learn* from them, they'll help you to grow and make Loving Choices.

Why Become Aware of Your Feelings?

Many participants in the Loving Choices Seminar have found this chapter offers a new beginning. Accessing and understanding feelings has resulted in changing how they relate to themselves and others. One of your Challenges is to become aware of your feelings so you can use them to help you make good choices, instead of allowing your feelings to control you. Your goal is to be in charge of your life. So, you want to avoid the three horns of the "feelings dilemma" — to be *unaware* of your feelings, to *deny* your feelings, or to allow your feelings to *control* you. These obstacles keep you from making loving choices.

Because this is such an important topic, we are going to move slowly and — we hope — gently. It's easy to get overwhelmed when you first begin to access your feelings. So, we'll start by exploring just one feeling: your *anger.*

Can Anger Ever Be a Good Thing?

We have observed in our classes that anger is one of the most challenging feelings that often arises in this inner process of exploration. Getting in touch with your anger gives you much more choice about your relationships with yourself and with others. In terms of the rainbow, anger is most often experienced as the hot and passionate color: red.

> *Anger helps you tear down the walls in your relationships*
> *so you can build bridges with the rubble.*

When we give ourselves permission to access and express anger it opens the channels for all the other feelings to be accessed and expressed. Many participants in our classes have shared how anger can be an emotion that creates a pitfall in relationships with yourself and with others. Here are some situations where angry feelings were in control:

Helen was talking about her past love relationship: "George and I never had a fight until the day we decided to separate and divorce." The Challenge might be for George and Helen to deal with emotional conflicts when they arise instead of avoiding the issues that need to be resolved in their relationship. The ignored and denied feelings contributed to their emotional distance and eventual separation.

Joe stated during the Fisher Rebuilding Seminar, "Why do we have to wait until after we are divorced to talk about the events that happened five or ten years ago?" The Challenge is to discuss the issues at the time they arise, instead of waiting until the pain of divorce motivates you to finally deal with them. It may take a crisis, such as a divorce, to uncork all of the feelings that people have been denying for years.

Jane confides that she doesn't want to be touched by her husband or have sex anymore. When asked how she expresses anger, she states she has never been able to be openly angry at her husband. Not dealing with angry feelings controls your behavior. Sometimes this contributes to distancing others. The Challenge is for Jane to learn she is uncomfortable with her angry feelings, and to find constructive ways of accessing and expressing them. Since she finds it difficult to express her anger, she distances her partner by avoiding sex.

When a couple seeks relationship counseling, usually the "fight-or-flight" approach to conflict has been operating. Steve wants to express his feelings of anger and be done with it (fight). Joan wants to avoid anger because it never solves anything in their relationship (flight). The angrier one person becomes, the more the other retreats, and vice-versa. The Challenge is to find a way to communicate the strong feelings so that the couple can become closer emotionally instead of distancing each other.

When Bill was in the seminar, we asked him if he had been feeling a lot of anger. He said, "No, but I have been feeling depressed a great deal of the time." The Challenge is to learn that anger that is not dealt with appropriately may result in feelings of depression. Bill's Challenge is to learn that it is better to express anger in an appropriate manner than to be depressed.

Paul was very rational and intellectual. He prided himself on never being emotional or "out of control." When his son expressed anger at the dinner table, Paul grounded him for a week. His discipline was irrational and out-of-proportion for the feelings his son expressed. *The person who attempts to be rational without accessing feelings sometimes behaves irrationally.* Paul may have had angry feelings that affected his method of discipline, causing him to be irrationally strict, but he wasn't aware of the feelings. Paul's Challenge is to learn to access his feelings instead of acting them out irrationally.

What about you? What is your color for anger? How do you deal with feelings of anger? Are you aware of your feelings or are they controlling you? Have you made decisions that were the result of strong feelings affecting you? We invite you to learn to access your feelings so that you can make Loving Choices. The result will be valuable for you in your relationship with yourself and with others.

What Did You Learn in Your Formative Years About Feelings?

You started out your life as a baby, being able to express feelings with innocence and with no inhibitions. What happened in your formative years? Did you continue to express feelings naturally and easily? Or did you lose your ability to be aware of what you are feeling?

We've asked the participants in our seminars to share what they learned about expressing feelings from their family of origin in their formative years. We think you'll enjoy reading some of the responses we have heard from the participants, and the Challenges that we gave them.

Anger — "All I See Is Red!"

Gary says it was okay for his parents to be angry, but when he became angry he was sent to his room. He learned it was okay for adults to be angry but not okay for him. It was very confusing for him.

Amy said her parents never talked about anger or admitted they were angry, but sometimes they would go several days without talking to each other. She learned that it was inappropriate to express anger but was confused when her parents didn't talk to each other.

Barry saw his parents angry a great deal of the time. They were continually throwing things and poking holes in the walls of his home. Shouting was the normal tone of voice. Often someone was likely to become emotionally or physically abused. He learned to keep his anger stuffed because he didn't want to be out of control like his parents.

Do you see red when you are angry? If not, what is the color of anger in your rainbow? Your Challenge is to access and express your feelings in a way that won't hurt you or anyone else.

Joy — "Sunshine and Light!"

Caroline shared in the seminar that when she was a child her grandmother was diagnosed with cancer. As the cancer progressed, Grammy came to live with Caroline's family in her home. Being a healthy three-year-old, she felt light, blissful, joyful, and expressed these feelings. Often she was told not to be so happy when Grammy was so sick. Caroline remembered, with tears in her eyes, that at three she began to feel that there was something wrong with her. As a result, she believed that she should dim her "light" because it upset and hurt other people. Caroline carries remnants of these memories and often dims herself down rather than expressing the joy and happiness that she feels. Does this ever happen with you?

What color is your joy and happiness? The Challenge is to allow yourself to stay open and light when you experience joy. You have a right to be happy!

Fear — "Oh, I Can't Do This!"

In Jim's home, there was a tremendous amount of fear, yet it was never expressed. As Jim grew up, he often experienced anxiety attacks and never knew why. His unexpressed fears affected all aspects of his life in a negative way.

Beth was never allowed to share her fear with her mother. As a child she consistently had nightmares. She would often attempt to talk about them. Whenever that happened she was told that she was "being a baby" and should "grow up."

What color is your fear? The Challenge is to understand that fear can assist you and can be a teacher.

Grief — "My Heart Is Broken"

When Audrey's grandfather died, her parents didn't show any emotion around the children because they didn't want the children to be upset. It is still difficult for Audrey to grieve today when she suffers an emotional loss.

Keith was taught that "big boys don't cry." When his father was killed in a car accident, he was not equipped to deal with this enormous loss. Because he could not express his deep pain, he ended up sick in bed for nearly six months and missed a year of school.

What color is your grief? The Challenge is to feel the grief and to allow yourself to cry.

Humor — "Laughter Really Is the Best Medicine!"

Nancy grew up with an older sister who was very beautiful. Nancy always felt like the "ugly duckling" around her sister and their friends. To compensate for her pain, Nancy learned to become the clown — to make everyone laugh. Inside she was feeling deep pain and hurt.

As she grew into adulthood she realized her pattern and she stopped being the clown to compensate. In fact, she even became irate when her children would tell jokes and laugh among themselves. During the seminar, she became aware of this new pattern and how much her lack of humor was controlling her. With this new awareness she was able to learn how to balance and utilize authentic humor and make Loving Choices.

What color is your humor and laughter? The Challenge is for your humor to be authentic and good medicine for yourself and those around you.

Rejection — "Nobody Wants Me!"

Bob found himself the scapegoat in his family of origin (growing up). Whenever anything went wrong, it was his fault and he was rejected. It was safer not to show any emotions. The pressure on him to take responsibility for any problem in the family increased when he showed emotions.

Nina's daughter Kim learned a lot about this feeling when she was quite young. One summer morning when Kim was six years old she invited two other little girls over to spend the day. Later that morning, Kim was found sitting under the apple tree looking lonely and with big tears streaming down her cheeks. When Nina asked what was wrong, she responded quietly, "Whenever there are three friends playing together someone *always* gets left out. I'm taking my turn at being left out, and it really hurts!"

What color is your rejection? Are you aware of the vibration of abandonment? The Challenge is to recognize that rejection is your own feeling and to use this feeling as an avenue into yourself.

Guilt — "I Am Bad!"

Mary had a "martyr mom" who did everything for her. Whenever Mary felt irritated and tried to do something for herself, her mom would lay a guilt trip on her. "Why don't you appreciate what I have done for you? I've tried to be the best mom I could be, and my kids don't even like me." Mary learned to feel guilty when she tried to do something for herself.

Robert was seven years old when his sister drowned. He was supposed to be watching her. He was told that it was his fault. No matter what he does he almost always feels bad and guilty.

What color is your guilt? Guilt is a feeling that seems to permeate every cell in the body. The Challenge is to explore and reflect on what is really going on. Many people, especially those who are sensitive, take on themselves the criticism and negative opinions of others. It's important to question why you may have been feeling responsible for everything bad that happens. We urge you to allow yourself to work through your guilt; you'll find the process very freeing and healing.

Love — "What Is This Thing?"

Of all the feelings in this chapter, this is the one that has given Bruce and Nina the most fertile ground for self-inquiry and discovery. Both of us spent our lives exploring, questioning, struggling, and stymied by this incredible, powerful, magical feeling called love. Both of us learned that love means hurt, abandonment, heartache, disappointment, and pain. We also learned that love means truth, freedom, consciousness, peace, and that true love expressed means more love received. We both grew up believing that loving ourselves was selfish and wrong and bad. Now we know better: the only true way that we can know ourselves is to love ourselves. What's more, we found that the degree to which we can love others and our planet is directly related to the degree that we accept and love ourselves. For us, love is all the colors of the rainbow inside us. What color is love for you?

The Challenge is to make the Loving Choice to access, express, and own all of your feelings as your teachers.

Emotional Blocks to Feelings

Throughout our growing years, we learn emotional blocks to expressing our feelings.

George learned to be the "nice guy." Living up to that image kept him from being emotional. Betty learned that females cried to be manipulative and get their own way. She had trouble shedding tears around her husband.

During a therapy session, Paula told us about the abuse she had suffered as a child. We expressed our anger that these things had happened to her, and asked if she could express some of her anger with us. She said, "No. I'm too afraid. I can't because you will hurt me if I do!" She so feared someone hurting her if she expressed her emotions that she blocked those feelings even with her therapists. Paula had terrible fears which prevented her from making Loving Choices.

Often it is the things that you fear most and do not express that come to fruition. We suggest to seminar participants that they do this exercise: Make a list of the things you are afraid of. They might be fears for your physical safety, relationship fears, fears of failure or success. Identifying the fears makes them less fearful. Share your list with a friend. Sharing them makes them even less likely to happen.

During the seminar, after we fill the flip chart with the fears of participants, we ask them what they have learned in their lives about expressing feelings — specifically some *positive* ways they may have learned to express feelings. We usually find only one or two people who can list anything positive. Our conclusion is that few people learn positive and productive ways of expressing strong feelings from their family of origin.

You've also learned about dealing with feelings from schools, churches, radio and television, movies, and other societal influences. Many of us, when we were children and got into a fight on the playground, had to stay in for recess. When our son Rob got into a fight in elementary school, the teacher sat the two boys down and helped them talk through their feelings. We think this is a much better solution for recognizing and dealing with feelings.

Sometimes what you are taught about grieving or not grieving becomes a block. Many people have trouble crying. Whenever you suffer an emotional loss, such as the death of a loved one, it will help for you to feel the sadness, to let yourself experience your emotions and grieve the loss. Without doing your "grief work," you may carry the emotional loss around inside you for a long time. As a result you experience the added pain of denial, depression, and physical illnesses. You may also feel emotionally and physically tired much of the time.

Have you any emotional blocks to expressing feelings? What happened in your childhood when you expressed strong feelings? Did you — do you — protect yourself by not expressing feelings?

Illusions About Feelings

You may have learned many illusions about feelings. Which of these statements do you believe to be true and which are illusions?

- Expressing feelings is a sign of weakness.
- Some feelings are more acceptable than other feelings.
- It is not masculine for males to express feelings.
- If you express anger, you will become out of control.
- Feelings are less important than thoughts.
- Intimacy is experienced only when you're making love with another person.
- People who don't talk about feelings do not have any.
- It's not okay to be angry with those you love; this means you don't really love them.
- Your father must not have loved you because he never told you so.
- If you express feelings, you will be hurt, criticized, misunderstood, or rejected by others.

Can you add some of your beliefs about feelings to this list? Do you still agree with the items on your list, or can you see that they are possibly illusions?

Positive Ways to Release Feelings

This chapter is subtitled, "A Feelings Is Neither Right nor Wrong, It Just Is." Do you agree?

We have discovered a powerful motif in our classes that we would like to share with you. *Anything you can talk out, you won't have to act out!* Talking things out decreases depression, frustration, guilt, shame, feelings of rejection, inadequate or low feelings of self-worth and confusion.

What you *do* with your feelings is important. What do you typically do when you start experiencing an uncomfortable feeling? Do you get busy? Do you start thinking so you won't have to feel? Do you crack a joke or laugh? Do you change your thoughts into something more pleasant? Do you analyze what is happening? There are many ways you can avoid feeling feelings.

Depression affects many people — in fact it is one of the most common reasons people enter therapy. As with all other human feelings, the causes of depression can be difficult to ascertain. One cause of depression is not accessing and expressing feelings, especially feelings of anger. When you are feeling "down in the dumps," expressing anger in a constructive way can make you feel much better.

Depression can be a positive feeling. Can you remember a time in your life when you were on a path that was not good for you? You probably reached a point where you knew something was wrong, and it seemed useless to continue in the same way. You may have experienced feelings of depression. If you listened to those feelings, you may have decided to change your thoughts and behavior. Maybe it was even a turning point in your life. Depression is a painful feeling that may have motivated you to make positive changes in your life.

It is crucial that your feelings not be denied or ignored and, at the same time, that they not be indulged. The key with feelings is to allow yourself to *experience* them. It's like cooking food on the stove. The Loving Choice is to keep the feelings consciously "cooking" inside you, to learn from them, and to grow through them. You must keep them "on your burner" long enough to allow them to heal. We suggest that you learn to *be* with your feelings, to neither ignore nor to indulge them. Experiencing your feelings will help you discover who you are.

Other People Can Teach You About Feelings

We all learn from each other. In the seminars, we've asked participants to share how they have learned to express and release strong feelings. The approaches are many and varied — and sometimes surprising!

Jane spends a good deal of time cleaning her house. Timothy jogs daily. Betty is inventive; she buys drinking glasses at garage sales and breaks them in her fireplace, where it's easy to clean up the broken glass. Others find that shouting and screaming help. Leslie noticed that, when she was becoming "gritchy" (*griping* and *bitchy*), it was helpful to her to scream while driving in her car out in the country where there was no traffic. Her kids observed that she was more fun to be around after she had been to her "screaming place." When they felt her becoming gritchy, they would suggest, "Hey mom, it's time for you to go to your screaming place again."

Jim's favorite way of dissipating strong feelings was to go into a big room, turn on some loud music, and dance through his feelings. He had to remember, as he performed some unorthodox movements, that dancing is not how you look but how you feel. He experimented with different movements in order to discover what felt the best and was the most healing. He learned that the dancing helped him work through feelings of anger, grief, and chaos in his life.

What about you? Do you think you would like to dance, or scream, or break glass as a way to heal and become more healthy? What have other people taught you about joy, peace, and love? Are the people in your life today the teachers that you want to assist you in this journey into your Self? You'll find that learning from others will help you make your own Loving Choices.

Your Feelings Help You Know Yourself

A little more about anger, that powerful feeling teacher. "Mirroring" is a very helpful tool. When you find your partner making you angry in the same way one of your parents made you angry, you might use your partner as a mirror for looking at yourself more closely, for finding out what you are feeling. If you are angry at a parent and haven't finished working through those feelings, this may be reflected in your relationship mirror. Perhaps what you see and what you don't like in the other person reflects something about yourself that you need to look at. (Someone who knows you well can be such a good mirror that you'll want to blow on the mirror, to cloud it, so you don't see yourself more clearly than you want to!)

Have you learned that when you can work through your anger with another person, you feel more intimacy and emotional closeness? The old cliché is, "Having a fight with another person is worth it, because making up feels so good."

Anger can tear down the walls between you and another person so you can build bridges with the rubble. Anger is the great cleanser that keeps the rubble from accumulating on your relationship bridges. Owning that you have angry feelings and accepting that they are part of you will lead to finding internal peace and feelings of forgiveness toward yourself and others. All of the energy you spent trying to control your anger is now available to love and forgive. You can be appropriately angry and keep your relationships clean. You can let go of the burden of carrying around all of your stockpiled anger, which has used up a great deal of your time and energy. You will have improved feelings of self-worth. You'll be better able to live in the present and to be appropriately assertive. Dealing with your anger allows you to be more loving. Anger — expressed positively and constructively — can be an ally of love. Ultimately, it will assist you to make Loving Choices.

Who Owns Your Feelings?

Who's responsible for the way you are feeling? Do you blame others for making you feel the way you do? Do you make statements using such "you-messages" as, "You make me angry"? (Instead of taking ownership of your feelings with an "I-statement": "I'm angry with you for doing that.") Is your personal power diminished by the actions or opinions of other people? Is someone else determining how you feel about yourself?

One of the many ways people give up their power is through their fears of rejection and abandonment. The fears you haven't dealt with are more likely to control you. For example, do you fear being rejected and abandoned? How have you been dealing with that fear? Have you been taking care of everyone else, thinking that if you do enough for them, they won't reject you? Have you been a people-pleaser, trying to please them so they won't leave you? Have you been the "nice person," hoping that if you are nice *enough,* they'll like you? Would it surprise you to learn that most of these behaviors will motivate people to *distance* you instead —to *reject* you? Your choice of behavior may have contributed to bringing about the very thing you feared most. Can you think of other ways you may have contributed to your own rejection and abandonment?

Ownership is an important concept in relationships. Taking ownership of your feelings allows you to be in control of them. Lack of ownership allows your feelings to take control of you. If you believe other people are responsible for your feelings, you have given them power over you. We encourage and support you in choosing to consciously take more responsibility for your feelings. We encourage you to allow your feelings to help you know yourself better, regain your personal power, and become free to make Loving Choices.

Your Emotional Buttons

No one can *make* you feel sad, mad, or glad if you don't have those feelings inside you. Another person may *trigger* feelings that you already have with comments that are unfair, critical, judgmental, domineering, or aggressive. They may "push your buttons," which results in bringing up your feelings in response. Remember, how you respond is your choice and your responsibility. *You own your feelings.*

Here's a suggestion. Any time someone says or does something that pushes your emotional buttons, ask yourself what you can learn from that interaction. The person who has pushed that emotional button has become a relationship teacher for you. Why not use the occasion to learn what you can about yourself, instead of blaming the other person for the way you feel?

Any feeling you can own can be worked through and made your friend. Is there any behavior or specific word(s) that pushes your buttons and trigger feelings inside of you? Why not use that as a chance to go inside and learn more about yourself?

What happens when someone interrupts you? What do you feel? Maybe it creates the same feelings you felt as a child when no one would listen to you? You'll find it interesting to learn about yourself by using triggers as an avenue into understanding yourself better. You'll learn that the feelings underneath can be accessed, accepted, expressed, worked through, and healed.

Breathing Assists in Accessing Feelings

Feelings are a form of energy, and your greatest source of energy is your breath. There is a direct connection between your breathing and your feelings. We encourage you to pay attention to your breathing, especially at times when you are aware of strong feelings. Notice what's happening with your breathing as you experience the various feelings we discussed earlier in this chapter.

What happens to your breathing when you are angry? Do you have a tendency to hold your breath? Or perhaps you find yourself breathing heavy and hard? Breathing deeply while "cooking" your anger often allows the feelings to be released. Deep breathing may help you to go deeper and perhaps to discover another feeling that has triggered your anger.

When you are experiencing joy and happiness, notice your breathing. At these times you may find that your body is open and flowing in a relaxed manner. Your breathing will be solid and deep during times of joy, lightness and laughter.

How about when you are experiencing grief? Most people find themselves sighing a lot when they are grieving. This is the body's way of moving heavy painful feelings out. Once again it is the breath which assists in healing.

When you are genuinely laughing at a humorous situation — maybe even at yourself — how are you breathing? Laughter brings more oxygen and energy into your lungs. Your whole body relaxes. You feel uplifted.

When you are experiencing fear, notice what is happening with your breathing. Have you stopped breathing in that moment? Can you feel the contraction in your body and perhaps in your lungs? A conscious effort to breathe deeply, slowly, and fully when you are afraid will most likely move the feeling through your body.

When you feel loving, notice your breathing. Love is the glue that holds life together! Love allows the breathing to be natural, calm and clear. When you are feeling love in your body, in your heart, and in your thoughts, it's reflected in your actions. Love helps in healing, wellness, and wholeness. Being "in love with love" results in growth and expansion. We encourage you to breathe in love for yourself and breathe out love for others.

In Appendix A of this book you'll find more material on breathing, which will help you to discover what a profound vehicle it is in accessing and expressing your feelings. Deep breathing assists in centering and healing. We Challenge you to become aware and utilize your breath — the life force within you. To consciously connect with your breathing is a very Loving Choice.

Feelings Assist You in Being Empowered and Loving

Assertiveness — honest self-expression — keeps you from "stockpiling" your feelings. It's not the same as *aggressiveness* — which is an attempt to impose your feelings on another person. *Passivity* allows others to erode your identity by denying yourself appropriate expression of your feelings. Acting assertively and establishing appropriate boundaries will allow you to maintain your identity — to be the person you really are.

Verbalize your feelings. Develop and use good communication skills, and improve your ability to express your feelings. When you utilize the communication exercises described in this book, you can express your feelings and learn about yourself. When you use the communication skills with another person, you will learn that "anything you can talk out, you don't have to act out."

You have a whole rainbow of colors inside of you — your feeling world. This rainbow of feelings helps you access and express the full spectrum of your colors — who you are. Feelings can be a source of strength. How much energy have you been spending keeping your feelings stuffed or denied? How often have your feelings been in control? How much energy have you spent on internal battles between your conflicting feelings? Can you accept your feelings as a part of you and allow them consciously to influence your actions and behavior? Your thoughts and feelings working together can be a powerful team. Balancing your head and your heart allows you to become centered, clear, integrated, and free from internal conflict. Instead of fighting yourself, you become an empowered, whole, loving person.

Are you ready to make Loving Choices about expressing your feelings in your relationships with yourself and others?

HOW ARE YOU DOING?

The following statements are designed to help you internalize and integrate the material in this chapter. Place a check mark beside the ones you have learned.

1. *I am committed to accessing and expressing my inner rainbow of feelings.*

2. *I have made a list of my beliefs about feelings and identified which are true and which are illusions.*

3. *I am living in the past in certain areas because I have not been expressing the feelings I need to express.*

4. *I've had certain traumatic experiences in my life that have stunted my personal growth, perhaps because I have not expressed my feelings about those incidents.*

5. *I am putting into practice the concept, "Anything I can talk out, I don't have to act out."*

6. *I am able to keep feelings "cooking on my stove" until I have worked them through.*

7. *I believe I can heal a past trauma by learning to talk about my feelings.*

8. *I've found ways to express my strong feelings in ways that will not hurt me or others.*

9. *I own and take responsibility for what I am feeling, rather than giving others responsibility for my feelings.*

10. *I'm finding that owning and expressing feelings can be empowering.*

11. *I'm working at having my thoughts and feelings work together in my relationship with myself and others.*

The Family Inside You

GETTING TO KNOW YOUR CRITICS, ADAPTIVE-SURVIVOR PARTS, INNER CHILDREN, AND WISE NURTURER

*The **challenge** is to recognize your inner voices, and to discover which of them is in charge as you deal with life situations.*

*The **loving choice** is to become as balanced as possible by integrating your inner voices.*

*Y*ou're probably a lot more complex than you realize. Most of us think of ourselves as individual personalities, with lots of different thoughts and feelings and behavior patterns. But did it ever occur to you that those different thoughts and feelings and behaviors might actually be "organized" into subsystems of their own? That you might be carrying with you a whole "family" of personalities?

No, we're not talking *schizophrenia* here — just looking at who you are from a different perspective. And we're quick to admit it's not the accepted view of scientists who study and analyze the human personality. It's just an easy-to-understand "working model" of the complex being that is you — and me (us).

Working with thousands of seminar participants over almost twenty-five years, we've identified four key inner parts or voices: the *Critics* — *Inner and Outer,* the *Inner Children,* the *Adaptive-Survivor Parts,* and the *Wise Nurturer.* In this chapter you'll get acquainted with each of them, discover their unique individual voices, and begin to learn how you can put them to work to help you make better Loving Choices.

Are You Crazy If You Hear the Voices?

> *I had imaginary friends that I talked to when I was a child. I didn't tell anyone about them because I was taught that it was childish and silly. Now you are suggesting that I start talking to my childhood friends again. It was so enjoyable to talk to my imaginary friends that I am glad you are giving me permission to do it again.*

"You're not doing it right! You should spend more time reading this book! You should be doing your homework. You paid good money for this book and this class; why aren't you working harder at it? Oh, never mind. You'll never do it well enough, anyway, so why try? You are really dumb and lazy!"

Sound familiar? Most of us have a voice inside saying words like these. Of all of the mixed messages we carry inside, this is the most common one. Remember in chapter 1 we talked about Old Nagger? We call Old Nagger your "Inner Critic." Most of your internal conflicts involve this part.

You've gone to bookstores and brought home arm loads of self-help books, right? You put them on a shelf, vowing to read all of them. After a week you have yet to open even one. Your Inner Critic comes along and says, "Why did you buy all of those books? You *know* you're never going to read them. What a waste of time and money!" Suddenly there's another voice, saying "I intend to read each one of them. I want to know as much as I can about relationships. Don't tell me I won't read them! I will eventually."

Meanwhile yet a third voice pipes up: "When are we going to have some fun? I'm tired of this internal fighting all of the time. Let's go veg-out in front of the TV. I want to escape. I sure don't want to have to keep listening to you shouting at each other."

Your internal conflict may be somewhat different, but we're certain you have several different messages speaking up inside you — often in disagreement with each other. Many of your conflicts with other people are actually your own internal conflict projected out into your relationships with others. If you haven't recognized it already, you'll find it's almost impossible to find peace in your relationships with others unless you create internal peace within yourself. Think about it on a global level: world peace begins with each of us finding internal peace.

If you're like most folks, you've experienced periods of loneliness in your life. One way of looking at loneliness is that you are separated from yourself. You haven't gotten to know your various inner voices. After you access, listen to, and learn that each of these inner voices is your friend, your chances of feeling lonely are greatly diminished.

The ideas we are talking about in this chapter may not be "mainstream," but they're not unique to our work. Roberto Assagioli was an Italian psychiatrist who developed the theory called "Psychosynthesis." He worked with Sigmund Freud in the 1930s, but his work did not become well known until around 1960. Much of his work focussed on helping people integrate and synthesize their various inner voices.

Hal and Sidra Stone have written several books, the best known one titled, *Embracing Yourselves.* They suggest that you access and listen to each of your voices until you have embraced and accepted them. They call their work "Voice Dialogue." If you give audible expression to the voices — talking out loud from each — you'll find that your voice will change to reflect the inner message you are accessing. For example, your Inner Critic voice will sound loud, critical, and parental. The voices of your Inner Children are often soft and speak of feelings reflecting vulnerability. We highly recommend the Stone's book if you want to learn more about your many internal voices.

Let's start our process of getting to know the many voices inside you with your Inner Critic. For most of us this is the loudest voice. It may be the one that has been making many of your choices. If you want to make more Loving Choices, you may need to tame this voice so you can hear some of the other voices that have been "out-shouted" by your Inner Critic.

The Critics — Inner and Outer

Each of us has both an Inner Critic and an Outer Critic. Your Inner Critic is critical of you, and your Outer Critic is critical of others. Both the Inner and Outer Critic have elements in them expecting perfection. You'll never completely please your Inner Critic because you are human and *not* perfect. We suggest you realize that and let go of continually trying to please this part of you. You can never do enough.

The Critics even seem to battle each other within us for top position. Some people have a louder Inner Critic, and some have a louder Outer Critic. If your view of yourself and others reflects an *"I'm okay—you're not okay"* belief, you have a louder Outer Critic. Denise's loud Outer Critic took on the entire Universe: "Even the stars are not located right. I could do a better job of locating them!" On the other hand, those who believe that *"I'm not okay—you're okay"* are expressing a bigger Inner Critic. "Charlie," the developmentally challenged hero of the poignant story, *Flowers for Algernon,* often labelled his everyday mishaps as "pulling another Charlie Gordon" — a put-down which clearly reflected his not-okay self-concept.

These attitudes are complex, and were created in your early developmental years when you were adopting the beliefs that built your self-concept. We'll talk more about this when we consider your "Inner Children" later in this chapter.

When people with a big Outer Critic feel pain, they project the responsibility and believe others are responsible for their pain. In contrast, when those with a big Inner Critic feel pain, they introject and believe they are responsible not only for their own pain, but for the pain of others as well. Usually the projector finds an introjector for a partner, and vice versa. Are you a "projector" (with a big Outer Critic) or an "introjector" (with a big Inner Critic)? Which is your partner?

We have found both the Inner Critic and the Outer Critic are there to protect some emotional and psychological pain inside of you. In this book, we will focus on the Inner Critic because we want to help you create a better relationship with yourself. You can make internal changes but it is difficult — if not impossible — for you to change things outside of you. We will not forget about the Outer Critic, however, and will talk about it from time to time.

Can you think of someone who reminds you of your Inner Critic? Maybe you'll think of an important person from your childhood who had great expectations of you and wanted you to be perfect. For most folks, this will be Dad or Mom. How did you react to that critical person? Did you believe the criticism? If so, it probably has affected your sense of self-worth. Did you tune out the critique, perhaps saying they were born in the Middle Ages and don't know anything? Did you rebel against the criticism? Are you still rebelling against authority?

You'll find that you usually treat your Inner Critic the same way you treated the critical person from your childhood. You may listen to it and believe you are unworthy. You may tune it out. You might rebel against it. Whatever you are doing, you probably do not like to listen to that voice. You want to get away from it. If you have an alcohol or addiction problem, you may be trying to "drown out" that voice with drugs or addictive behaviors.

Do you have a big Inner Critic voice? If so, which of your parents was a perfectionist? Did you create your Inner Critic in order to help you deal with that parent's expectations for you to be perfect? You may respond by identifying both of your parents as perfectionists. You could say your Inner Critic is continuing their demands for perfection, even though they may no longer be living.

Can you imagine an empty chair next to you with an imaginary person in that chair? How would that person act if you ignored her, acted with distaste toward her, or turned your back to her? You've probably done that a lot with your Inner Critic, so it doesn't feel listened to or heard, and it tries harder and harder to get your attention. If you keep ignoring it, it may get your attention through aches and pains in your body. The energy of the Inner Critic seems to grow when you ignore it. It shouts louder and louder and will figure out how to affect you in one way or another. How many people do you suppose are seeing medical doctors or going to hospitals because they haven't made peace with their Inner Critic?

Why not turn to that "empty chair" next to you and *listen* to your Inner Critic? You may have to force yourself to listen, since it's a voice you don't like to hear. If you listen to it until it begins to feel heard, it will begin to soften. You could even use a tape recorder to record the Inner Critic voice, repeating out loud what you hear it saying. Or maybe you'll want to get out a piece of paper and write down the words you hear. A good friend or a therapist would be willing to listen to what your Inner Critic is saying if you want to share.

You may notice when you start listening that the Inner Critic uses lots of "you-messages." For example, "You're really dumb and lazy." If you listen to it long enough, you may notice that it is changing from "you-messages" to "I-messages." For example, "I suggest you read this book so you will be more knowledgeable."

Take a minute to go into yourself and feel your feelings. Did you react emotionally to the "you message" you just read about being dumb and lazy? Did you react differently as you read the "I-message"? Think about it. As you tame your Inner Critic, you may begin to feel more internal peace. It may take you days or weeks of listening before your Inner Critic changes to "I-messages," but it's truly worth the time and effort.

There's another important benefit of taming your Inner Critic. If you have identified your Inner Critic with one of your parents, or another significant person in your childhood — perhaps even using that person's name for the Critic — you can actually make peace with that person as you make peace with your Inner Critic. You internalized messages from that person earlier in your life, and she or he is, in some ways, still controlling you (even if no longer living). It is exciting to make peace with that internalized parent, even though the person is not involved and doesn't know it. What a wonderful Loving Choice to make peace with your family of origin and your childhood!

Let's take it a little farther. Maybe the critical person in your life was not able to nurture himself or to receive nurturing from others. One reason that person was so critical is because he did not feel loved and accepted. We suggest that you not only listen to your Inner Critic voice, but that you also learn to nurture, accept, and love that part of you. It may not be easy at first, but eventually you will be able to make that Loving Choice. When you do start accepting and embracing your Inner Critic, it will continue to soften and may even transform into a good internal parent, helping you to gain greater self-discipline, motivation, and commitment to accomplish your life goals.

An important side benefit of listening to your Inner Critic in the empty chair is that it will help you put the Inner Critic in its place. *You are not the Inner Critic;* it is only one of the many voices inside of you. By separating and differentiating yourself from your Inner Critic and the other inner voices, you are developing internal boundaries. The more you get to know your various inner voices, the clearer your internal boundaries will become. Instead of looking at yourself as a blur, you will be able to identify and separate your inner voices. "I recognize that voice; it's my Inner Critic. Is there another view I want to hear as well?"

The goal is for you to identify and listen to as many of your inner voices as possible. It is important to be able to hear what each one is saying. Answering an important life question by listening to your inner voices is like having a "committee meeting" and making sure you hear from each member of your committee. After hearing from all of your parts, you, the Chairperson of the committee, make the Loving Choice about what to do next with your life.

The Adaptive-Survivor Parts

There are other powerful inner voices that need to be identified and described. We call one group of them your *adaptive-survivor parts*. These are voices that you may have not thought about or identified. You may be surprised to find parts of yourself that are so important that you wonder how you could have ignored them all these years. In this section, we'll try to explain how you created these parts to help you adapt and survive in your formative years.

Let's start on a positive note. You have done a lot of thinking about negative traits—now we want you to start thinking about what *healthy* traits you would like to have. Here's a partial list of healthy personality traits:

- awareness and expression of feelings
- sense of humor
- honesty and openness
- ability to nurture yourself
- creativity and spontaneity
- good communication skills.

This short list is just a beginning. We encourage you to continue adding to the list on your own. It will motivate you to further develop your own healthy personality traits and to expand your awareness of healthy traits.

Were many of these healthy traits acknowledged and supported in your family of origin? Which ones were affirmed and encouraged? We have found a wide variety of reactions, but most people find only one or two healthy behaviors that were affirmed and supported in their family of origin. Many people in our society did not receive much affirmation for being healthy. No wonder some choose an unhealthy relationship instead of a healthy one! The unhealthy one is more familiar.

Chances are that during the early years you developed patterns of *adaptive-survivor behavior* which allowed you to feel more loved, get more attention, and be happier. The more unmet needs you had as a child, the more evolved these adaptive-survivor parts are.

What kinds of adaptive-survivor behavior did you choose? One of the more common is to become *over-responsible* (OR) — more concerned about meeting the needs of others than about meeting your own needs. The OR person became a rescuer, a caretaker, an enabler, a person — in the extreme — who is attempting to save the world.

We have listened to many people describe their adaptive-survivor parts. We are impressed that when the list of possible behaviors you could have chosen is identified, it appears you chose the best one for your situation.

Paul came from a family with alcoholic parents, and his environment was at times very chaotic. He learned to be the OR person who saw to it that everything was taken care of. He was the caretaker for his siblings. And he received several payoffs for his care-taking, even though at the time it didn't seem that way.

Adaptive-survivor behavior works well in the formative years, however, when you reach adulthood and start looking for love relationship partners, there's a tendency to connect with someone who will support the adaptive-survivor behavior. If you learned to be OR, for example, you look for someone *under-responsible* (UR). If the person is not UR enough, you may *train* him or her to be more UR. The caretaker finds a receiver. The person with an "urge to help" finds someone who needs help.

Jane was responsible for carrying out the garbage. She began to feel resentful about being the "garbage person," and insisted that Peter take his turn. When he missed a couple of wastebaskets, Jane was infuriated. Then he failed to get the garbage cans to the curb before the garbage truck came, angering her even more. "If you want something done right, do it yourself" is OR vocabulary. Peter gave up on doing the job right and Jane was back at her old task. She had taught Peter to believe that he couldn't do it "right." The irony is that Peter had lived alone for several years and never had a problem with taking care of the garbage until he lived with Jane.

After a while, OR people become resentful of their UR partners. The OR may have chosen a UR partner because she saw the UR was having so much fun. Eventually, however, you have difficulty liking the part in the other person that you don't like in yourself.

Bruce's paternal grandparents were critical German people. His father realized he couldn't do anything right so he gave up trying and became a UR person. That's one way people develop a adaptive-survivor part of UR. Do you know anyone like that?

In the Rebuilding Seminar at least 80% of the participants identified themselves as OR in their relationship that ended. Where are the UR people? Why aren't they taking the seminar? Maybe they're out fishing and having fun someplace. We believe over- and under-responsibility to be a major cause of love relationships ending.

There are many other adaptive-survivor behaviors. You may have chosen to be the *perfectionist* as your adaptive-survivor behavior. You learned to do things perfectly so you would not be criticized by the perfectionist adults in your childhood. It worked as a child, but with whom do you create an adult relationship? Maybe *"Pig Pen,"* as the late Charles Schulz called his always-dirty *Peanuts* cartoon character. Such a person refuses to do anything perfectly, of course, but you don't give up easily. You continue to encourage your Pig-Pen to be perfect, as your significant adult encouraged you to do as a child. Maybe a *"people pleaser"* who can always please you and your perfectionist expectations. Or perhaps someone who is always *"rebelling."* You criticize, he rebels, and vice versa. Or perhaps you choose another *perfectionist* so the two of you can continue to criticize each other the same way you felt criticized as a child! It may not be fun, but it's certainly familiar!

You may have decided that the only way to survive in your chaotic family of origin was to be *logical* and never show any feelings. Everyone around you was "off the wall" and you had to be rational and intellectual and consistent in order to hold the family together. The significant adults around you may have had some additions. Maybe you're a male who learned from his father's example never to show feelings.

With whom does the logical person connect? Someone who is very *emotional*. Stereotypically, this would be a male-female polarization, with the male logical and the female emotional. The logical person becomes more and more intellectual as the emotional person becomes more and more emotional. We call that process *polarization*, and we'll talk more about it in the Power Struggle chapter.

What unmet needs and feelings are underneath your adaptive-survivor part? Maybe you felt *rejected* if you weren't over-responsible.

Perhaps you do things for others so you won't feel *guilty*. Sometimes you take care of others because you are *angry* and want to control them. If you have low feelings of *self-worth*, you may feel better about yourself when you are acting as a caretaker. If you don't do everything perfectly, perhaps you are *fearful* of being criticized. Your adaptive-survivor part may have one or more of these feelings underneath it.

Maybe you learned adaptive-survivor behavior because you thought that was what males or females were "supposed" to do. Men are breadwinners, right? Strong and dominant? Women are family caretakers, aren't they? Weak and compliant? Stereotypes such as these lead to many of our adaptive-survivor behaviors, as we live out the expectations of society or gender roles.

We'd like to suggest some homework for you, to help you minimize the power of your adaptive-survivor part. Ask yourself which of the above feelings you experience when you do these homework activities for each of your adaptive-survivor parts. For example: emotionally, *over-responsibles* are good givers and poor receivers, often giving to others what you wish they would give to you. If you are an OR, your homework is to say "no" when someone asks you to do something for them. The other part of the homework is to ask someone to do something for you. What feelings do you have when you do this homework? This homework is designed to help you stretch yourself beyond your usual patterns, to become more balanced, to be able to give and receive equally well.

Here are other assignments for various adaptive-survivor styles:

- If you are *under-responsible,* we suggest you take over the check book for three months and pay all of the bills — on time and without being overdrawn!

- If you are a *perfectionist,* try *not* making your bed for a week when you awake in the morning.

- If you are *Pig-Pen,* make your bed every morning.

- If you are a *people pleaser,* do something to make someone mad this week.

- If you are *logical,* write ten "I-feel" messages.

- If you are an *emotional* person you may not know what you are feeling. You may be using emotional outbursts as a way to avoid expressing your feelings directly.

Perhaps you may also need to write "I-feel" messages because you have been avoiding direct expression of your feelings.

- If you are *living out the expectations of others,* question whether you want to continue living up to those expectations.

Think of other homework for your special adaptive-survivor parts. (Hint: If your first reaction is, "I can't do that," you've discovered the right homework for you!)

After you have done your homework and identified some of the feelings underneath your adaptive-survivor behavior, try some exercises designed to help you deal with those feelings.

- If you feel *rejected,* make a list of twenty things you like about yourself. If you can improve your self-worth enough, you might be able to say, "Anybody that rejects me is missing out on getting to know and be with a wonderful person."

- If your feeling is *guilt,* write "I'm not responsible" on a sheet of paper and post it where you can read it until you believe it.

- If your feeling is *anger,* write as many times as you need to, "I am angry at you because _____." After you have written all you can write, go back over it and change each "I am angry at you because _____" to "I am angry because _____."

- If your feeling is low *self-worth,* have several of your friends or loved ones write a list of what they like about you. Read the list until you begin believing it.

- If your feeling is *fear,* make a list of things you are afraid of. Share your list with a person you feel safe with and can trust. The fears you can talk about will diminish.

Adaptive-Survivor Behaviors — A Partial List

There's a partial list of adaptive-survivor parts on the next page. Do you identify with any on the list? Put a check mark beside those that might describe you.

ADAPTIVE-SURVIVOR PARTS

over responsible	under responsible
logical	emotional
perfectionist	people pleaser
parental	rebellious
helper	I need help
emotional	stoic
enmeshed	indifferent
superman	helpless
aggressive	passive
superwoman	do it for me
martyr	I can do it myself
competitor	I'll let you win
caretaker	take care of me
I know it all	I don't know how
criticizes others	criticizes self
flame thrower	asbestos suit
optimist	pessimist
righteous	complacent
fighter	placater
blamer	blamed
clown	serious
judger	guilty
do it myself	can't do it right
do it now	procrastinator
work-a-holic	let's take the day off
treadmill	spontaneous
complainer	compliant
it's your fault	it's my fault
risker	play it safe
whiner	suffer in silence
organized	disorganized
life of the party	wallflower
center of attention	withdrawn
confronter	avoider
enabler	drug abuser
saver	spender
kids need discipline	kids need to be listened to

You tend to create relationships with people who have adaptive-survivor parts that are the opposite of yours. Do you recognize any adaptive-survivor parts that describe a person with whom you have a relationship? Put that person's initials beside those parts.

There can be many combinations of the parts we've listed. For example, many perfectionists will create a relationship with another perfectionist. This may result in both expecting the other to be perfect, similar to the way a perfectionist adult in your childhood expected you to be perfect. Wouldn't it be a Loving Choice to become as balanced as you can?

Ours is only a partial list of adaptive-survivor behaviors — there are many more. We suggest you keep looking for more of your own adaptive-survivor parts. The number is unlimited, since you chose one or more of these behaviors to help you survive, adapt, or to make the most of your unique childhood situation.

As an adult you've probably needed to become more balanced — almost all of us do! You're probably in a relationship with a person who has one or more adaptive-survivor parts from the opposite list, to provide you with more balance. For example, you thought you chose a love partner because you fell in love. Maybe what you really fell in love with is a behavior in another that you have not yet developed in yourself. After the honeymoon period in your love relationship is over, you may come to dislike in your partner a behavior that you've not yet learned to like and accept in yourself. Stick around, you probably have some growing to do!

Each of these adaptive-survivor behaviors can be healthy. If there was pain, anger, and hurt in your early environment, for example, you needed to find ways to protect yourself from that hurt. Many of these adaptive-survivor parts were like a protector for you. It's only when they take over "driving your personality car" that they become a problem.

The process of taking charge of your life begins with your awareness of your adaptive-survivor behavior. Because this behavior often started when you were feeling pain, you may feel pain when you start recognizing and owning these parts of you. Healing usually occurs when you embrace your pain and decide to learn from it.

Doing the communication exercises will be very helpful in your healing process. It is important to learn how to nurture yourself. Later on we'll talk about the Wise Nurturer. The wisdom of the

Wise Nurturer diminishes the need for strong adaptive-survivor behavior.

To summarize, awareness will help you identify your adaptive-survivor parts, which will lead to your owning and becoming responsible for your behavior. Embracing any pain you may feel will help the pain become your teacher and help you discover your need for nurturing. The end result is that you will learn to make Loving Choices instead of the adaptive-survivor behaviors making your choices for you.

The Inner Children

Is there really a bunch of kids running around inside you? Who are your "Inner Children" anyway? Is there any limit to the number of them? How old are they? What are their names?

Let us begin by acknowledging that the concept of a variety of Inner Children is not universally accepted in psychology. Many skeptics doubt the existence of Inner Children because they are not easily accessed from the conscious thinking brain. Nevertheless, many therapists have found it relatively easy to go into an altered state, such as under hypnosis, and "remember" your birth, your first birthday, and all of your early childhood experiences — memories you don't have with your conscious mind. While researchers of differing views study what "really" happens, we've found the concept of Inner Children very useful as a way to understand aspects of our personalities that are not easily understood in "traditional" academic terms.

As we learn more about the child part of ourselves, we recognize how complex that child part is. In fact, there are many different kinds of Inner Children within you: the *vulnerable* children, the *wounded* children, the *playful* children, the *sensitive* children, the *creative* children, and many more. We will go into more detail about this in chapter 10. Your Inner Children were developed largely during the first three years of your life. They have continued to develop since that time. They will keep building, learning, and developing throughout the rest of your life. They represent, among other things, the spontaneous, creative, feeling part of you. Inner Children are not "childish," in the sense of being immature or underdeveloped. They are "childlike" and can assist you to have fun and live in the present. Inner Children don't care much about the past or the future. They are spontaneous and want to be first. Not surprisingly, Inner Children want to be cherished and loved.

In the very early months of life, we humans take in most of the information from our environment through our bodies. We don't have an intellectual mind developed yet, so we don't learn intellectually but through feelings and experiences. You adopted many important beliefs in those first few months. You decided whether you were wanted or not. You decided whether the world was a trustworthy place, and if there were people who would care for you. You developed your basic sense of self-worth. You decided if you were "okay" or "not-okay." You decided if it was safe to be intimate with another person, if it was safe to feel vulnerable. You decided if you were lovable or not.

In order to get in touch with these fundamental feelings and beliefs you hold about yourself and the world, we suggest a very profound process. Sit quietly. Relax and go inside. Pay attention to your breathing. Have someone state out loud the following statement. "You are a very special and lovable person". What did you feel in your body? If your Inner Children believe you are lovable and special, your body probably felt comfortable and you were able to believe the statement. If your Inner Children disagree, you probably felt discomfort or pain somewhere in your body.

Do you remember the 1970s "pet rock" fad, when everyone received the perfect pet for Christmas? You didn't have to feed it, change its diapers, or do anything to take care of it. When Danny, one of the class participants, heard about the "Inner Children" concept, he asked if it was a fad like the pet rock. Later he had a therapy session where he was able to access one of his wounded Inner Children. He found himself curled up on the floor, crying, in a fetal position. Many people have an emotional and powerful experience when they connect with their Inner Children. During this experience he discovered the feelings and beliefs residing in his Inner Children. After Danny realized how much he had been influenced by his Inner Children, he stopped joking about it.

Many women who have had more than one pregnancy are aware of the different personalities of their unborn children. Some are active, some are passive. Some appear to have a connection with the mother and respond when she is angry or sad. It appears you started developing a personality before you were born!

Sam experienced healing one of his vulnerable Inner Children. In his own words, "An important piece of my personal work has been discovering this new part of me called my 'Inner Children'. It has been exciting and rewarding to get to know this little boy inside of me. It was largely created before, during, and after my birth, and it has been altered somewhat since that time. I have found the decisions I made in that pre-verbal stage have been far more influential in my adult life than I had formerly believed."

The Wise Nurturer

There is a wise, intuitive, and nurturing voice within you that you may not yet have accessed or become aware. It is the voice spoken aloud by the writers of those wonderful greeting cards that seem so wise and supportive. After you learn to listen to and access this voice, you will be able to write your own greeting cards. Some of you may call this voice your "Heart Space" or your "gut feeling." It does not come from your logical mind but appears like a bolt of lightning as a sudden new insight.

Many people who are able to nurture others have trouble nurturing and affirming themselves. If that describes you, find the part of you that nurtures others and simply start saying and doing the same things for yourself. Bethanne knew that her boss, the store manager, was not going to tell her that she did a good job. After she had done the vegetable display, she stood back, looked at it, and said to herself, "I did a good job displaying those vegetables." She knew that the only way she was going to get any affirmations in that job was to give them to herself. How long has it been since you have affirmed yourself in a meaningful way?

The development of your Wise Nurturer is enhanced if you had someone who was wise and nurturing to you in your formative years. Can you think of a person who supported and accepted you? Who frequently praised you with affirmations and compliments? A person who believed in you and your worth? A person who inspired you to be all that you could be? You may even want to name your Wise Nurturer part after that person.

If you didn't have the good fortune of having a relationship with such a person, you may find it helpful to develop some relationships with a person or persons who will help you develop your Wise Nurturer now. You might find that an older relative, someone from a support group, a neighbor, a friend from church, or a member of a relationships class will be nurturing. You might find a special relationship with a therapist or spiritual advisor. You might develop a love relationship or a deep friendship with a person who nurtures you. Hearing an external voice that is affirming and nurturing of you will assist you in learning to listen to the wise nurturing voice inside. Ultimately, you will find this voice inside of you.

Gary, one of the participants in the seminar, was very affected when he learned about the Wise Nurturer. In his own words, "I had not accessed this voice during most of my life. I began to listen to it when I was remodeling my house, of all things! I would be outside working and needed a hammer from the basement tool room. A voice would come and tell me to bring a pair of pliers. I would ignore that voice because, after all, I knew what I needed and it wasn't a pair of pliers! With much chagrin I would discover as I was using the hammer, I did need pliers to finish the job. After making several extra trips to the basement, I began to listen to this wise voice who seemed to know what tool I needed better than I did. Surrender became an important word for me. I needed to surrender, to let go of my ego, and to allow another part of me to become a nurturing and supportive internal friend — even when I felt independent and in control of my life. I have learned to appreciate this new friend inside of me, and have been impressed with how much difference it has made in my life."

As we listen to people accessing this part, we too are impressed with the wisdom of the Wise Nurturer. It knows all of your other sub-personality parts. It can share information about these other parts that your conscious mind may not have accessed. It has suggestions that are very beneficial to listen to and accept.

The Wise Nurturer is the part of you that can say to you, "I like you," or "I love you." It can give you all of the nurturing and love you didn't feel you received as a child. It is detached, objective, caring, nurturing, compassionate, and mature. It knows what your Inner Children want and need. It knows how to nurture the Inner Critic, and also how to nurture any of your other parts.

The most important thing is that your Nurturer can give you the love, support, and nurturing that you thought you needed and wanted from someone else. Your Wise Nurturer gives you unconditional love and affirmation. With this support from within, you can let go of being dependent on someone else to do this for you. What empowerment to let go of the expectations you have been placing on your friends and loved ones!

It is a beautiful part of you. You will be a more loving and free person as you learn to access, embrace, and listen to the Wise Nurturer.

Summary

Most likely you have been very aware of the critical voice inside we are calling the *Inner Critic*. Most people try to ignore this voice because it often has hurt. However, it can be transformed into a valuable inner parent, full of self-discipline, and can assist you in accomplishing your goals in life.

You may have been controlled by one or more of your adaptive-survivor parts. You have not been aware of how many choices that part of you has been making in your life. Identifying and describing those parts is the beginning of taking charge of your life. They have been important in your earlier life. They helped you to grow and develop. You needed them in your formative years. Now they have outgrown their usefulness. They can cause problems and stress in your adult relationships. We suggest you give them new job descriptions. You decide what their role and function is in your life. You choose when you want them to emerge. The choice is to use them instead of being controlled by them. Homework: *keep a journal and write down your reactions to the various concepts described in this chapter.*

Your *Inner Children* often have been shut in a disowned and unused closet in your life. They may have made decisions for you from a place of neediness because they were wounded, hurt, scared, and felt so alone. They've probably tried to get your attention, and may have acted out and expressed their pain, both internally and externally. The acting out has often been a "cry for love." You may have ignored this vital creative part of yourself. Painting, writing, making music, sculpting, gardening — all these and other creative activities are freeing and healing. Allowing and encouraging your innate creativity will expand this aspect of your child-self. How long since you have played on a playground and swung on a swing? Your Inner Children wanted to have fun, but you remained serious and wouldn't allow them to come out and play. Homework: *do something spontaneous, healing, and fun as soon as possible!*

As you begin accessing your *Wise Nurturer* part your discovery will be that you can nurture yourself better than anyone else. It knows your Inner Children and knows what they need better than anyone. When these two parts start talking to each other you'll be amazed at the healing you can do by yourself. Homework: *take a walk by yourself and let your Wise Nurturer say to your Inner Children all that you wanted your parents to say to you when you were little.*

We have introduced these parts to you so you can start getting to know them better in the next chapter. The Self-Encounter is a method designed to help you get to know your inner voices better. This powerful communication tool will assist you in sorting out and making friends with the many voices inside you.

HOW ARE YOU DOING?

The following statements are designed to help you internalize and integrate the material in this chapter. Place a check mark beside the ones you have learned.

1. *I am aware of my Inner Critic voice.*

2. *I have identified the inner conflict that I have been having between my Inner Critic and some of my other inner parts.*

3. *I want to learn how to make more Loving Choices by listening to my inner voices.*

4. *I want to identify, separate and get to know my inner parts.*

5. *I have identified whether I have a bigger Inner Critic or Outer Critic.*

6. *I have identified one or more people that I can name my Inner Critic after.*

7. *I have discovered that I am reacting to my Inner Critic the same way I reacted to the critical people in my childhood.*

8. *I am learning to listen to my Inner Critic so I can make it feel heard and understood.*

9. *I am ready to learn how to tame my Inner Critic by listening to it instead of trying to ignore it.*

10. I am committed to accessing my Inner Children and learning to be more spontaneous and have more fun.

11. I have identified at least one of my adaptive-survivor parts and am doing the homework needed to assist me in making Loving Choices.

12. I will choose to let my adaptive-survivor parts assist me instead of allowing them to be in control of my life.

13. I am motivated to keep looking for new and different adaptive-survivor parts inside me.

14. I am intrigued with the idea of learning to nurture myself.

15. I think it would be wonderful to be able to write my own greeting cards.

16. I want to take a walk and have a conversation between my Inner Children and my Wise Nurturing part.

17. I want to spend more time thinking about the concepts in this chapter before I continue reading.

18. I am motivated to learn how to communicate with myself by doing a Self-Encounter.

19. I think the Self-Encounter may assist me to get to know my various inner voices better.

20. I am exploring whatever resistance and hesitation I have about the various concepts described in this chapter.

21. I am keeping a journal and writing my reaction to the various concepts described in this chapter.

22. I want to face the Challenge of learning more about my internal mixed messages so I can make more Loving Choices in my life.

SECTION TWO

Communicating with Yourself and Others

COMMUNICATION BEGINS with learning to communicate with yourself first. The next four chapters describe four different aspects of our communication model.

First is the **Self-Encounter** (chapter 4), whereby you'll learn to access the important voices within you. We consider this process one of our most important gifts to you in this book.

The second communication tool in this section (chapter 5) is the **Repetitive Self-Encounter.** This is a powerful method to employ when you realize that a single Self-Encounter doesn't finish the work you need to do. You can repeat the Self-Encounter in order to take a deeper journey into yourself.

Chapter 6 takes the inner communication process a step further yet, allowing you to access three or more members of your "Internal Family" in your Self-Encounter, and learn to bring them together in an **Internal Family Conversation.** This inner dialogue may become an important self-healing exercise, resulting in a remarkable feeling of inner peace.

The fourth method, introduced in chapter 7, is the **Healing Encounter.** Now you're going to begin to apply — in a relationship with another person — what you've learned in communicating better with yourself. The Healing Encounter is a two-way process, involving an **Initiator** Self-Encounter shared with another person, and a **Respondent** Self-Encounter back to the initiator. We have come to view the Self-Encounter as the "main course" and the Healing Encounter as the "dessert." Just as Grandma told you years ago: *eat your dinner first, then you may have dessert.* Please learn how to do the (main course) Self-Encounter before attempting the (dessert) Healing Encounter.

We know you're going to enjoy getting to know yourself better, and using that knowledge to improve your relationships with others.

CHAPTER FOUR

The Self-Encounter

LEARNING TO COMMUNICATE WITH YOURSELF

*The **challenge** is to learn the Self-Encounter in order to
learn to communicate with yourself.*

*The **loving choice** is to continue to do solo time first
before attempting to communicate with another.*

The Self-Encounter involves listening to the self-talk voices
you hear inside your head and body, and helps you to get
to know and understand your various parts, behaviors, or
voices. You truly encounter yourself.

The Self-Encounter is a time efficient process. It will take you a
little more time and effort at first because it's like learning a new
language. Eventually you will be impressed with how much you
progress in a short period of time.

Take a look at the elements in this outline to get an idea of where
your Self-Encounter journey will take you:

- **Topic**
  - logical importance
  - emotional charge
  - motivation
- **Facts and Observations**
- **Thoughts or Interpretations**
- **Body Sensations**

- **Feelings**
- **Survivors**
- **Inner Critic**
- **Inner Children**
- **Wise Nurturer**
- **Wants, Needs, and Intentions**
- **Summary and Conclusions**

We have found the most effective way of teaching the Self-Encounter is to actually describe one. Here is a Self-Encounter that Mike tried. You too may find this a relevant topic.

Mike's Time Management Self-Encounter

The topic of my Self-Encounter is: time management.
(Now Mike will rank the following three items from 1 to 10, with 10 being the highest.)

The logical importance of my topic is: 3.
   "I know my grades will improve if I get my homework done when I'm supposed to."

The emotional charge for my topic is: 3.
   "I'll be more relaxed and happier if I'm not always rushing around."

My motivation is: 5.
   "I want to be able to manage my time better."

My facts and observations are: *Yesterday I did my homework in the car on the way to class.*

My thoughts or interpretations are: *I am constantly doing things at the last minute. I think I could plan ahead more and do things a few days ahead of time. I think planning ahead would make my life less stressful.*

My body-sensations are: *I am experiencing some tightness in my shoulders and neck.*

My feelings are: *I feel rushed most of the time. I feel stressed by doing things at the last minute.*

My Adaptive-Survivors say: *My busy-holic part says life goes along pretty good as long as I keep busy.*

My Inner Critic says: *You should do things on time. You should plan ahead. You should do things right.*

My Inner Children say: *Who cares if the homework gets done? I just want to play.*

My Wise Nurturer says: *You might benefit from paying attention to what you are feeling, instead of just keeping busy.*

My wants, needs and intentions are: *I want to change this pattern of doing things at the last minute. I want my life to be less stressful.*

My commitments are: *I will schedule time to organize my life better. I will look into books, tapes, and classes on time-management. I will do more Self-Encounter exercises on this topic.*

Summary and conclusions:

- The idea of getting to know myself better by doing a Self-Encounter is a new topic for me. I don't think I know myself very well.

- I realize that I don't have the foggiest idea of how to manage my time better.

- I have been hearing my Inner Critic voice the most.

- I didn't know I had such a wise, nurturing voice; I need to listen to it more.

See how quick and easy it is to do a Self-Encounter? Are you ready to try it? We encourage you to try at least one — you probably will find it fun! (See the Self-Encounter form at the end of the chapter for help.) We suggest you practice doing Self-Encounters until you can do one without using the form.

Your Inner Critic may be telling you that you can't do a Self-Encounter. Our Wise Nurturer says you can do as many Self-Encounters as you choose. It's up to you!

Discussion of the Self-Encounter

You will probably have difficulty picking a *topic* at first. We suggest you start out with simple topics such as:

- I'm tired of picking up dirty clothes that some else has left on the floor.
- Shall we go out to eat tonight?

- My resistance to doing a Self-Encounter.
- I want to learn why I became so angry at the clerk in the grocery store.
- My reactions to being stuck in traffic on the way home from work.

Later, you may want to tackle such big topics as:

- How can I learn to deal with my anger better?
- How can I be more happy?
- How do I feel about my teenage son or daughter being in so much trouble in school?
- I want to overcome my drug addiction problems.
- Should I separate and file for divorce?

You may discover that the topic of your Self-Encounter evolves into another topic. If your topic changes as you are working through your encounter, it may indicate that the encounter is helping you learn more about yourself. If a new topic emerges, discipline yourself to stay on the identified topic, but make a note of the new topic so you can come back to it later and do another encounter.

- It is helpful for you to look at how important the topic is for you *logically*. We suggest you write a number from 1 to 10, with 10 being the most important.
- Do you have an *emotional charge* about the topic? Again, choose a number, with 10 meaning the topic is emotionally very important for you.
- What is your *motivation* on a 1-to-10 basis? The question we usually ask at this point is. "How motivated are you to learn how to do a Self-Encounter?" Then we ask for an explanation of your motivation. The explanation assists you in understanding your motivation.

These three questions — and the numbers you assign to them — help you focus on yourself and effectively communicate a great deal of information in a quick and easy manner. Think of how helpful this will be when you share an encounter with another person.

You might discover that the numbers for these three questions increase as you work on the topic. Often people realize the topic is much bigger and more important than they originally thought. As you reach closure with the encounter, the numbers often decrease, and may be lower than when you started.

• The facts and observations may be a new idea for you. You have made interpretations like, "That person is angry." What facts did you use to make that interpretation? Did the person talk loudly? Was her face red? It is helpful to identify the facts used in your interpretation. Remember, facts and observations are like newspaper reporting: they are descriptive, non-emotional and non-judgemental.

We suggest you access your facts through one of your five senses. Often you can state your facts with "I saw _____," or "I heard _____." Observations that *don't* come from one of your five sensory inputs may be thoughts or feelings.

• Your *thoughts and interpretations* may be more subjective than you want to admit. One of the benefits of the Self-Encounter — and one that can make your relationships healthier — is to realize that you see the world not as it is, but as you are. You take in your facts and observations, and make sense of them with thoughts and interpretations that are affected by who you are: your age, your ethnicity, your culture, your family of origin, your religion, your politics, your attitudes and beliefs, and your education. It is easy to become righteous and believe your thoughts are absolute truth, and any that disagree with yours are absolutely wrong. It is a step toward healthy relationships to realize that your thoughts are subjective and reflect who you are; they are not facts. Thoughts are like computer data. As you put in new information, your thoughts can change just as the computer output changes with new data. Today's thoughts may be different than tomorrow's thoughts. It is healthy if your interpretations are changing; it means you are growing. It may be helpful to write "I think _____," or "My interpretation is _____," rather than "I think you _____," which is a "you" message. If you have written some "I think you" statements in your interpretations, go back and change them into "I think I" statements.

• Mike had not been aware of his *body sensations* because he had not been listening to one of his most important teachers — his body. The body doesn't lie! The higher your number for your emotional charge, the more likely you will experience some body sensations. When you begin to learn about body sensations, you may discover a pathway to understanding yourself better. Think of some of the phrases you have often heard that validate this statement, such as, "that person is a pain in the neck." When you ignore angry feelings, your neck becomes like a cork in a bottle, keeping all of your angry feelings bottled up. It may take some emotional and physical energy to keep that cork in place. When someone does something that triggers angry feelings in your body, you may experience a pain in your neck as you put more energy into keeping your "bottle-neck" in place. Instead of saying: "That person is a pain in the neck," you might say, "Thank you for doing something to catalyze my anger. My neck is informing me that I need to work through positive ways of dealing with anger, instead of continually denying it." It is helpful to talk about where in your body you experience the sensation. This will help you separate body sensations from feelings, which may be hard to pinpoint to a specific place in your body. You might access this inner voice by saying, "I am experiencing _____ in my _____," (a specific part of your body).

• You have accessed observations and facts through only one of your senses; you thought about the facts with your brain, and those facts may have stimulated some body sensations. Now let's access some of your *feelings*. Where in your body do your feelings reside? Many people experience feelings in their stomach and chest. Body sensations may help you determine what you are feeling. For example, "I experienced tightness in my stomach, which helped me realize *I was feeling fearful*." It is interesting that you can't talk about future feelings. These would be considered thoughts because they are what you think you *might* feel in the future. Thus, feelings reside in the past or in the present. When you express a feeling, the third word in your feeling statement is an emotional word. You may want to turn to page 69, "Feeling Words," to help you access your feelings. Write your feeling statements with "I feel _____," or "I felt _____ when you were late for dinner." It may be helpful to explain your feelings after the using a feeling word in the sentence.

• Did you identify some *adaptive-survivor* parts when you read chapter 3? Sometimes we refer to them as *coping strategies*. Are you a caretaker or a taker? Are you perfectionist or pig-pen? Are you a people-pleaser or are you arrogant? Are you always a boring intellectual, or an off-the-wall feeling person? Where do you hear this message in your body? Adaptive-survivor parts may be a new concept for you. Until you've thought about it for a while, you may have trouble identifying — or admitting — that you have adaptive-survivor parts. Be patient. You will eventually be able to make a long list of your adaptive-survivor parts. We keep finding more we evolve and learn more about ourselves.

• Your *Inner Critic* voice is easy to access because it's probably the voice you hear the loudest and the most frequently. Most people hear this voice in or around the head. Accessing this voice and letting it talk is new behavior for most of you. This may be difficult, and your natural tendency is to avoid listening to it. In order to tame this voice — and to transform it into a good internal parent — you will need to listen to it until it feels heard. Usually when you first access this voice it will be using "you-messages." If you keep listening long enough, it will change to "I-messages," indicating a transformation into a more desirable internal parent. The Self-Encounter is a good way to learn to listen to this part of you.

• Many people experience their *Inner Children* voices in their stomach or diaphragm. If you have a tendency to "stuff" your feelings, you may have also stuffed these child voices, because many of your feelings represent your Inner Children. Your Inner Critic may be shouting at you not to let these voices out because the Inner Critic's job description includes protecting your Inner Children. It may be saying that you will become vulnerable and get hurt if you let these voices out. Most of your internal conflicts are between your Inner Critic, your Inner Children, and adaptive-survivor parts. Sit quietly, breathe deeply, and take time "To Be." Allow your Inner Children out of the closet. They may have been shut in for eons. They may be anxious to play, need to be healed, desire to be heard, want to be seen, or perhaps are fearful they may be abused again.

• How long has it been since you said something wise and nurturing to yourself? Maybe it is time to access your *Wise Nurturer* voice. Many people find this voice difficult to locate in the body. It may come from out of nowhere, like a bolt of lightning. Usually when your Wise Nurturer speaks, you feel better. Can you access any self-nurturing comments that will make you feel happier, more peaceful, or more confident? For example, "You are doing a good job of reading and understanding how to do a Self-Encounter," or "I'm proud of you for trying this."

• You have been traveling through your body, finding the various voices. Now you are ready to verbalize and speak about your *intentions, wants,* and *needs*. These might be called your *assertive voices*. If you don't ask for what you want or need, you're not likely to get it. Some folks can tell you what everyone around them wants or needs, and yet find it difficult to speak about what they want or need themselves. Try saying out loud, "I intend to spend the time and effort needed to learn how to do a Self-Encounter."

• After listening to your voices and having a meeting with your various parts, what are you — the Chairperson of the Board — going to do? It's easy to talk about what you want or need, but what will your *commitments* be? It's time to put your money where your mouth is and talk about your specific responsible behavior. Try putting your name in the commitment messages. That may help you take more responsibility to carry out your commitments to make Loving Choices. Saying "I am committed" out loud results in you feeling internal strength and more empowerment.

"I, (*your name*), am committed to do one Self-Encounter per day for the next week."

Feeling Words

LOVE	*JOY*	*ANGER*	*FEAR*
accepted	adventurous	alienated	aching
adequate	airy	angry	afraid
alive	alert	annoyed	anxious
amorous	at ease	anxious	bent down
appreciated	at home	betrayed	bleeding
attracted	blissful	bewildered	crushed
awake	bursting	bitter	dark
bright	cheerful	blamed	depressed
bubbly	contented	boiling	dismal
captivated	giddy	bothered	distressed
caring	dashing	boxed-in	down
charmed	delighted	burdened	fearful
clever	ecstatic	closed	fragmented
comfortable	elated	cold	frigid
compassionate	electrified	combative	gloomy
confident	excited	critical	grieved
cuddly	exhilarated	dejected	heartsick
enchanted	frisky	disgusted	hollow
enthused	funny	exasperated	horrible
fantastic	glad	fed-up	hurt
flirtatious	happy	frustrated	immobilized
fulfilled	humorous	furious	inadequate
gentle	jolly	grouchy	insecure
giving	joyful	grumpy	miserable
hopeful	jubilant	harassed	pained
intimate	lively	hateful	perturbed
loving	lustrous	heavy	scared
moved	mellow	hostile	suffering
passionate	merry	irritable	threatened
protective	peppy	irritated	trapped
romantic	playful	low	unhappy
sexual	sparkling	mad	upset
sympathetic	terrific	mean	uptight

Summary and Conclusion of the Self-Encounter

When you begin doing the Self-Encounter, you may discover that you have been using one or more of your parts most of the time, and using some of the other parts very rarely. Learning to use the Self-Encounter will help you become more well-rounded and balanced. It will encourage you to use *all* of your parts, instead of just one or two.

You also may learn something about yourself by doing the Self-Encounter. Maybe you will find that you have difficulty talking about and accessing your feelings. Perhaps you will learn that you have trouble identifying what you want or need. You might discover that you have trouble following through with responsible behavior and commitments. The Self-Encounter can assist you in becoming more balanced, internally *and* externally.

We have observed many people who use the Inner Critic as one of their primary voices. Many have not accessed their Wise Nurturer and have not nurtured themselves. Some have not learned to access their Inner Children, and some have not been able to access and share feelings.

What parts have you been accessing the most? What parts do you seldom access?

Are you aware of any *new topics* that you thought about as you were completing your Self-Encounter? Often the couple whose relationship is undergoing stress has not been talking about other unresolved issues in their relationship. It may be difficult to stick with the original topic. If you jump to a new topic, you may never complete the original topic. Make a quick note of a new topic that you became aware of while doing the Self-Encounter, then continue trying to reach closure on the original topic. When you have time, do another Self-Encounter on the new topic.

An example of a new topic from Mike's original encounter might be, "Learning to complete my homework on time."

What did you learn about yourself as you did your Self-Encounter? A valuable Self-Encounter often has new information that you had not thought about before. Take a minute to think about what you have learned about yourself, or any new information that emerged while doing the encounter.

Signing and Dating the Self-Encounter

Will signing your name motivate you to do a better job in completing the Self-Encounter? If you share this Self-Encounter with another person with whom you are in a relationship, a signed Self-Encounter will probably be more meaningful to them. Usually signing the Self-Encounter indicates more commitment and ownership of your thoughts, feelings, and behaviors.

It also is helpful to date the Self-Encounter. If you refer to it in the future, you will have a record of when you completed it.

Do You Resist Doing a Self-Encounter?

You may have a voice, or voices, that will resist learning how to do a Self-Encounter. Do you have a voice saying you feel confused? Is your Inner Critic telling you that you have to do it perfectly? Are you in a process of transition that leaves you feeling too over-whelmed to learn how to do a Self-Encounter? Do you rebel against anything that looks or feels like a "should"? Are you afraid of finding out something about yourself that you don't want to know? Do you really want to get to know yourself better? Do you have other activities that are more important than completing the encounter? If you are experiencing resistance, we suggest your first topic be, "My resistance to doing a Self-Encounter." It might be a way of learning more about yourself.

People don't often think about using the Self-Encounter to share a happy experience. Did you just experience a wonderful weekend, an exciting vacation, or some other beautiful experience that you want to share and describe? Doing a Self-Encounter and sharing it with another person is a great way of conveying your feelings. Try doing a "happy" Self-Encounter.

We have discovered that the journey into self is exciting, fulfilling and transforming. Changing challenges into Loving Choices is one of the greatest gifts you will ever give to yourself.

Completing a Self-Encounter

When you begin learning how to participate in a Self-Encounter, you may have some difficulty deciding in which section your statements belong. It may be helpful to jot down a list of ideas, phrases, and key words without worrying about where they fit, and then go back through your entire list and put your statements into the "proper" section of the Self-Encounter.

We strongly suggest that you write out your Self-Encounter when you are first learning how to use the model. Writing allows you to determine if you have weak or missing parts, and also allows you to set the Self-Encounter aside for a while, coming back later to review it. Eventually, when you are doing a two-way Healing Encounter, you may choose to share your written encounter with the other person.

As we said earlier, learning to use the Self-Encounter is a little like learning a foreign language. When you begin to think in that language, chances are you have mastered it. Practice doing the Self-Encounter until you can think in the language of the model. If you have a statement in mind, and then have to stop and think about which section it belongs in, you will find doing the Self-Encounter awkward. When you automatically know where the statement belongs, you will find using the Self-Encounter easy and comfortable. Many people discover they have internalized the encounter and do it automatically, without writing it down.

Changes in Your Speaking Voice

When you say your encounter out loud, your voice will often change as you go from part to part. For example, your Inner Children voices might be soft and little. Your Inner Critic voice may sound loud and critical. Other people listening to you may be more aware of the changes in your voice than you are.

Do You Have Other Inner Voices?

Yes! You have a number of parts or voices beyond what we have identified, including many *different* adaptive-survivor parts and Inner Children. We have only identified what we believe are the most common.

For example this book comes from what we call our "teacher part." It is different from the thoughts and feelings of the other parts we have identified. What other parts do *you* have that are important in your personality? Are they affecting your adult relationships? What parts do you identify with? What parts do you deny?

Our experience is that most people can heal by recognizing their many parts, embracing them, and integrating them into a whole person. Imagine yourself as a picture puzzle with many parts entitled "Who am I?" You have identified some of your parts and put them into the puzzle, but there are likely to be other parts you haven't integrated. Take a minute to get the big picture. Aren't you a sum of *all* of your parts? Could you call the total of all your parts consciousness? Awareness? Identity? Being?

You are *so much more* than your parts. The avenue to wholeness begins by becoming aware of all of these parts and roles. It's an ongoing life process. You're a special, unique human being, and Self-Encounters can help you bring your head and heart together so you'll get to know yourself better and progress rapidly on your journey to becoming a whole and balanced person.

HOW ARE YOU DOING?

Write a number for how many Self-Encounters you are committed to do this next week. _____

The following statements are designed to help you internalize and integrate the material in this chapter. Place a check mark beside the ones you have learned.

1. *I am able to differentiate between facts, thoughts and feelings.*

2. *I have determined which of the inner voices I have been using the most.*

3. *I have determined which of the inner voices I have not been using.*

4. *I am able to stay on a topic by identifying another topic when it emerges and by making a note of the new topic.*

5. *I am able to do a Self-Encounter without my Inner Critic telling me I am not doing it well enough.*

6. *I am committed to listen to my Inner Critic until it changes to "I-messages" and becomes a good internal parent.*

7. *I am able to see how important the Self-Encounter can be as I change my Challenges into Loving Choices.*

8. *I am practicing the second breathing and centering exercise in Appendix A of this book.*

The Self-Encounter Form

Follow this form while you complete your Self-Encounter. You may want to use an extra sheet of paper in order to have enough room to write. (Do not limit yourself to the examples given.)

My **topic** for this Self-Encounter is:

The **logical importance** of this topic for me is (1 through 10, with 10 being extremely important):

The **emotional charge** of this topic for me is (1 through 10, with 10 being highly emotionally charged):

My **motivation** for doing this Self-Encounter is (1-10, 10 being highly motivated):
Briefly explain your motivation or lack of motivation.

My **facts and observations** are: (Write "I saw _____," or "I heard _____," or "My observation is _____.")

My **thoughts or interpretations** are: (Write "I think _____," or "My interpretation is _____.")

My **body sensations** are: (Write "I am experiencing _____ in my _____," describing a specific part of your body.)

My **feelings** are: (Write "I feel _____," or "I felt _____ when _____," and explain your feelings.)

My **adaptive-survivors** are: (Over-responsible, under-responsible, perfectionist, people-pleaser, rebellious, intellectual, emotional, etc.)

My **Inner Critic** says: (Examples of "you" and "I" messages. "You should do it right." "You can do better." "You really are dumb and stupid." "You should know better." "I have the following suggestion for you to think about." "I want you to pay attention to what is happening.")

My **Inner Children** say: (Examples of Inner Children messages. "I feel scared and alone," (vulnerable child); "I hurt," (wounded child); "I believe in angels," (magical child); "I want to have fun," (playful child); "I like to draw and color," (creative child), etc.)

My **Wise Nurturer** says: (Be intuitive, creative, wise and nurturing.)

My **Intentions, Wants and Needs** are: (Be assertive)

My **Commitments and Actions to Make More Loving Choices** are: I, (*your name*), am committed to:

Summary and Conclusions:

What parts have I been using the most?

What parts do I need to use more often?

What did I learn about myself while doing this Self-Encounter?

What new topics came up while doing this Self-Encounter?

_____   _____

Sign your name here   Date

CHAPTER FIVE

The Repetitive Self-Encounter

GOING EMOTIONALLY DEEPER INTO YOURSELF

*The **challenge** is to learn the benefits of continuing
to do the Self-Encounter in order to go emotionally
deeper into yourself.*

*The **loving choice** is to be committed enough
to learn all you can about yourself from this
Self Therapist Repetitive Encounter.*

Sometimes after a self-encounter, you don't feel "finished." You may have a sense that you could learn more about yourself if you went a little deeper. Why not? It's possible to repeat a Self-Encounter — we call it a *Repetitive Self-Encounter*. In this chapter, we'll show you how to do it.

Take the Self-Encounter you've completed and determine if you can make any additions to it. Most likely the topic you started with has changed. The original topic is sometimes like a smoke screen, covering up the real topic. You don't have to follow the same order of accessing inner messages in the Repetitive Encounter, and you don't have to start with the facts or observations — unless they've changed significantly. You may also add a new message at any place in the Repetitive Encounter. However, it's still very important to do all ten parts.

Mike's Self-Encounter was explained in the last chapter. (You may want to review it.) He didn't learn as much about himself as he thought he could, so he decided to do a Repetitive Encounter. He was impressed with how much more he learned. Isn't it interesting the way a small topic can lead you to a deeper issue?

Here is his Repetitive Encounter, expanding upon his "Time Management" Self-Encounter.

Repetitive Encounter Number One

I thought about my original topic on time management, and decided I needed to expand the topic to include taking a look at my priorities.

My **topic** expanded to: *time management and my priorities.*
- My **logical importance** changed from 3 to 5.
- My **emotional charge** changed from 3 to 5.
- My **motivation** changed from 5 to 7, and I added that *I want to determine and define just what my priorities are.*

I added to my **facts:** *I was rushing around yesterday from 8:00 a.m. to 10:00 p.m. with no time off.*

I added to my **thoughts:** *I think setting priorities would help me manage my time better. I think I scheduled too many activities yesterday. I think this is a pattern for me. I think there are many other things I would like to do with my time.*

I added to my **body-sensations:** *I am experiencing tightness and heaviness in my head.*

I added to my **feelings:** *I feel frustrated at not being able to find time for IMPORTANT activities.*

I added to my **Adaptive-Survivors:** *My over responsible voice tells me to plan some more activities for tomorrow.*

I added to my **Inner Critic:** *You sure do have your priorities messed up. When are you going to get things right?*

I added to my **Inner Children:** *I feel scared. Who cares about priorities?*

I added to my **Wise Nurturer:** *I think you have the courage and strength to take a serious look at your priorities.*

I added to my **intentions, wants** and **needs:** *I want to make a list of my priorities and schedule my time to include doing those activities which are important to me.*

I added to my **commitments:** *I will spend one hour Tuesday evening setting up a regular, weekly schedule of activities that will include my top priorities.*

Summary and Conclusions: *I am learning more about myself. I think I need to continue doing this Repetitive Encounter.*

Repetitive Encounter Number Two

I became aware of an underlying issue and began my second Repetitive Encounter with some additions to my *thoughts: I think I avoid being left with unscheduled time. I think I am avoiding being alone with myself and thus I am avoiding getting to know myself better.*

The **topic** remained the same.

- The **logical importance** increased from 5 to 7.
- My **emotional charge** went to a 10.
- My **motivation** went from 7 to 8.

I added to my **facts:** *I observed that I seldom take time to be by myself.*

I added to my **body sensations:** *I am experiencing a knot in my stomach.*

I added to my **feelings:** *I feel afraid to access and talk about my feelings. I feel afraid to take a look at who I really am!*

I added to my **Adaptive-Survivors:** *My busy-holic part began shouting louder than ever that I needed to keep busy to avoid feeling emotional pain.*

I added to my **Inner Critic:** *You surely have blown it now. Why didn't you leave well enough alone?*

I added to my **Inner Children:** *You have kept so busy that I never get any attention. I never have felt lovable! Nobody ever listens to me. I feel sad, lonely, ignored, unimportant and disconnected from you.*

I added to my **Wise Nurturer** (nurturing my Inner Children): *Now is the time to let your feelings keep cooking so you will learn as much as you can about yourself. You are a special person. You will feel more and more loved when you feel listened to. You are lovable.*

I added to my **intentions, wants** and **needs:** *I want to spend more time alone and get to know myself better.*

I added to my **commitments:** *I will spend time alone each day. I am committed to taking time to listen to my Wise Nurturer and allow it to nurture my Inner Children more and more each day.*

Summary and Conclusions: *The Self-Encounter exercise can be very helpful in getting to know myself better.*

Repetitive Encounter Number Three

I began my third Repetitive Encounter with these additions to my *feelings: I felt healed and transformed after the Wise Nurturer talked to my Inner Children. I feel good when I spend some time alone with myself.*

My new **topic** is: *finding time alone so I can improve my feelings of self worth.*

- My **logical importance** decreased from 7 to 5.
- My **emotional charge** decreased from 10 to 3.
- My **motivation** to do more Repetitive Encounters increased to 10 because I am learning how I can do my own therapy.

I added to my **facts:** *I observed that I have spent only about one hour doing these four Repetitive Encounters.*

I added to my **thoughts:** *I think I received many messages when I was a kid that I was "not-okay," which contributed to my feelings of low self-worth. I think my busy-holic part began to grow and develop about the same time that I received those not-okay messages. I think I didn't feel very worthwhile if I didn't keep busy.*

I added to my **body sensations:** *I experienced a great weight being lifted from my head and shoulders after my Inner Children shared so many painful messages.*

I added to my **Adaptive-Survivors:** *I don't hear as many messages from my adaptive-survivors. Their job description was to protect the Inner Children from painful feelings. Now that the Inner Child is being listened to, my adaptive-survivors are not so much in control. I can still choose to access an adaptive-survivor voice if needed. For example, I may choose to be over-responsible when my parents are ill.*

I added to my tamed **Inner Critic** some helpful **internal parent** voices: *I suggest you continue to pursue this journey into yourself by doing more Repetitive Encounters.*

I added to my **Inner Children:** *It feels so good to be seen, heard and felt. Thanks. Now can we go out and play?*

I added to my **Wise Nurturer:** *It is never too late to have a happy childhood.*

I added to my **intentions, wants** and **needs:** *I want to continue to improve my feelings of self-worth by allowing my Wise Nurturer to nurture my Inner Children. I intend to do more Repetitive Encounters in the future.*

I added to my **commitments:** *I will make a list of 20 things I like about myself and post them in a prominent place where I can read them until I believe them. I will do an affirmation in my car on my way to work every morning. I will stop beating myself up emotionally for not learning to manage my time better.*

Summary and Conclusions: *I can expand the Self-Encounter exercise into Repetitive Encounters. I can heal myself by improving my feelings of self-worth through using the Repetitive Encounter.*

Discussion of the Repetitive Self-Encounter

Did you notice how the logical importance, emotional charge, and motivation went up and down? It is typical and desirable for the numbers to start low, increase as you do the encounters, and then diminish again as you begin to reach closure and healing.

Take time to go into yourself. Did you notice any changes in how you felt as you read the Repetitive Encounters? Did your body sensations change? Did your internal numbers for logical importance and emotional charge go up and down along with Mike's numbers with each encounter?

Did you notice how the topic changed? As Mike went into the topic, he was able to get to a deeper level and discover the real issue was self-worth, not time management. This deepening of the topic is typical and happens often in a Repetitive Encounter.

Did you do an internal encounter as you read Mike's? Did his encounter relate to you in any way? What feelings might you have if you did a Repetitive Encounter looking at one of your adaptive-survivor parts? What would you call Mike's adaptive-survivor part that kept him busy so he wouldn't feel the pain of low self-worth? Do you have a similar adaptive-survivor part? We have found that many people keep busy so they won't feel any pain from their Inner Children.

The Repetitive Encounter does a good job of explaining the healing that can take place as you access your Inner Children. Mike's Inner Children had not been listened to, and they had "stuffed" all of their pain. When Mike slowed down and spent some time with himself, he was finally able to listen to his Inner Children. It is important to point out that when the Wise Nurturer supported the Inner Children after the Inner Children had shared their pain, more healing took place. Are you aware that talking about your pain is healing, and that being affirmed by your Wise Nurturer continues the healing? Mike's Encounter shows how you can learn to heal and nurture yourself, instead of expecting other people to do it.

Notice how interconnected the various parts are. As the Inner Children share feelings, the body sensations change, the adaptive-survivor relaxes its protection of the Inner Children, and the Inner Critic begins transforming itself into a good internal parent. All of the parts act as a system. When one part changes, it affects the rest of the system.

The Repetitive Encounter is a step towards the *Internal Family Conversation,* as explained in the next chapter. These "family conversations" between your different parts — as you have seen in the Repetitive Encounter — can be helpful and effective. We support and encourage you to do your own Repetitive Encounters. The rewards of going deeper into yourself can be immense.

How Are You Doing?

The following statements are designed to help you internalize and integrate the material in this chapter. (Place a check next to the ones you feel you've mastered.)

Number of Repetitive Encounters I am committed to doing this next week: _____

1. *I am able to continue accessing various messages and voices until I feel complete with Repetitive Encounters.*

2. *I am able to heal and experience personal growth by doing the Repetitive Encounter.*

3. *I have identified which of my voices I access the most.*

4. *I have identified which of my voices I need to access more.*

5. *I am learning to access all of my various internal messages so that I can find more balance in my life.*

6. *I am learning to identify when my topic needs to be changed or altered as I complete the Repetitive Encounter.*

7. *I am learning to let my Inner Children and my feeling parts talk long enough to heal and transform.*

8. *I am learning to nurture my other parts with my Wise Nurturer.*

CHAPTER SIX

Conversations with Your Internal Family

ASSISTING YOU WITH INNER PEACE

*The **challenge** is to discover your Internal Family.*

*The **loving choice is** to learn how to dialogue between your Inner Critic, Inner Children, Wise Nurturer and Adaptive-survivor Parts. This will result in creating a healthy and nurturing Internal Family to assist you in experiencing inner peace.*

*Y*ou may not be aware that you have already been having Internal Family Conversations! If you are able to under stand what you have been doing, you can use it as a process that will allow you more integration and assist in healing.

Instead of each part talking once, as in the Self-Encounter, we suggest you have a conversation among the various parts. Allow each part to talk whenever you hear that particular voice. You will know you are finished with your Internal Family Conversation when you experience a feeling of inner peace.

The First Phase of the Conversation

You might have already had a two-member Internal Family Conversation between your Inner Critic and one of your Adaptive-Survivor parts. Your adaptive-survivor learned that part of its job description was to protect your Inner Children.

Imagine each of your inner-message parts sitting in a chair. Arrange them to represent the way they have been interacting. From

Mike's Self-Encounter, we can speculate that he had an Internal Family Conversation that looks like this illustration.

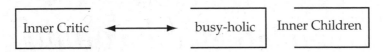

His adaptive-survivor part could be called "busy-holic" because he kept busy so his Inner Children would not have to feel pain. Mike started this dialogue in his adolescence, while he was still living at home. The busy-holic part came about so he would feel less criticized. Notice how the adaptive-survivor part is sitting in front of the Inner Children, protecting against the Inner Critic.

The conversation might go like this. The Inner Critic says: *You are wasting your time reading comic books all of the time. You should learn an occupation so you can survive as an adult. You should do something that makes you a better person.*

The busy-holic responds by finding things to do to keep Mike busy so the Inner Critic will be less critical. It knows the vulnerable Inner Children are feeling hurt and criticized by what they hear from the Inner Critic. Keeping busy keeps the children from feeling hurt and wounded. The busy-holic might say: *Let's make sure you keep busy this week. The mean old Inner Critic has been nagging you about spending too much time with your comic books. You'll feel restless and uneasy if you don't keep busy. Go clean your room. Maybe that will keep him off your back.*

Mike's Inner Critic might come back with: *What does cleaning your room have to do with planning a career? You should be doing something more worthwhile. You just keep busy so you don't have time to decide what you want to do with the rest of your life.*

Have you had a similar internal conversation between your Inner Critic and one of your adaptive-survivor parts? Take some time for reflection in the next few days to determine if you have been doing this kind of Internal Family Conversation.

This two-part dialogue probably caused Mike a great deal of grief. He had to keep busy in order to tune out the internal war.

The Second Phase of the Conversation

Mike has started doing Self-Encounters. His Wise Nurturer has begun nurturing his Inner Children. It feels so good that he wants to continue. He realizes he can add the Wise Nurturer to the internal dialogue. He has named his Wise Nurturer "Gramps" after his grandfather. The interaction might look like this.

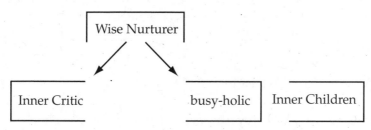

Gramps might say to the busy-holic adaptive-survivor part: *You have done a great job of protecting little Mikey. I appreciate you keeping him from feeling too much pain when he was little. He couldn't protect himself at that time. Of all the adaptive-survivor parts that could protect little Mikey, you were probably the best one for the job.*

However, Mikey doesn't need you to protect him in the same way now. He is ready to grow up and learn to meet his own needs for love and attention. I want to give you a new job description. When Mike has homework due for next week, you can help motivate him to do it when he is feeling confident and ready to learn more about himself.

Gramps might say to the Inner Critic part: *You were right about Mikey needing to prepare for a career. Planning and preparing for a career would have been very helpful for him. As long as you were placing expectations on him, his father would lay off and not be so judgmental and critical of Mikey. You did a good job!*

Now he is learning to actively search for what he wants to do with his life. He doesn't need your "you" messages at this time. Maybe you could learn to give him some "I" messages to support and motivate him on this difficult journey of discovering himself.

Notice the Wise Nurturer is not nurturing the Inner Children, but is nurturing the adaptive-survivor part and the Inner Critic. As both of them feel listened to, accepted and nurtured, they relax and the adaptive-survivor lets go of protecting the Inner Children. The Wise Nurturer is able to nurture the Inner Children without the busy-holic part protecting and being in the way. The interaction may look like this.

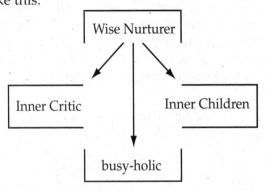

This will most likely be the type of interaction you choose when you start conversing with your internal family. The four chairs will allow each of your parts to be heard. This also allows the Wise Nurturer to nurture the other three parts. You should feel the healing and experience more inner peace than you have in the past.

Gramps may now be able to say to little Mikey: *"Many times you did not understand that your father only wanted the best for you. Criticizing you was the only way he could show you love. You may not have thought about how little nurturing he got when he was young. He often was saying the same things to you that his father said to him. He thought that was how fathers talked to their sons.*

Your busy-holic part came in to protect you from your father's criticism. It seemed to understand that you needed some assistance at that time. Keeping busy was sure better than other types of coping strategies you could have chosen. Using drugs, dropping out and doing nothing, or becoming angry and rebellious would have been some other choices.

Now you are ready to heal the old wounds. You will find your Inner Critic and busy-holic part are much better friends than you formerly realized. Keep on growing and learning to meet your needs.

There is one more phase that many of you may learn if you continue practicing the Internal Family Conversation.

The Third Phase of the Conversation

You now have flexibility and can make choices concerning the type of Internal Family Conversations you wish to create. You are able to make a Loving Choice about which of the four parts you want to use in the interaction. Typically the following interaction occurs.

The Inner Children access, feel, and share any painful or wounded feelings they have been denying. Usually this is childhood pain of some sort from being wounded, abused, or overly frustrated while young. The Wise Nurturer gives the children any guidance, direction, support, affirmation, or love they need.

It is usually not an intellectual decision for the Inner Critic and adaptive-survivor parts to withdraw. They seem to have a sense that the Inner Children are having their needs met and they can stop acting as protectors.

Little Mikey might talk like this: *I had so many feelings of worthlessness when I was a child. It seemed like no matter what I did, it wasn't enough for my father. I felt so inadequate. It helped to keep busy so I could avoid feeling worthless. Many times I just wanted to cry, but that would have made things worse.*

Gramps says loudly and lovingly: *It's okay to cry. Tears can wash away some of the old feelings of not being enough for your father. I commend you for being strong enough to choose to cook your feelings so they can alter and transform.*

Mikey says: *You are saying things to me that I wish someone had said to me when I was young. It feels so good to discover that someone understands and accepts me, even when I am feeling worthless and inferior.*

I believed that when my father did not say loving things, I would never hear anyone say them to me. I thought keeping busy was the only way to keep from feeling the pain. Now I am amazed that you understand me and are able to nurture me. Thanks, Gramps.

It is interesting to note that when Mike completes the internal dialogue and is beginning to feel more inner peace and contentment, his close friends also became aware of it. Perhaps you also felt the inner peace that Mike was feeling.

At this point Mike has begun to heal his Inner Children and let go of being busy as a way of avoiding painful feelings. He can make Loving Choices about how busy he wants to be, instead of having to be busy to protect his Inner Children. He has made some peace with his external father. It is a beautiful healing process.

Our wise nurturing part says you can do the same healing process that Mike did. It's up to you to decide if you want to.

Naming Your Family

It may be helpful to name each member of your internal family, and can allow the dialogue to flow more smoothly. You can call each part by its name, which tends to make it feel acknowledged just as you are acknowledged by your own name. When you call it by name, it responds. The Inner Children names you select are often names you were called when you were little. For example, Mike reported that he was called "Mikey" when he was little. Ask your little child when you are conversing what it likes to be called. It will usually tell you. Remember that there are a number of Inner Children and they all may want their own special name. Be aware, however, that naming your parts may become limiting. Sometimes the names will change as your grow in your process.

Can you think of a person who reminds you of your Inner Critic? You might name your Inner Critic after an ancestor — maybe your mother or father. One woman's critical significant person was her maternal grandmother, so she called her Inner Critic "Screaming Grammy."

Naming the Wise Nurturer is important. Can you think of a person to whom you were connected emotionally as a child? A person who nurtured you and made you feel important? A person who taught you about unconditional love? You have probably known at least one person like this. You may have had a role model you looked up to such as a minister, priest, rabbi, teacher, or coach. Maybe you want to name your Wise Nurturer after this person who was nurturing in your childhood. Don't worry if you can't think of a name at first. It will come to you when the time is right.

Creating a Healthy Internal Family

When you were a child, your parents were responsible for nurturing and helping you meet your needs. Sometimes your parents were able to give you the support and love you needed. At other times, they were not able to meet your needs for a variety of reasons. If your parents weren't able to meet your needs, you may have experienced some hurt and pain. Adults often carry that childhood pain around in their Inner Children parts, affecting their adult relationships.

It's common to treat your Inner Children the way you were treated by the significant adults in your childhood. If you were taught that kids should be seen but not heard, you probably have not listened to your Inner Children. If you were told to shut up and stop crying, then you might not comfort your Inner Children when they are sad. If you were abused as a child, you're likely to abuse your wounded child. If your Inner Children did not emotionally bond and attach with a significant adult, you may have trouble emotionally connecting and bonding with your Inner Children.

You may expect your love partner, close friends, or even children to meet those needs which your parents were unable to meet for you. Adult relationships are often formed in an attempt to complete your unfinished growth from childhood. It is important to be aware of this process.

When you fall in love, you may be attracted to someone who gives you what you didn't receive as a child. New lovers say, "I've never been loved like this before!" It may be true that your Inner Children have never been loved in this way. The Inner Child says, "Wow! I finally have the support I've always needed. Don't let it go." You cling to this other person because you don't want to lose this love and support which you have longed for since you were a small child. It feels so good, you want it to last forever. This results in giving your power away by believing someone else is responsible for your happiness. You feel loved as long as the other person is loving you. What happens if the other person leaves through death or divorce?

It is helpful to develop your internal family so you can learn to love yourself. It is healthy to let go of expecting others to do things for you that you can do for yourself. The internal family is a form of intra-dependency — depending upon yourself. The key is finding a balance between your head and your heart, both internally and externally.

When we were teaching the Internal Family Conversation, Sam expressed his apprehension about doing it. We asked him to talk about it. He said, "The Self-Encounter was easy. It was like a committee meeting with each committee member saying a few words as they went around the table. I could remain in my linear, intellectual left brain and keep it logical. Now you are asking my parts to sit in three or four chairs facing each other and have a conversation. That means my parts will have to face each other without a table or anything to hide behind. It is a free-flow interaction with very little structure. I want to learn how to do it, but it seems like it will take much more courage than doing a Self-Encounter."

We agreed that it is a big step going from the Self-Encounter to the Internal Family Conversation. However, we believe that you will find doing the Internal Family Conversation very healing and worth the effort. We have heard many say that it is much easier to practice the Internal Family Conversation than they first thought it would be.

A List of Adaptive-Survivor Parts

It may be helpful for you to hear about other adaptive-survivor parts that protect Inner Children. Ed, an engineer, had a mechanical solution for everything. He used this technique to avoid any Inner Child pain. Ginny had an angry adaptive-survivor part, which developed from her childhood abuse. The angry part kept everyone emotionally distant from her Inner Children. The sad part is that it kept her Wise Nurturer distant also. Gary, the therapist, had an "other-centered adaptive-survivor" that kept attention on someone else, while avoiding giving any attention to his Inner Children. Dora, "the doormat," had an adaptive-survivor that allowed everyone to wipe their feet on her. In this way she was able to hide her scared little girl inside. Don had so much denial that his adaptive-survivor looked like a big wall between his Inner Children and Wise Nurturer.

Can you identify some of your adaptive-survivor parts that have kept your Inner Children isolated and lonely while protecting them? Can you do some Internal Family Conversations to help bring more balance and harmony into your life?

The Inner Critic Finds Renewed Vigor

We have found that when people make some important changes and do some healing and transforming, the Inner Critic can rise up with renewed vigor. It can be disconcerting to think you have it tamed, only to discover it is still attacking you. This critic has at least as much strength — and maybe more — than it had when you first started your process.

There are many possible explanations for an uprising. When an animal is cornered, it attacks because it is feeling fearful. Sometimes the Inner Critic is afraid it is being exterminated, or is not needed anymore. This leads to a Loving Choice for you to consider: *Nurture the Inner Critic and reassure it that it is not being exterminated.* It has a new job description and is needed just as much now as it ever was.

As you access your Inner Children, you become more vulnerable, causing the Inner Critic to become more protective. The Loving Choice is to keep creating and developing broader and more effective boundaries as you become more vulnerable.

It seems the Inner Critic likes the attention it is getting. Maybe it is becoming more critical in order to get more attention? You may not want to nurture it because it is becoming too obnoxious. It is a Loving Choice to *keep nurturing it,* rather than ignoring it is because you feel it is too critical.

While you are gaining more confidence and emotional strength, it is possible to delve deeper into yourself. Each time you delve a little deeper, you find more of the dark side of the Inner Critic waiting to be transformed and healed. You might find that at about six to eight weeks into this process, your relationship seems to have more stress than before you started Loving Choices. *It is helpful to note that your extra stress is a result of increased emotional strength; you are not back to square one of your process.*

Sharing Your Conversation with Another Person

When you feel ready, you may want to have an Internal Family Conversation while another person is observing. It is a chance for your partner, or anyone you feel safe with, to get to know you better. Many individuals have found this to be another experience in intimacy and healing. Sometimes this sharing will be a valuable step before you begin doing Healing Encounters with another person.

The observing person can often help if you find yourself stuck and not able to hear another voice. They might be able to ask a question or make a comment that will help keep the conversation going. *A word of caution to the observer:* It is easy to come from *your own thoughts and feelings*, which may be detrimental — and confusing — to the other person. Remain as detached and objective as possible. Stay with the other person by actively listening, instead of offering suggestions or advice.

A Variation on the Internal Family

We've learned to respect how much wisdom the Wise Nurturer has. It will choose many different ways to interact with the internal family in order to help in the healing process. For example, Glen had a very demanding, disapproving, and condemning Inner Critic — an echo of his father. This voice led him to develop an achieving adaptive-survivor in an attempt to please the Inner Critic and his father. Glen went to Vietnam as a pilot and returned home with many decorations and ribbons. He showed them to his father, finally expecting to feel accepted and affirmed, but his father simply said, "If you had done a good job, your co-pilot would not have been killed."

When Glen talked with his internal family, his Wise Nurturer emerged as a powerful force of love. It met the Inner Critic nose-to-nose and toe-to-toe in a two-way dialogue. During this Internal Family Conversation, the Inner Children remained silent.

Some observers began to wonder why the Nurturer was not nurturing the Inner Children. Gradually it became apparent that the Nurturer was doing exactly what the Inner Children needed. It met the Inner Critic head-on, which prevented the Inner Critic from inflicting more hurt on the Inner Children. After it had met the Inner Critic with love, the Inner Critic began to transform and let go of its criticism. Glen realized that his Wise Nurturer had given the echo of his father more nurturing than his father had ever received in his whole lifetime!

We have learned how versatile the Wise Nurturer is. It will find creative ways of healing you that you may have never thought about.

Conclusion

We invite you to learn and practice the Internal Family Conversation. You can give to yourself all of the love and nurturing that you thought others would — or should — have to give you. You can overcome co-dependency and let go of your expectations for others to heal you. It truly is never too late to have a happy childhood!

HOW ARE YOU DOING?

Place a check mark after the following statements to indicate you are ready to move on.

1. *Write a number for how many Internal Family Conversations I am committed to do this next week.*

2. *I understand how my Inner Critic, Inner Children and Wise Nurturer can interact and converse between themselves.*

3. *I understand how my adaptive-survivor parts were created to protect my Inner Children.*

4. *I have identified which of my adaptive-survivor parts have been interacting with my Inner Critic in the past.*

5. *I am naming my various parts so that I can converse between them more easily.*

6. *I am finding that naming my inner parts makes them feel more accepted and listened to.*

7. *I am making a Loving Choice to access my Wise Nurturer so it can heal my other parts.*

8. *I am willing to let my Wise Nurturer play whatever role it needs to in order to help me heal myself.*

9. *I am thinking about the ways my Inner Children were hurt and wounded during my formative years.*

10. *I am becoming aware of the many different Inner Children I have within me.*

11. *I believe I can heal myself by doing the internal family exercise.*

12. *I am willing to let go of expecting others to love me in a way that my family of origin did not.*

13. *I believe it is never too late to have a happy childhood.*

CHAPTER SEVEN

The Healing Encounter

USING THE SELF-ENCOUNTER TO COMMUNICATE WITH OTHERS

*The **challenge** is to learn to communicate effectively with another person using the Self-Encounter.*

*The **loving choice** is to practice doing an "initiator encounter" and a "respondent encounter" until both people are proficient at using the communication tool.*

*M*ike was so excited about his growth and insights that he wanted to share his experience with his partner, Judy. He decided to try a *Healing Encounter* — basically an *initiator encounter* and a *respondent encounter*, each following the same format as the Self-Encounter we've discussed in chapters 4 and 5. In this chapter, we'll take a look at the elements of the Healing Encounter, beginning with an example of an initiator encounter.

Mike's Initiator Encounter

- My **topic or issue** is *sharing my exciting personal growth with Judy.*
- My **logical importance** is a 10.
- My **emotional charge** is an 8.
- My **motivation** is an 8 because I want to talk about my growth as a way of gaining a better perspective on what happened.

Judy actively listens and gives feedback of what she has heard so far. This lets Mike know he has been heard, and lets Judy know she has heard the topic correctly.

I hear your topic is telling me about your personal growth experiences of the last week. The importance is a 10; the emotional charge is an 8; and your motivation is an 8 because it would be helpful to discuss this experience with me so you can gain a better perspective.

Mike replies that Judy has heard him correctly and that it feels good to be understood. He now continues his initiator encounter without interruption from Judy.

My **facts and observations** are:

- I first did a Self-Encounter about doing my homework at the last minute on the way to class.
- I did a repetitive encounter and changed the topic to the way I keep busy so I won't feel worthless.
- I next did an Internal Family Conversation, which helped me heal my Inner Children. The end result of this was to be able to nurture and heal my Inner Children, instead of having to be busy all of the time.

My **thoughts and interpretations** are:

- I think these communication tools really do work for me.
- I think I was able to solve some of my emotional issues without seeing a therapist.
- I think I will have greater freedom to better manage my time because I won't have to stay busy to avoid feeling painful childhood feelings.
- I think the changes I have made are permanent and long-lasting.

My **body sensations** are:

- experience less tension in my neck and shoulders.
- experience more energy, and my body feels much lighter.

My **feelings** are:

- feel excited about the growth I have been able to accomplish.
- feel joyful and happy.
- feel more loving towards Judy.

My **Adaptive-Survivors** are:
- Much less powerful and controlling. My busy-holic isn't driving my "personality car" anymore. I can make a Loving Choice about what part of me is out and talking.

My **Inner Critic** says more "I-messages" now.
I suggest you keep doing Self-Encounters and Internal Family Conversations so you don't fall back into your old patterns.

My **Inner Child Mikey** says:
I like having Mike spend more time with me instead of being so busy all of the time. I feel loved and cared for.

My other **Inner Children** say:
We feel scared and shy. Everything is so different. We're not used to being seen. We also feel relieved; we've been waiting for a long time in this closet.

My **Wise Nurturer Gramps** says:
I congratulate you on having the strength and courage to take this journey into knowing yourself better.

My **wants, needs and intentions** are:
- I intend to do more encounters and internal dialogues to resolve some of my other issues.
- I want to share my written encounters and dialogues with you, Judy.
- I want Judy to learn how to use these communication tools if she is interested.

My **commitments** are:
- I am committed to doing more Healing Encounters with Judy.
- I am committed to doing at least three Self-Encounters each week.
- I am committed to continue my personal growth process.
- I feel finished with my initiator encounter. I would like to hear your responses to my encounter, Judy.

(We suggest you not do the summary and conclusions listed on the Self-Encounter form. It can interfere with the flow of the Healing Encounter.)

Judy affirms Mike by saying: *I want to thank you for sharing this important experience with me. I think you did a great job with your encounter.*

Judy now does a respondent encounter without any interruptions from Mike.

Judy's Respondent Encounter

I want to refer to your written encounter, Mike. May I borrow it? (Mike agrees to share it.)

My **topic** is *my response to your sharing your recent personal growth experience with me.*

- My **logical importance** is an 8.
- My **emotional charge** is a 3.
- My **motivation** is a 10 because I want us to grow together instead of you outgrowing me.

My **facts and observations** are:
I heard you say you did three different communication exercises.

My **thoughts and interpretations** are:

- I think I can be more comfortable with you when you are calmer and less emotionally scattered than you were two weeks ago.
- I think I would like to experience more calmness by doing my own personal growth work.
- I think it is important to our happiness for both of us to do this work.
- I think our relationship will be stronger and deeper as we continue doing this emotional work.

My **body sensations** are:

- My heart feels open.
- My face feels warm.
- I experience my palms being sweaty.

My **feelings** are:

- I feel joyful and excited about our personal and relationship growth.
- I feel somewhat threatened that you might outgrow me.

My **Adaptive-Survivors** say:

- My caretaker part says I am glad you are managing your

time better so I don't have to keep after you to get your homework done on time.

- My caretaker is concerned about whether you will need me as much now that you have become more independent.

My **Inner Critic** says:
You should be doing encounters on why you are so often late for appointments.

My **Inner Children** say:

- I want to play with Mikey!
- I feel warm and cuddly and all soft inside.

My **Wise Nurturer** says:
Judy, you don't have to feel threatened by Mike's growth. You are doing a good job learning about the Self-Encounters.

My **wants, needs and intentions** are to learn how to do more encounters and internal conversations.

My **commitments** are to set aside thirty minutes a day, three times a week, to learn how to do the communication exercises better. I am also committed to listening to Mike share his encounters and conversations with me.

Free-flow time for questions and clarifications.
Mike, you stated you did some healing of your Inner Child with the internal family. I would like to know what that healing was like for you.

Mike replies: *I remembered many times that my father was critical of me. I realized I felt "not okay" in many areas. My healing consisted of learning to nurture myself with my Wise Nurturer.*

Mike asks Judy for a **change in behavior,** knowing that it is okay for Judy to agree or not to agree to the request. *Judy, I would like you to spend more time this week doing Self-Encounters instead of spending so much time writing in your journal.* Judy agrees with the change of behavior for the next week.

Mike states that he is feeling **closure**. He asks Judy if she is. She also feels finished with this topic. It is understood by both that they will spend time talking and sharing encounters this next week. They are feeling emotionally close and spontaneously hug each other.

Discussion of the Healing Encounter

Maybe the Healing Encounter felt strange to you. It is an unusual form of conversation. Do you fear that your partner might not agree to take part? Do you fear revealing your feelings in such a direct way? Can you see how the Healing Encounter might benefit you and your relationship?

It is common for those observing or reading encounters to be doing an encounter internally. Did you do an internal encounter of some sort while reading Mike and Judy's? Perhaps you want to make a date with yourself to put it down on paper.

The initiator of the Healing Encounter — Mike, in our example — has spent time writing down his part before sharing it with the other person. The respondent — Judy — has to respond spontaneously. This can be challenging until you have become proficient at doing Self-Encounters. Healing Encounters are simple if both parties have done several Self-Encounters.

Structure of the Healing Encounter — Step-by-Step

Step 1: Do the initiator encounter by yourself (as a Self-Encounter), without involving the other person. You don't even need to share with the other person that you are doing it. Often, the problem you thought would not be solved until the *other person* changed is resolved when you are able to work through *your own* internal conflict.

Your topic may have changed as you completed your Self-Encounter, which is one reason you do your Self-Encounter first. Have you ever tried to resolve an issue with another person when you weren't clear what the issue was? It probably ended up as unproductive communication; you were not talking about the issue you needed to talk about. You can see that there are many advantages to doing the Self-Encounter first.

Step 2: As the initiator, make an appointment with the respondent to share the initiator encounter. You'll want to allow at least an hour to complete most encounters. The communication should be a time without interruptions from telephones, doorbells, and kids. Good communication between the two of you is your top priority.

There is an important challenge for the initiator concerning the topic to be shared with the respondent. You can share the topic either when you ask for an appointment or when you share your Initiator Encounter. Sometimes it is better to share the topic at the time of making the appointment, so the respondent can be thinking about it. Sometimes it is better to wait until the appointed time to share the topic, because sharing it may result in such an emotional response from the respondent that the Healing Encounter will start right away. The decision as to when to share the topic becomes easier after you have more experience with Healing Encounters. Here are a couple of examples on how to share the topic.

- "I would like to share with you my Self-Encounter this evening at 9:00 o'clock after the kids are in bed. Would that be a good time for you? I don't want to share the topic with you at this time."
- "I would like to share with you my Self-Encounter about going to the party Friday night. Would this be a good time to do it?"

Step 3: The initiator shares her encounter without interruption.

Sometimes the initiator needs to make sure the other person is really hearing what she is saying, and will therefore request that the respondent encounter be focused completely on *active listening.* Sometimes she is more interested in hearing the respondent's *feelings.* Most people find it valuable to respond with a balance of active listening and sharing feelings.

An example of a request for an active listening response would be: "I often feel that you do not hear me when I talk to you. I need you to actively listen and repeat back to me what you are *hearing* me say." An example of a request for sharing feelings: "I have usually felt heard by you so I don't need you to show me you're actively listening. Instead, I want to know what your *reaction* is to my topic and my initiator encounter. Please respond to my Self-Encounter with your honest feelings."

Step 4: The respondent affirms the initiator's Self-Encounter. A healthy relationship includes more affirmations than you may be accustomed to giving. The initiator has spent time and effort on doing the Self-Encounter. It is appropriate for the respondent to acknowledge the work done by the initiator.

Step 5: The respondent shares his respondent encounter response, again, *without interruption.*

Step 6: This is the free-flow time. After the foundation of good communication has been laid by both parties, talking from all of your parts with Self-Encounters, the next step is to ask questions of each other, and respond to any statements that need clarification. The two of you do not need to follow the form for the Self-Encounter, but instead you can talk from whatever part you choose. It may still be helpful to identify a statement such as, "I'm aware of another feeling. I felt good when you said you wanted to go to the party with me."

The goal of the Healing Encounter is for each party to find ways to better understand the other, to offer new solutions to the topic, and to keep learning from the other relationship teacher. A Healing Encounter is not designed for one person to win and the other to lose — which may have been your pattern of communication in the past. Rather, it is a chance for both of you to win by increasing intimacy and emotional closeness, and providing new information, new solutions, and joint agreements for future behavior or actions.

Step 7 is to ask for a change in behavior, either in the initiator or the respondent. Asking for change in the other person is permitted, and the other person has the right to agree or not agree to the change. In a relationship, one person may try to get the other to change, or may manipulate and control the other person in an attempt to bring about change. Why not ask openly for change, and communicate more honestly? Put your cards on the table and let the other person know what you would like to have changed!

Time-Out!

Sometimes it is appropriate for one or both parties to take a *time-out* during a Healing Encounter. You may be overwhelmed by new information, become emotionally and physically tired, or need a drink or a bathroom break. One or both of you may have become angry or hurt, or need to be alone for a while. We encourage you, as part of your Healing Encounter, to call for a time-out if needed. Using the sports signal of making a "T" with your hands is an effective way to call a time-out.

A time-out is not a cop-out. The person calling for a time-out is expected to make a commitment for a time to continue. It might be ten minutes or it might not be until another day. "I am feeling very angry right now. I don't want to use 'you' messages, so I will need a ten-minute time-out to cool down emotionally." Another example:

"I feel emotionally drained and need time to recuperate. I would like to commit to finishing this encounter tomorrow evening after we have the children in bed. Is that okay with you?"

When a time-out is called, you may find it beneficial to do another Self-Encounter before finishing the two-way encounter. The initiator may choose to do a Repetitive Self-Encounter on the same topic. The respondent may choose to do a solo Self-Encounter on the topic before doing a respondent encounter.

It's Not Over Till It's Over

Hopefully the two of you can reach closure with the Healing Encounter. Feeling "finished," solving the problem, reaching a compromise, or beginning to feel intimate are signs of closure. A different kind of closure occurs when the two of you "agree to disagree."

Occasionally one person will feel closure and the other won't. There are several options at this point, such as:

- continuing the free-flow time until both of you feel closure.

- expressing as many feelings as you can until you both reach closure.

- commitment by the person who doesn't feel closure to doing another Self-Encounter on a topic such as, "I want to understand why I don't feel closure." (It may be that both parties need to do another Self-Encounter.)

It is important to reach closure if possible. Many couples will be pleasantly surprised to reach closure if they haven't been able to resolve an issue in the past.

It is preferable that one party takes ownership for feeling closure. For example: "I feel closure," or, "I feel finished. How about you?" It is better to state *your* position first, instead of saying, "Are *you* feeling closure?" Asking the other person to take a stand before you do is poor communication.

An interesting paradox often occurs at this point. Many times closure results in a profound "opening" of a whole new area to explore and discover. This is a very beautiful occurrence, and can further continue the healing process. We suggest that you recognize this and then make the choice as to how much longer you will communicate at this time. You may want to identify new topics and do another solo Self-Encounter first.

Other Helpful Hints

The Healing Encounter is simple — there are very few rules — and easy to learn. Practicing the Self-Encounter is the best preparation for the Healing Encounter. The rule of doing the entire Self-Encounter without interruption is important. If you interrupt each other, it will be difficult to reach closure and communication might begin to resemble your old pattern of relating.

Audio- or Videotaping of the Encounter

Recording the Healing Encounter, either with an audio or video recorder, can be very helpful. It allows the participants to hear and see themselves, and to learn from and critique their own encounter. If the encounter has not been healing, and one or both of you feel wounded and hurt, it is valuable to listen to the tape to understand how the hurt occurred. Sometimes the person who has been hurtful does not realize how they were hurtful until they listen to the tape. Many people are surprised at how they sound on tape.

Ken and Jeanette felt hurt and wounded after their first Healing Encounter. They recorded it and chose to play it back a day or two later while rubbing each other's feet. They learned they had not been listening to each other because they were feeling so much hurt and pain. It was a positive learning experience for them to listen to the tape. They were actually doing a second encounter when they listened to the tape. In their third encounter they were able to really listen and hear each other; it truly became a "healing" encounter.

Sharing Written or Taped Encounters

Some couples, especially those in a power struggle, will have difficulty presenting an entire Self-Encounter without interrupting each other. In these situations, it may help to make an audio or video recording of the Self-Encounter, and then share the tape with the other person. The respondent may also choose to do the respondent encounter on tape. You can also write a Self-Encounter and share the written encounter with your partner. Writing or taping the encounter eliminates interruptions and allows the couple to develop new patterns of interaction, instead of continuing the old power struggle type of interaction. Eventually, however, your goal is to develop direct, face-to-face communication.

One Initiator Only

Sometimes *both* parties will do an *initiator* Self-Encounter and then attempt to do a joint Healing Encounter. This is difficult to do and requires more skill and persistence in reaching closure. Two initiators complicates the Healing Encounter and limits the couple's ability to listen to each other. We suggest there be only one initiator, especially when you are learning to do a Healing Encounter.

Overcoming Deadlock

Sometimes you'll find you get to a "stuck place," where you don't know how to reach closure with the encounter. Here is a simple suggestion that may be helpful: *stand up behind your chairs.* Discuss from this vantage point what is going on with each of you. Talk about yourself and share your motives, feelings, and hidden agendas that you have not shared with your partner. It may be very helpful to access your Wise Nurturer at this point.

You may have reached a stuck place where you both want your own way. The initiator says, "I feel angry because you always get your way." The respondent says, "I have gone to the movie you've chosen for the last three times. This time I am going to the movie *I* choose."

Time for both to stand up. Now the initiator says, "I think what I am doing when I am being stubborn in the chair is acting like a teenager, arguing with my parents. They treated me as though I were still very immature. I felt capable of making up my mind without them telling me what to do. I don't want you to tell me what to do like they did."

The respondent answers: "I think my stubbornness is similar. I am the laid-back one who is always agreeable to what you want to do. I reached my limit and this time I decided I was not going to be a wimp, rather I would do what I wanted to do." As both share their feelings, most likely the deadlock is broken.

Can I Do a Healing Encounter with Anyone?

Over the years we've heard people say, "I thought the Healing Encounter was only useful for my love-partner and me. However, I found myself using it with my parents, my children, and my co-workers." The tool works in all of your relationships. How do you do a Healing Encounter with someone who is not familiar with the procedure? First of all, you can disguise it. Talk in the vernacular, such as: "I noticed a certain behavior on your part that I thought was interesting. It made me feel great inside. I have an inner voice that would not allow me to have so much fun, but I heard another voice say I could do it if I wanted to. I want to follow your example and am committed to trying the same behavior myself." The other person won't realize they have just had a Self-Encounter laid on them!

We have also found use of the Healing Encounter to be contagious. After you have shared your encounter, the other person will tend to mirror and reflect back a respondent encounter, even though without reading or studying this material. We think will be pleased to see how well this tool works in all of your relationships.

Topics for Healing Encounters

Here are a few examples of Healing Encounter topics:

- Aging and how it affects our relationship
- My survivor parts
- Getting more humor in our relationship
- My lack of sexual desire
- I realized a co-worker was stuffing anger with me like I do with you
- How I am healing my childhood abuse
- Choosing where to live when you work in one town and I work in another
- Taking care of my aging mother
- Planning our vacation together instead of me planning it
- Working on a project together (As co-authors, we did a number of Healing Encounters while writing this book.)

HOW ARE YOU DOING?

The following statements are designed to help you internalize and integrate the material in this chapter. Place a check mark after the ones you have learned.

1. *The number of Healing Encounters I am committed to do this next week: _____ .*

2. *I understand the difference between a Self-Encounter and a Healing Encounter.*

3. *I understand the difference between an initiator and a respondent encounter.*

4. *I am able to actively listen to my partner's satisfaction.*

5. *I am able to do a Self-Encounter without using the Self-Encounter form.*

6. *I understand the steps in doing a Healing Encounter.*

7. *I am able to listen to my partner's encounter without interruption.*

8. *I am aware of the choice to share my initiator's topic either at the time of making the appointment or at the time of sharing the initiator's encounter.*

9. *As a respondent, I have learned to actively listen to the initiator's topic, logical importance, emotional charge and motivation.*

10. *I consistently affirm and validate my partner's encounter when she is finished sharing it.*

11. *I understand how to complete the encounter by doing free-flow time.*

12. *I am able to ask for a change in myself or in my partner's behavior.*

13. *I have learned how to take a time-out without it becoming a cop-out.*

14. *I have learned how good it feels for both of us to reach closure.*

15. I am willing to record my encounter with an audio- or videotape, if appropriate.

16. I can do an initiator encounter whether my partner is doing a respondent encounter or not.

17. I have been able to figure out ways to continue the Healing Encounter when we become stuck.

18. I am doing Healing Encounters in many of my relationships and not just with a primary love partner.

Your Relationship with Others

EACH CHAPTER IN Section Three briefly describes a major challenge facing relationships. We could write a whole book on each one of these topics, but instead we'll give you just a sampling of life challenges. If a particular challenge is presenting a major problem for you, you may want to go to the Bibliography and find a book to help you change that challenge into a Loving Choice.

The older you get, the more powerful your **Family of Origin** influences may seem to be. You probably keep saying and doing the same things to your children that you hated your parents for when they said and did them to you. The goal of chapter 8 is to help you understand some of those influences better so you can make peace with them.

If you are making a life-course correction and are **Seeking Your Identity,** your relationships with others are likely to be under a great deal of stress. In chapter 9, because there is so much difference in the process for the person seeking identity and for the partner, we have written special sections to each of you. We have received a great deal of positive feedback from previous readers of this chapter. It is a very important chapter for many readers.

You probably are not aware of or connected with **Your Inner Children.** In fact, the concept of "inner children" may be new to you. As a result, you may be controlled more than you know by denied and/or unknown parts of yourself. Chapter 10 may help you to integrate those parts so you can become more whole and self-actualized.

We have found the challenge of **Power Struggles** very difficult for most people to resolve. Like a pot of stew on the stove top, power struggles have many ingredients within them, and a fire that keeps the pot boiling. The most powerful steps toward resolving a power struggle are for you to take *ownership of your feelings* and *responsibility for your own happiness.* By recognizing that "how you feel is up to you," you'll begin to resolve many internal conflicts that cause your external power struggles with others. Chapter 11 will show you how.

We have often heard people say that they "lose their identity" in relationships. They blame the relationship for this problem and so avoid getting into another relationship. Chapter 12 will help you learn to create appropriate **Boundaries and Ownership,** which will assist you in finding your true identity.

Chapter 13, **Relationships Are Your Teachers,** applies all of the concepts from the book into creating health and happiness in your relationships. Several special types of conflicts are described to help you better understand and resolve each of them.

The final chapter, **Loving Choices,** is about looking back on the personal growth journey you started when you began reading this book (or perhaps even at some previous time). Now is the time to practice decision-making that brings your head and your heart together. You are ready to create and appreciate the joy and happiness that you so richly deserve. We believe the communication tools we have described will assist you to change most of your life challenges into Loving Choices.

CHAPTER EIGHT

Family of Origin

CREATING PEACE WITH YOUR PARENTS AND YOUR CHILDHOOD

*The **challenge** is to become aware of the many influences
from your Family of Origin and childhood upon your
relationships with yourself and others.*

*The **loving choice** is to utilize both the "gifts of love"
and the "gifts of pain" from your Family of Origin.
This will assist you in becoming the whole human being
you are capable of being.*

The wedding was beautiful, wasn't it? The bride was radiant, the groom dashing. Now take a look at their families. Can you imagine the groom's significant parent married to the bride's significant parent? In most cases the significant parents would be the groom's father and the bride's mother, although it could be a variety of people including grandparents. It is difficult to imagine how this imaginary relationship would ever work out.

Interestingly, most relationships have a tendency to be like that imaginary relationship! We tend to create relationships like the ones we observed in childhood, yet most of us don't want that kind of relationship. One of your Challenges is to create a relationship different from that imaginary relationship.

Here is another Challenge. We have asked lecture audiences and seminar groups the following question. "If you would like to have a marriage basically like your parent's marriage, raise your hand." Only about five percent of the people raise their hands! You learned more about marriage and love relationships from your parents than anywhere else. You also have a tendency to create relationships similar to your parents' relationship. If you don't want a marriage like your parents, what kind of marriage do you want? The Challenge in this chapter is to learn as much as you can about how your family of origin is affecting your adult relationships, and then learn how to make Loving Choices, instead of living out your past.

Family of Origin Traits

Our observation is that many people do not realize how influential their families of origin are upon their present lives and relationships. Some of the family of origin influences are easy to see and understand. We all tend to belong to the same political party as our parents, to have the same religious beliefs, to live in the same locality or setting, and to have the same socio-economic level.

(Hold on a minute. We've been talking about "family of origin" as if everybody is familiar with the term. But maybe you don't know its meaning. It's actually a label that sociologists cooked up years ago to designate the family you grew up in: you, your parent(s), your siblings (if any), your aunts and uncles and cousins, and your grandparents and other ancestors. The social scientists often compare and contrast your "family of origin" with your "family of orientation" — you, your love partner, your children. We won't dwell much on the terminology here, but will use "family of origin" a lot, so now you know what we mean.)

Below is a partial list of traits that can be passed on to you from your family of origin. It is designed to stimulate your thinking about these traits. Place an initial for the significant adult from which you learned that trait, such as "F" for father and "M" for mother, "GF" and "GM" for grandparents, and so on for other significant people. Leave blank those traits that are not important to you.

addictive use of drugs _____ or abstain from drugs _____
birthdays important _____ or not important _____
boys and girls treated differently by parents _____ or treated
   the same_____
conflict: avoid _____ confront _____ resolve _____
crying: okay _____ not okay _____
household chores: sex roles _____ or shared _____
education important _____ or not _____
emotional closeness _____ or distant _____

exercise important _____ or couch potatoes _____
extended family important _____ or not _____
family secrets _____ or open sharing _____
fearful _____ or trusting _____
feelings expressed _____ or not expressed _____
financially careful _____ or carefree _____
hard working _____ or lazy _____
healthy _____ or sick _____
touching _____ or non touching _____
live in past _____ present _____ or future _____
matriarchal _____ or patriarchal _____
medical treatment sought _____ or resisted _____
moved a lot _____ or seldom moved _____
nicknames important _____ or not _____
observer _____ or participant _____
openly angry _____ or anger denied _____
optimistic _____ or pessimistic _____
organized _____ or disorganized _____
other-directed _____ or inner-directed _____
pack rats _____ or discarded things _____
parents dominant _____ or passive _____
parents fought openly _____ or never fought _____
perfectionism _____ or laid back _____
prejudiced _____ or accepting of others _____
punctual _____ or tardy _____
reading important _____ or not _____
religious values important _____ or not _____
sexuality discussed _____ or kept secret _____
smoking _____ or non smoking _____
stingy _____ or generous _____
strict discipline _____ or listening important _____
things _____ or ideas _____ more important
under _____ or over _____ responsible

Can you add some other traits that were important in your family of origin? Make a note of the traits that have in the past or in the present have caused difficulty in your relationships with others.

Adult Relationships

Many of your adult relationships reflect patterns in childhood relationships. Many of your adult Challenges are in actuality an echo of childhood experiences which are unresolved. Becoming aware of this phenomenon can help you to take more ownership and responsibility for your adult relationships, and lead you to more healing and health in all your relationships.

Many times we create relationships to learn lessons about unresolved childhood patterns in our lives. We observed this first hand when Nina's daughter Kelle and her boyfriend Gardner were participants in the Loving Choices Seminar. It was interesting and very healing for both Kelle and Nina when the large group discussion was about family of origin and influences from the family. You have a Challenge and an opportunity to finish growing through unresolved issues. Perhaps what appeared to you to be a disaster is in reality a wonderful chance to finish some unfinished business.

Parenting Your Inner Children

If you didn't receive enough good parenting in your childhood you may tend to make your partner responsible for that lack. There is a part in you that wants your love partner to give you the love and acceptance you don't believe you received from your mother and father. In some people this part is small — in others it may be large enough to cause stress and unhappiness in a love relationship. It is not possible for your love-partner to make up for the love and attention you didn't receive when you were a child.

This may lead to another problem: You thought you were involved with someone who could parent you; you discover instead that you are being your partner's father or mother In your formative years, you learned to adapt when you didn't get all of your needs met. Often the adaptive behavior was to become a "father" or "mother" to the other members of your family of origin. This resulted in your learning, as your survivor behavior, to be a caretaker.

You needed to be the caretaker, so you wound up with someone who needed care. Underneath the caretaker part of you is a little child who needs to be nurtured and loved. Gretchen said it very well in a seminar session: "I married my father and he married his mother, and together we lived out their lives."

You'll find the Internal Family Dialogue we discussed in chapter 6 will be helpful if you married someone like one of your parents. It is a way for you to learn to "become your own parent" and to nurture your Inner Children yourself. Start the dialogue by accessing your Inner Children and asking what they want — perhaps more love and attention when you were little. Next access your Wise Nurturer and ask it to talk to your Inner Children. You may be able to keep the dialogue going between those two parts to allow the Wise Nurturer to begin to heal your Inner Children. This will diminish the need for your caretaker survivor part to protect and care for your Inner Children.

Pam described her Inner Children needs quite succinctly. "It is much easier for me to focus on your needy little child. When I do this I ignore my own needy Inner Children. I want to focus on the needs of my Inner Children, rather than continuing to ignore them by taking care of others."

Dealing with Conflict

There are many other more subtle influences coming from your family of origin. Nina comes from a family of powerful females where the males often disappeared one way or another leaving the females in charge. In Bruce's family of powerful male ancestors, several of the first wives died. The German farmer male ancestors would remarry and have more children to help work their many acres of farm land. These influences from the past sneak into our relationship on an unconscious level.

Early in our relationship, for example, we were unloading the clean dishes from the dishwasher and putting them in the cupboard. We got into quite a power struggle. Nina's grandmother would say "there is a place for everything and they belong in that particular place." If someone told Bruce's father where to put something, he would rebel, become independent, and put them in another place. Nina was deciding where the proper place was for each dish. Bruce was being stubborn and independent putting them wherever he wanted to. Nina was still trying to please her grandmother. Bruce was continuing his father's pattern of rebellion against Bruce's grandmother.

Suddenly we looked at each other and realized our conflict was between Nina's grandmother and Bruce's father. We were able to laugh at ourselves and to break the influences controlling us from the past.

You may have learned from your family of origin to fight when there was conflict. Others learned to withdraw in order to avoid conflict. Isn't it interesting how many relationships have a fight/ flight match-up? During this incident, Nina was the "fighter" and Bruce was the "flighter." It seemed to Bruce the argument over the dishwasher was at least thirty minutes long because it was so uncomfortable for him. Nina — perhaps a little more detached — was probably more accurate when she said it was about three minutes long.

Does this story have any meaning for you? Have you and your partner ever had an argument that was really your ancestors in conflict? If so, we suggest you do a Healing Encounter. Your topic might be, "Our dining room table is getting crowded, with so many ghosts from the past coming to have dinner with us!"

Leftovers

A leftover is a conditioned response that continues even after the stimulus has been removed. Leftovers can occur at times you least expect. They are an opportunity to grow and to heal and to live more in the present.

Annie, a participant in the Loving Choices Seminar, became aware of a leftover that had been controlling her and preventing her from making choices in her relationships. In her childhood and then again in her first marriage, she had been very open with her feelings. Usually she would share her deepest thoughts and feelings from a very vulnerable place. Later, when there was some kind of conflict with the person she had shared with, her sharing would be thrown in her face and used as ammunition against her. This was very painful for Annie. She learned that it was not safe to be vulnerable, honest, and intimate.

Her leftover began to display itself in her relationship with her best friend Janet. Annie was sure that Janet would do the same thing if she shared with her. It affected her trust. Annie didn't trust Janet — or herself — and began to withhold her feelings. The leftover controlled her and created distance and conflict in her friendship. It was painful for both of them, and other conflicts started happening.

During the seminar, Annie became aware of this dynamic and the leftover that was controlling her. She did a Self-Encounter, then two repetitive Self-Encounters, and then was able to share a Healing Encounter with Janet. The end result was growth and transformation for both of them.

There was an unexpected side effect later on in the seminar. Janet was able to get in touch with some of her leftovers that had also been affecting their friendship in a negative way. Annie's willingness to explore her leftovers inspired Janet to do the same thing. A Loving Choice for both of them resulted in an even deeper friendship.

The question for you is, "How many leftovers are you carrying around? Are you able to recognize what they are? Are you willing to explore what is really happening? Are you committed to communicating about them?

It's time to do another Self-Encounter. The topic might be, "How can my leftovers assist me in my growth?" When you are able to let go and work through a leftover, you open up the possibility of transforming that leftover into a life giving and creative part of you. You are then able to live more in the present and not be controlled by old patterns. You have more choices.

The Domino Effect

One of the most discouraging aspects of being family therapists is to see destructive aspects of family interaction being passed from generation to generation. It's an example of the "domino effect." For example, if parents abused their children, the children often abuse the grandchildren.

Bruce was working with a family as a Juvenile Probation Officer. The father had the "smiling Buddha face" common among angry people who are masking their suppressed angry feelings. His daughter Elena shared in a private session that she had been physically abused by her father, then remembered a time when she was baby-sitting and become so angry she hit one of the children with her hand. She recognized that she had hit the child the same way that her father had hit her. Elena cried and cried when she realized that she had behaved and acted out the same way that her father had. She was hit, fell over, hit the next one, causing it to fall over — much the way dominoes do.

On the other hand, one of the most rewarding aspects of being family therapists is to see a "person-domino" remain standing when there are several generations of dominoes trying to push that person down. It takes great courage, awareness, communication and commitment to change a pattern that has been operating in the ancestral family for many generations. We salute all who have been able to "stand up and be counted" by changing inherited patterns of behavior and thinking. We Challenge you to use this book to help break the domino effect in your personal life and relationships!

Gifts from Your Family of Origin

Gifts from your family ancestors come in various sizes and shapes. You can't always tell by the wrapping paper how valuable the gift is, or how you will use that gift. Elena, who stopped her family "dominoes" of abuse, had a special kind of gift. As she became more aware and decided to stop the abuse, she found an inner strength and courage she didn't know she had. Learning to deal with her "abusive gift" helped her to learn how to make Loving Choices instead of continuing the old pattern. Maybe some of the gifts of pain you feel you received from your family of origin are more positive than you had previously thought. Maybe you haven't opened the gifts and explored the benefits within them.

Two key things help determine your life: the events that happen to you in life and the way you interpret and react to those events. Sometimes you can't do much about what happens to you. (Although as we work through our own processes, we have become aware we are creating more of what happens to us than we thought). However, you *can* do something about how you react to the events in your life. When the card game of life deals you a difficult burden, you can react like a martyr and suffer the burden silently and passively. You can react with denial and never learn anything. Or, you can learn to experience the pain, let it be your teacher and motivator and use it to help you become the person you want to be.

We have observed that the "favorite" son or daughter is most likely to internalize the inherited gifts and continue the domino effect. If the inherited gifts are healthy, the favorite child most likely will be healthy. If the gifts are unhealthy, the favorite child often will have a very difficult time escaping the domino effect.

We have also observed that the son or daughter who is not the favorite and may even be the scapegoat of the family, is most likely to avoid the domino effect. These children have to struggle in their childhoods and yet the struggle helps them become strong and take control of their lives. Their childhood may be more difficult, but their adult lives can be free of the domino effect.

Gifts of Pain from Your Family of Origin

You probably did not get all of your needs met in your formative years. You may still be accessing and healing some abuse and trauma you experienced in childhood. We encourage you to re-frame your pain; let yourself explore the positive side. Many of the painful experiences you had can be worked through and become gifts. You don't have much choice about accepting or refusing them. Your environment, internal motivation, and personality will determine to great extent how you use these painful gifts.

When you are experiencing the pain it may be hard to see any benefit or value from the gifts. The process of self-actualization and transformation is often one of learning from pain. Some of your relationship teachers are teaching you through pain. The pain you received from your family of origin may assist you to develop strength of character and have a deeper understanding of yourself and of life. The result can be that you become stronger and more vulnerable, sensitive, caring, compassionate, empathetic , understanding, and loving.

Of course this does not always happen. We know many people who carry a burden of anger and hurt around from their past family experiences. Do you know anyone like that? You may still be controlled by the painful experiences of your childhood. This pain may be expressed as discomfort, agony, anguish, suffering, distress, or perhaps grief when you have internalized the pain. You may be into blaming and projecting. You may be in denial that anyone else has emotional pain because you have not accessed and learned from your emotional pain. You may be carrying anger that could be called "childhood rage."

Accessing and using your healthy "internal family" will enable you to heal whatever dysfunction you experienced in your family of origin. Imagine being able to create internally the kind of mother or father you wished you had had as a child. Learning to utilize the internal family will help you transform the gifts of pain into gifts of awareness and wholeness.

Many of the friendships that you value are with people who have worked through their childhood pain and are more mature, objective, aware and loving. We have observed many people who have used the communication tools and the awareness you've gained from this book to change their family of origin gifts of pain into gifts of love. Isn't it exciting to think about healing your past pain?

Making Peace with Your Parents

All of these ancestor issues may leave you at odds with your parents. How do you make peace with your parents? There is an internalized part of you that is like your parents. If you still have anger and resentment towards your parents, you may have transferred that anger and resentment toward your internalized parent. You may not be feeling internal peace.

We suggest you use the Self-Encounter, Healing Encounter, and internal Family Dialogue to work on making peace with your internalized parent. During your formative years, you internalized parts of your parents. In spite of yourself, you say the same things now to your children that you hated your parents for when they said them to you. We all tend to parent the way we were parented. You can make peace with your internal parent, and you can do that even if your parent is deceased.

Do you find this confusing? After all, your parents now may not be the same as they were years ago when you internalized them. Parents tend to mellow out as they get older. But the beauty of this healing process is that, after you have made peace with your internalized parent, you may find you have made peace with your real parent as well!

We need to point out that your parents may never be ready to make peace with you because of their unhappiness. That is the sad reality. Don't let that stop you from making peace with your internal parent. You can do important healing with your internalized parent whether your actual parents respond or not.

Some of you will need to be angry at your parents while you are working through family of origin issues. Please remember, this is *your* anger. More often than not, it is most healing to share and express these feelings in a safe setting rather then to "dump" the anger on your parents. The more unmet needs you had from your parents, the more anger you are likely to feel. The goal is for you to work through the process. The end result can be forgiveness of yourself and then forgiveness of your parents.

Emotional Bonding and Attachment

Developmentally, the early formative years are the time when you emotionally bond and attach to your parents. Most bonding takes place in the first year of life. Your Inner Children develop beliefs about intimacy, trust, personal self worth and feelings of self-love as part of the bonding process. If you bonded and attached in your first year of life, you are probably confident, trusting and able to give and receive love easily.

If you didn't emotionally bond and attach in your family of origin, you may be attempting to complete this process in your adult relationships. You place expectations upon your relationship partner to help you feel safe, intimate and loving. If you don't feel these things, it is easy for you to blame your partner. This is one of the ingredients in a "power struggle" that we will talk about in chapter 11.

We have observed an interesting interaction many times in a couple counseling situation. The couple reaches a point of intimacy where the two are feeling emotionally close to each other. Suddenly one of them cracks a joke, changes the subject, or does something to break the intimacy. You probably have longed for intimacy and want to create as much of it as possible in your relationships. Why would one partner sabotage intimacy when it occurs?

If you did not emotionally bond and attach as a child, intimacy can feel uncomfortable and fearful. Often this results in trust issues. You come to expect a negative consequence of some sort after feeling intimate. You may be fearful of getting hurt because that often happened in your family of origin. If you haven't bonded and attached, you expect your partner to make you feel intimate. If this does occur and you feel emotionally close, you run from it and blame him or her for not being there for you.

Your partner cannot make you feel intimate and emotionally close if you have not learned to bond and attach. You may feel lonely because you are separated from yourself. You haven't learned to be intimate within yourself.

Do you have any ideas for a solution? Do a Self-Encounter with the topic, "Did I emotionally bond and attach as a child?" Do an Internal Family Dialogue and practice bonding and attaching between your inner parts, especially your Inner Children and Wise Nurturer. Then do a Healing Encounter with another person on the topic of, "I want to share how I learned to emotionally bond and attach with myself." Give yourself ample time to accomplish these three important steps in your healing process. And remember, "It is never to late to have a happy childhood."

You may be pleasantly surprised to discover that when you emotionally bond and attach with yourself, you feel more emotionally close and intimate with everyone else.

Ancestors and Survivors

Have you thought about what survivor parts your ancestors exhibited? You may want to go back to the list in chapter 3 and think about your father, mother, grandparents and other significant adults. Did they have any of those survivor parts? Your ancestors probably did not get all of their needs for attention and love met in their families of origin. Make a mark on the list to identify which survivor parts go with which ancestor. What effect did their survivor parts have on you?

Did you find yourself "polarized" with any of your ancestors? Usually when one or both of the people in a relationship have survivor parts, it leads to polarization issues. Ron says his father was under-responsible as a way of dealing with both of his parents, who had perfectionist survivors. Ron developed an over-responsible survivor part in order to compensate for his father's under- responsible survivor part. What survivor part did you develop to compensate for one of your ancestor's survivors?

Appreciating Your Ancestors

While you are looking at your family of origin, are you only aware of the "pebbles in your shoes" that are causing you discomfort? Have you thought about where the *shoes* came from? You were given many gifts from your family of origin during your formative years. Your parents did the best they could. They gave you the gift of life and many other gifts that you can be thankful for. We suggest you put some time and effort into becoming aware of the many positive gifts you received from your ancestors. You couldn't be the wonderful and special person you are if you hadn't been given some very special gifts from your family of origin.

Here is a sample Self-Encounter illustrating how you can change a gift of pain into a gift of awareness and healing.

Topic: *Making peace with my critical external mother.*

Facts:

1. I heard my mother yell at me many times when I was growing up.
2. I saw my mother involved in therapy for many years.

Thoughts:

1. I think my mother was unhappy.
2. I think she was critical of me because she was critical of herself.
3. I think my mother had a loud Inner Critic voice which she had never tamed.

Body Sensations:

I would experience stomach pains when she yelled at me. I still experience them when my relationship teachers yell at me.

Feelings:

I felt discounted, criticized, not okay, sad, depressed, angry, resentful when she continually criticized me.

Survivor:

My suit of armor survivor told me to keep quiet so she wouldn't yell at me so loud.

The old Inner Critic named "Icky-Witch":

"You always were misbehaving. You deserved to be yelled at. Somebody had to keep you in line." (This kind of vocabulary could go on for a long time before the Inner Critic will feel heard and listened to. Taming the Inner Critic is usually a lengthy process. Please be gentle and patient with yourself during this healing process).

The tamed Inner Critic named Gladys (which was my mother's name):

"I suggest you do some breathing exercises when you experience stomach pains. It would be a way you could learn to relax and feel better."

"I was there to protect you by keeping you out of trouble. If I had not been helping you, you would have misbehaved more and been yelled at more."

"I didn't feel nurtured when you were a child, and I didn't know how to nurture you."

Inner Children:

"It was I who had the stomach pains. I hurt so much when she was yelling. I felt really, really scared. I just wanted to run away and hide. I felt so helpless because there was nothing I could do. I feel mad and sad."

Wise Nurturer:

"You did the best you could in a very difficult situation. You may have thought your mother wanted you to be unhappy. The truth is that she was unable to let you know how scared she was. Your mother projected her pain out onto you. I acknowledge you for embracing your pain and allowing yourself to feel your fear and hurt. I support you and love your willingness to heal."

Intentions:

1. I intend to continue to listen to my tamed Inner Critic. I feel much better when it suggests things with "I-messages" instead of criticizing me the way my mother did.

2. I intend to have weekly massages. I want to do all that I can to heal in every way that I can.

Commitments:

1. I am committed to learn to access and listen to my Inner Critic voice on a regular basis.

2. I am committed to do self-care such as a massage at least once a week.

3. I am committed to continue doing the Internal Family Dialogue so I can create as healthy an Internal Family as I can.

4. I am committed to balancing my head and my heart while I am choosing inner peace.

What topics emerged for you in this chapter? Did you find a new concept intriguing or fascinating? We suggest you do a Self-Encounter on a topic that was important to you.

Suggested Homework

Have you thought about doing some research into your family of origin? What patterns and style of interaction would you discover? We encourage you to do a history of your family tree. Is it possible for you to interview any of your ancestors on an audio tape? If they are not living, interview other friends and relatives who knew your ancestors.

The *Loving Choices Workbook* has a "Journey Back in Time" exercise to assist in creating peace with your childhood and a "Family of Origin" form to assist you in recording the information concerning your ancestors. We have observed that very few people under thirty years of age are motivated to complete their family tree. No matter what age you are, we know you will learn a great deal about yourself by learning about your ancestors.

HOW ARE YOU DOING?

The following statements are designed to help you internalize and integrate the material in this chapter. Are you ready to move on to the next chapter? Have you made some progress at making peace with yourself, your family of origin and your childhood?

1. *I believe after reading this chapter that my family of origin is affecting me more than I had realized.*

2. *I marked on the family of origin traits chart which identified traits were passed on to me.*

3. *I have identified which significant person in my family of origin passed on specific traits.*

4. *I recognize that in some ways I married a person like one of my parents.*

5. *I have completed a Self-Encounter about being in relationship with one of my parents.*

6. *I like the way I deal with conflict in my relationships.*

7. *I understand the concept of leftovers.*

8. *I have identified some of my leftovers.*

9. *I am a "person-domino" who has broken some domino effects in my family.*

10. *I understand the concept of changing gifts of pain into gifts of awareness.*

11. *I am changing, or have changed, some of my gifts of pain into gifts of love.*

12. *I am committed to do Self-Encounters on changing gifts of pain into gifts of awareness.*

13. *I am committed to do an Internal Family Dialogue to help me change gifts of pain into gifts of awareness.*

14. *I am making peace with my internal parents.*

15. *I am making peace with my actual parents.*

16. *I am becoming more bonded and attached with my internal family.*

17. *I have identified my parent's survivor parts and how they are affecting me.*

18. *I appreciate the many gifts of life that my parents gave me.*

CHAPTER NINE

Seeking Your Identity

GROWING FROM SHELL TO REBEL TO LOVE WITH HELP FROM YOUR INTERNAL FAMILY

*The **challenge** is to find an identity of your own separate from the expectations of family and society.*

*The **loving choice** is to create a working balance among all of your internal family voices. The result will be a stronger self-identity.*

*D*on't should on me" is common vocabulary for those seeking an identity of their own, separate from the expectations of family of origin and society. You're tired of doing what you are "supposed" to be doing. You want to behave in a way that pleases yourself rather than pleasing others. It could be called an "identity crisis," in the sense that you don't have a strong sense of who you are. You often know what you *don't* want, and you have difficulty determining what you *do* want.

We believe the process of developing one's own unique identity is positive and potentially healing and empowering. It's the way teenagers cut the apron strings and become free from the family of origin. It can be a process of finding more balance in your life when you have been out of balance. It is a way of taking control back from your Adaptive-Survivor parts that have become too strong and powerful. It's a way of healing your childhood abuse. We view it as a way to deepen your spiritual faith and find a closer relationship with your God.

There are people who go through the identity crisis and become stuck in the process. They never work beyond rebelling against everything around them. We have known a few who behaved in very destructive ways, causing pain and suffering for themselves and everyone around them. Some people begin the process of developing their own individual identity, become frightened, and regress back into the "shoulds" again. People who are already involved in committed partnerships may develop third-party relationships — often the beginning of the end of their primary relationships. Such involvements are often completely out of character, often resulting in confusion and depression. Then there are those people who don't grow in the process and have to repeat it several times in order to find their own identity.

Part of the problem is that you feel very independent and believe that you don't need any information or advice to work through this process. This independence is encouraged by the lack of support and understanding from those around you. There are plenty of people out there with a big outer critic who are eager to encourage you to conform and stop acting so immature. This chapter will assist you in working through the process instead of becoming stuck. Please put aside your "I've got to do this on my own—nobody understands me" part. We invite you, as you read, to explore and think about this Chapter with an open mind.

We've often heard from readers about the concepts in this chapter. Typically, it is the partner of the person in rebellion who reads the chapter first and believe the partner "should" also read it. Our standard suggestion is to simply tell your partner that you found some information that was very helpful for you and you would like to share it with him. We suggest you simply share *your experience* about reading the chapter. It may be a welcome change for him if you talk about yourself instead of telling him what he "should "do.

Rebellion is an attempt to become free. It is not the final step. Choosing to rebel can be as controlling as conforming. Doing what someone wants you to do is being controlled. Doing what someone doesn't want you to do is also being controlled. It is not until you learn to take control of your life and find your own identity that you become free.

Here is a helpful analogy to better understand the identity process. The fish that is hooked with a fish hook starts behaving very differently from other fish. It is attempting to become unhooked. The other fish wonder about its strange behavior. It looks like unusual behavior to them. To the one hooked, it makes sense as being the best way to become free. People in rebellion are attempting to get free of the fish hook of expectations from others. They are truly seeking an identity separate from the "shoulds" they have lived all of their lives.

Of all the people who have participated in the Fisher Rebuilding Seminar, approximately one-third of them identified their former love partner as being in rebellion. We perceive this as a process of seeking one's identity. The adult person in rebellion behaves much like a teenager trying to individuate — to be come a separate individual, free of parental and societal expectations.

After hearing so many participants in the divorce class talk about their partners being in rebellion, it appeared evident rebellion was a major cause of relationships ending. The feedback we have received indicates this chapter is tremendously helpful, both for the person in rebellion and for the partner. People say that we have put into words a process which they have observed in their own lives. Arlene, whose husband was in rebellion, told us this explanation helped her find some sanity in what appeared to be the insanity of her spouse's behavior.

Let's discuss this identity process in order to better understand what we are talking about.

A Theory of Childhood Growth and Development

Teenage rebellion is acted out mostly on the stage of the relationship between the parents and the teenagers. The way the process occurs is an expression of the relationships within each family. Children who are encouraged in the family to find an identity of their own have less need to create an identity by rebelling against the parents.

Part of the problem around rebellion in our society is the lack of formalized puberty rites. Sometimes the most important ritual signifying maturity is obtaining a driver's license. If a teenager could prove she was becoming mature by a recognized cultural ritual at puberty, perhaps the need to seek maturity by rebelling would be minimized.

The Shell Stage

During childhood you wanted to please your parents. They were bigger than you, smarter than you, more powerful than you. They rewarded you for proper behavior. The relationship between parent and child was — in the vast majority of families — clearly defined and understood—you were the little person and they were in charge. As we pointed out in the Family of Origin chapter (8), you very likely developed the same moral values, belonged to the same religious institution, and supported the same political party as your parents. Your attitudes and beliefs reflected their role modeling as you were growing up. Most parents say things like, "Don't rock the boat. Be concerned about what others think of you. Do things in the traditional way."

The relationship between you and your parents was usually stable. These are the golden years in many families because the family interaction typically was peaceful and tranquil. You seldom questioned your parents' authority.

External Rebellion

The rebellion process usually starts when the child reaches the teenage years. These days it seems to be starting even younger. You begin to question both your parents' and society's expectations. You begin to rebel, to experiment, to try out new behavior and to push against the limits established by your parents. You begin seeking an identity of your own, separate from their expectations. You begin questioning every "should" you ever learned.

The family interaction is often chaotic and stressful when the kids are rebelling. One minister said it well in his sermon, "It is a humbling experience to be the parent of a teenager." Communication in the family is difficult. The interactions result in power struggles. The common language is "you" messages. This scenario is not conducive to finding your identity. If anything, it perpetuates your lack of identity.

You also began to rebel against the expectations of society. You question why you should do all the things that society thinks you should do. You keep pushing for more freedom and less control.

It is easy for parents to believe children want complete freedom when they are in rebellion. Actually they need to push against limits.

As parents, it's our job to provide consistent and clear limits which give them the security they need to be able to explore their new thoughts and feelings. It can be scary and confusing when the hormones are changing, new feelings are occurring, and feelings toward the opposite sex are suddenly a primary force.

If the parents don't provide enough limits for the child to push against in rebellion, the child may feel insecure. Part of rebellion is gaining emotional strength by pushing against emotional limits. It is analogous to pushing physically against limits through exercise or physical hard work. You develop your strength by pushing against a strong force. If the parents don't provide this strong force, the children will have difficulty growing strong emotionally with an identity of their own.

Sometimes the search for identity is done in a less rebellious way. It is done internally because the pressures are minimal and the teenager has a pretty well-defined identity. On the other hand it can be like a volcano, with the internal pressures released rapidly through some acting out behavior. Some teenage delinquency is in reality rebellion against authority. Too much pressure from parents encourages teenagers to seek relief by acting out.

Internal Rebellion

Healthy teenagers begin to learn that the search for identity is an internal search. It is your own Inner Critic that is responsible for your being controlled. The battle usually takes place between your Inner Critic and your Inner Children. The Inner Critic has been winning the battle while you are in the Shell stage (usually early childhood). The Inner Children start winning when you are in the Rebel stage (usually during the teen years). The Wise Nurturer emerges in the Love and Forgiveness stage (usually adulthood). When you understand this internal battle, you can begin to create internal peace between your parts by conducting your rebellion internally.

It takes courage and strength, awareness and ownership, motivation, and commitment to do internal rebellion. It is easy to project your unhappiness upon someone else in the external rebellion. It is a Challenge to take responsibility for feeling trapped in the internal rebellion stage because you must take ownership for causing your own lack of freedom.

Forgiveness and the Love Stage

Although you began to find an identity of your own during your teenage years, the search can occur anytime in life. As you matured you began to appreciate your parents for doing the best they knew how. You began to love yourself and others from an identity of your own. At this point the relationship between you and your parents became one of equals, rather than of parent and child. There is usually a sigh of relief from everybody because now the family interaction allows each of you to be more accepting of others. Communication becomes more clear and the atmosphere is more peaceful. The final love stage may not be achieved until you physically move away from home.

In the Shell stage, you do what you *should* do. In the Rebel stage, you do what you *shouldn't* do. In the love stage, you choose what you *want* to do. It has been interesting to observe that the behavior in the love stage is very similar to the Shell stage behavior. The difference is that you consciously choose your behavior in the love stage. In the Shell stage you try to live up to someone else's expectations of what your behavior should be.

For example, many teenagers in the Shell stage follow their parents' religious affiliation. In the Rebel stage they might develop a religious affiliation different from their parents. In the love stage, they often go back to their parents' religious affiliation by choice, rather than by conformity to their parents' expectations.

Growing Beyond Your Parents

It is often difficult for the child to grow beyond the stage the parents are in. If the parents are stuck in the Shell stage, they have difficulty understanding the child's need to rebel. They are concerned about what other people think. They try to pacify their children, which allows the children to be in control. Inter-generational boundaries in the family are often weak and sometimes non-existent. This role reversal causes stress and discomfort in the family. The children's tendency is to go back into pleasing the parents and thus fail to go beyond the stage their parents are in.

Let's go to the next level of development. If the parents have not reached the love and forgiveness stage they can be threatened by the child's outgrowing them. They feel uncomfortable with the child who is not following tradition and behaving in the way they think the child should. They often try to control the child with oppressive limits. It may appear that the parent is picking on the child who is showing the most mature behavior. This is confusing to everyone. The child sometimes aborts the process and goes back to rebelling or to pleasing everyone else. Some children develop a strong enough identity so that the controlling parenting is the catalyst for them to have an even stronger identity.

This same malfunction occurs in adult relationships. It is difficult to grow beyond the stage your love partner is in. Partners may not understand your rebellion if they are in the Shell stage. They may rebel against you if you attempt to find an individual identity and grow into the love stage. If your partner is unable to be strong enough for you rebel against, you may have difficulty growing emotionally strong in the relationship.

Why Rebellion Is Sometimes Volcanic

You had the first opportunity to find your identity in childhood when you were two years old — remember the "terrible twos" stage? This is sometimes also called the "no" stage, since the child's response is "no" whenever the parent suggests or tells the child what to do. The child is making a first attempt to find a separate identity. "What is me and what is not me?" is the unspoken vocabulary as the child separates from the parent. If you were not successful in completing the first attempt at individuation as a two-year-old, the pressures build to seek your identity later on in life.

You have the second opportunity to individuate as a teenager, as described above. If you weren't successful finding an identity of your own as a teenager, the pressures continue to build until, at some point in your adult life (usually when you are going through a difficult time), you go into adult rebellion. If the first two opportunities to fulfill your identity were not successful, your need to rebel as an adult will be greater. There will be more difficulty and trauma in your adult rebellion process if you have unfinished business from your childhood. Those with childhood trauma often have a more volcanic rebellion.

One ingredient in rebellion is the need to question whether your parents care for and love you. The rebellion is a test to see if they care enough to provide limits and to prove to you that they do love you. Some adults who continue to rebel may need to find self-love, and let go of the expectation that their parents are going to make them feel loved. It is possible to do a lot of adult rebellion to test your parents' love before you find your own self-love. Doing the Internal Family Dialogue can help solve this need to test whether your parents love you or not. You can give yourself the love you are attempting to get from your parents.

The Adult Rebellion Process

The adult person in rebellion has a pattern of behavior that is easy to identify and describe. It's a paradox because the person is conforming to non-conformity. Following is a description of the process. We will make interpretations about what each of the behaviors means after we have described the behavior.

1. Your Need to Relieve Your Internal Pressures

The process starts when you experience internal pressures that motivate you to do something. You are tired of being the mythical Atlas carrying the whole world on your shoulders. You are tired of doing the "shoulds" you have been doing all of your life. If the pressures are great enough, you may feel as if you will explode. The alternatives might be an emotional breakdown, depression, or even suicidal feelings. It is a temptation at this point to separate from your partner in an attempt to relieve the internal pressures.

Like the baby chicken inside the eggshell (in the Shell stage) who is ready to hatch, you need to peck your way out of the shell — to rebel. All that matters to you at this point in your process is to get out so you can breathe, live and do all the things you have been "wanting to do." You are tired of doing all the things that you had learned you "should" do. It is easy to believe your partner is the eggshell, limiting your growth and causing your internal pressures. Hence your belief that you must separate from her (him).

Common vocabulary at this stage is, "I need emotional space." When you are trying to find your identity separate from other people's expectations, you need room to grow.

Interpretation: The reason the "shoulds" cause internal pressure is because they are someone else's expectations. It means you haven't found your own identity separate from the expectations of family of origin and society.

Often your internal battle has been a battle between your Inner Critic and one of your Adaptive-Survivor parts. Your Inner Children have become tired of watching these big people fight. They're saying — as children will — "it's my turn," and your process of seeking identity has begun.

2. Projection of Your Unhappiness

During rebellion you're likely to blame others for your unhappiness. "If only you would change and stop bugging me, I could be happy. It's all your fault." Your partner, or another person very close to you, usually becomes the main brunt of this projection.

Your partner, loved one, family member, or friend will often accept your projections and take the blame. He may walk around on eggshells trying not to upset you. The person in rebellion often leaves her spouse, when in reality she is trying to free herself from the expectations of someone in her past—usually her mother or father.

Interpretation: You are pushing against the eggshell, symbolized by the person closest to you. Your perception is that the other person is controlling you. You probably seek out the strongest person around you (emotionally) to rebel against, because a part of you knows you need something strong to push against. You want to be able to rebel while the other stays strong. If the other person simply gives in, it makes you feel bad for causing him so much pain. The stronger your love partner becomes emotionally, the more you will rebel against him. This is usually quite confusing to both of you.

In reality, the control you are feeling is within you. Often you are rebelling against your Inner Critic or one of your Adaptive-Survivor parts. You may be projecting your rebellion out upon the person who may have been using language or behavior which reinforces your Inner Critic or one of your Adaptive-Survivor parts.

3. If It Feels Good, Do It!

Of course, it feels so good doing whatever it is you want to do. You are determined to continue doing it, almost without regard for the effect it has on others. Your partner and loved ones around you wonder about this strange new behavior. They are accustomed to having you do what you "should" do. Typically they are quite critical of your behavior and wonder what has gotten into you.

Interpretation: Doing what feels good usually helps relieve the internal pressures. If everyone around you is critical, then you have a chance to develop a stronger identity while being criticized. What a perfect opportunity for you to work on your own identity!

4. Taking Control of Your Adaptive-Survivor Parts

The process of seeking identity is directly connected to your Adaptive-Survivor parts. One or more of your survivor parts has been very powerful in your life. It may have been the *over-responsible* part, which resulted in your taking care of others. This left little or no time to do your own self-care. It may have been your *perfectionist* part, which may talk up via your Inner Critic, with many expectations of how you should act. It may have been your *logical* part, which never allowed you to access and share feelings. Taking control of these various parts means seeking balance, by developing the opposite behavior of your Adaptive-Survivor part. If you've been over-responsible, you may be acting out under-responsible behavior. If you have been logical, you may be accessing your emotional side. If it has been difficult to be intimate, you may want to share and risk becoming vulnerable with someone. You may quit work and look for a less stressful job. Or, if you are a perfectionist you may do poorly at work because you are not motivated to do what you "should" do.

You may become a very under-responsible parent at this point, sometimes behaving more like one of the kids than the parent. Both you and your kids may be trying to find your identities at the same time!

You may be rebelling against a survivor part in your partner. The partner has almost always been controlling, parental, over-responsible, critical, or one of the many adaptive-survivor parts listed in chapter 3. It is not a coincidence that you rebel against them and their survivor parts. In fact, it may be appropriate.

Interpretation: It takes a great deal of time and emotional energy to let go of your survivor behavior. It is hard work to become more balanced and develop the parts that you had been suppressing or denying.

5. The Growing Relationship with Another Person

At this point, you probably will have found another person to talk to. Perhaps you are spending a great deal of time talking intimately with this person, who may be younger than you, of the opposite sex, and also be seeking her adult identity. Most likely it will be a nurturing person, who does a good job of listening and supporting you. You may say things like, "I can really talk to this person. She understands me and really listens. My partner doesn't understand me, doesn't listen to me, and doesn't support me." This other relationship may be very helpful to you in your attempt to find your own identity. However, it looks like an affair, especially to your partner. Because it is so important to you, you may not understand why everyone is so critical of this relationship. It provides you with what feels like the unconditional love that you are seeking.

Your partner, and others, may believe your relationship with this person is sexual. Sex is usually not important at this time. It is more important to you to be able to talk openly with someone you trust, and to discover your identity.

It is important to emphasize that the significant relationship you need to help you find your identity can be with *anyone*— it doesn't have to be a potential love partner. You can find a friend, family member, therapist, clergyperson, or anyone who understands the rebellion process and is willing to listen and support you. Anyone who is still in the Shell stage, however, may have difficulty understanding and accepting what you're going through.

Interpretation: A place to talk about your new thoughts and feelings is very important. If you're trying to find an identity, it is very helpful to find someone with whom you can talk, bounce ideas off and get reactions from. The development of your Adaptive-Survivor was partly due to your not getting some needs met in your growth and development process. This other relationship is probably a new attempt on your part to get those needs met. This will diminish the power of the Adaptive-Survivor part that has been in control of you.

A word of caution. It is easy to give away your power again by believing the other person is responsible for your finding an identity. Please remember, *you* are the one seeking your identity. The other person may be supporting and enhancing that process: however, you are learning to take control of your life. Don't give away your power by believing the other person — *any* other person — is responsible for your happiness.

6. I Don't Love You

In your process of seeking identity you may say to your partner, "I don't know if I love you, and I don't know if I ever have. I like you and care for you, but I don't know if I love you. I may not want to spend the rest of my life with you. I need emotional space, and I need to be away from you so I can find out who I really am." This usually devastates the partner, who takes it personally and feels rejected, abandoned and unloved.

Interpretation: Your top priority is finding your identity and self-love and becoming free. Loving another person is not on your list of priorities. You feel burdened with "shoulds" and are questioning them all. Loving another person feels like a "should."

7. No Parents Allowed

When you are in rebellion you do not want any authoritative people around. This includes a love partner, mom or dad, therapists, police, a boss.... "I don't need anyone to tell me what to do. I've got to do this myself." You're not likely to go for therapy, or to take personal growth workshops or classes. You don't want to talk to anyone who acts like a parent or criticizes you.

On the other hand, the rebellion process is very inconsistent and contradictory. Your contradictions are confusing to your partner. You may say you don't want a parent, but then you put others in a parental role and proceed to rebel against them.

Interpretation: You fight against the very thing you want the most. You want and need appropriate limits but don't want any parental figure telling you what to do. This puts your partner in a difficult and confusing position.

These seven aspects of the rebellion process put a tremendous strain upon a love relationship. The partner of the person seeking identity usually internalizes all of the above behaviors and becomes emotionally distraught. Let's look at how this is reinforced. The partner hears, "It's all your fault." "I need to do whatever feels good." "I can talk to this other person." "I don't love you anymore." "I need emotional space to be alone." "I'm not going for counseling or attending any classes, that's not what I need now." No wonder the partner becomes drained and the relationship often ends!

We want to affirm and support you if you are in relationship with a person in rebellion. There aren't very many warm fuzzies or rewards during this time. If you can understand the process, you may realize what a gift you are giving to the other person by being there while she goes through this process of healing.

Plato's Myth of the Cave

Let us illustrate this process by digressing and borrowing a teaching concept from Plato, the Greek philosopher, who wrote before the time of Christ. Isn't it amazing that something written over 2,000 years ago is still pertinent? We are referring to Plato's "Myth of the Cave." We'll give you the short paraphrased version of the story.

The people of the cave were shackled in such a way that they were facing the wall of the cave. Behind them was a transparent curtain, and behind the curtain was a fire. Other people were moving around the fire, casting their shadows through the curtain upon the wall in front of the people in the cave. These shadows were seen as "the truth" — the "real" people. (The Shell stage)

When a crisis occurred, some of the cave dwellers were freed from their shackles. They discovered that what they had believed to be real people — or "the truth" — were really only shadows on the wall. Consequently, they started searching for a deeper truth. They began climbing up the long trail out of the cave. (External rebellion)

At the mouth of the cave were green trees, blue skies, flowers and fresh air. This was indeed the real world. This new awareness overshadowed the imagined truth in the cave. The people felt joyful and excited with their new-found truth. They began to grow and find an identity of their own. (Internal rebellion)

They became acclimated to the beautiful colors, smells and sights that they had not been aware of before. They found happiness and contentment, something they had not known before.

After coming out of the cave they were able to internalize this new truth. They realized that they were able to make choices about their reality. They could choose to stay out of the cave or go back in and believe that the shadows upon the wall were real.

They began to feel comfortable with their new identity. They were able to forgive themselves for not being completely awake and aware while shackled in the cave. They forgave their ancestors and people from the community—the people whom they believed had shackled them in the cave. (Love and forgiveness stage)

There is a danger in all awareness and growth. It might be called the zeal of a new convert. The people are tempted to go back into the cave and tell their friends who are still shackled—"Hey people, there's a whole bright new world out there. These figures of people on the wall are just shadows and are not real people. I've found the real truth, if you would just listen to me." (Often these shackled people are your family of origin)

The response of the shackled people is predictable. "Have you lost your mind since you left the cave? Everyone can see the truth upon the wall. Don't bother me with your nonsense."

Interpretation: As you grow and discover new truths about yourself and the world, it's important that you remain grounded, centered, and aware, so that you are able to handle all of the new truth without becoming overzealous or confused.

Words of Support and Wisdom to Partners of the Person in Rebellion

It would be easy for you partners to play victim and believe there is nothing you can do. The truth is you probably are more empowered to be loving than your partner. She is attempting to relieve internal pressures and to find internal peace as best she can. You can be on the edge of the water with a life-supporting pole. But it won't be easy, or without pain for you.

The first thing we suggest is not to take things personally. The roots of this search for identity go way back into childhood. This started long before you knew this person or were in relationship with her. Her process has very little to do with you. Try to detach yourself from her process. Be a cheerleader for her if possible.

However, if you sit back and do nothing, your relationship may end. You have an opportunity to take this gift of pain and turn it into a gift of new life. The lesson she is giving to you, if you choose to take it, is to look at *your* Adaptive-Survivor parts. Most likely you are over-responsible, perfectionist, or exhibit some form of controlling behavior. It is not an accident she is rebelling against you.

On her side of the fence, she is rebelling in order to become free to be herself. On your side of the fence are some survivor parts that you may never have looked at if your partner had not given you this gift of pain. We suggest you take this opportunity to grow and become the most balanced person you can be.

Normally, you as the partner feel helpless and impotent. When you learn you have some important decisions to make, you can learn to feel more self-empowered.

The first decision you have to make is whether or not you will stay in the relationship. When the person who is rebelling is in one of the seven stages we described earlier, it is tempting for you to leave. Many of your friends and relatives will encourage you to leave. Think seriously about what you really want to do.

When you decide what you really want to do, act on that decision. There are some positive advantages of learning all the lessons you can learn from this experience. These lessons might include taking a look at your survivor parts. This could very well be a painful process for you. On the other hand, it will ultimately assist and empower you to discover your own potential — a Loving Choice for both you and your partner.

If you can understand this process, you can be supportive of your partner. If you don't understand the process, you will probably continue all the old patterns of behavior. You have an opportunity to make a Loving Choice about that.

You can decide to take the opportunity to do some self-care. How about having a full body massage occasionally? Maybe read some of those books that you've had on the shelf for months? Start writing in your journal and record this difficult time. Journaling is a wonderful way of recording your emotions and feelings. Find some supportive friends and take the time to ask for emotional support. You have several possible Loving Choices you can make for doing your own self-care.

You can make a decision about what you want to share with others. It would be easy to tell everyone about the terrible destructive behavior the person in rebellion is exhibiting. You may choose to talk only with trustworthy friends who will hold in confidence what you share about your partner.

What about that "other" relationship? Almost everyone in full-blown rebellion has found another person to talk to. It is easy for you to be threatened, jealous, critical, and deeply hurt by that extra relationship. If you are critical of that relationship and put your partner down for having it, you risk driving her closer to that person. If you are understanding, you may help her to start talking to you. Be the best listener you can be if you want your relationship to last. Remember, anything you can talk out, you don't have to act out.

Effect upon Adult Relationships

How does this business of rebellion relate to adult love relationships? Very likely both of you were in the Shell stage when the relationship started. When one of you began to rebel, the partner in the Shell stage tended to please the person in rebellion. This resulted in no limits for the person in rebellion. Consequently, the partner still in the Shell stage became "emotionally upset." The relationship became chaotic, with everyone confused.

If you are the partner, you need to take this opportunity to grow and develop rather than pleasing the partner in rebellion. Ask yourself questions like: "Why am I being rebelled against?" "How have I been parental, controlling, over-responsible, or critical?" "What can I do to make this crisis into a creative experience?" "What do I need to do so I can let go of my survivor parts and take control of my life?"

This book describes methods, tools, awareness and solutions that are designed to help you take control of your life. We have found that when both the person in rebellion and the partner read this book, it makes the resolution of problems in the relationship much easier. You will still have to do the hard work necessary for both of you to transform your life. It's also an opportunity to take control of your life!

Questions Frequently Asked

Here are some of the questions we are frequently asked about the process of seeking identity.

How long does the process of rebellion last? External rebellion can last the rest of your life. It is always expecting someone in the external environment to change, and that may never happen. There is usually a need for some external rebellion before one can get into internal rebellion. On the other hand, when one is able to grow and evolve into internal rebellion, the internal war and conflict may end in months. The process will always take some time, however. It is difficult to grow from the Shell stage into the Love stage; some Rebel time is needed. Awareness, ownership, Self-Encounters and Internal Family Dialogues can make a world of difference as to how long the process takes.

If so many relationships end, is there any hope for our relationship to continue when one person begins to grow? If the person in rebellion can grow into internal rebellion, and the partner can let go of controlling survivor behaviors, there is a good chance the relationship can survive. The success depends upon how committed both of you are to transform and to let go of the old patterns of behavior. If the partner says "My partner is in process. I will wait and do nothing because she is the problem," the chances of the relationship surviving are greatly diminished. If the person in external rebellion continues the seven external rebellion behaviors described above, the relationship will probably not last.

Bruce began developing this identity theory in 1971. After observing this process for nearly thirty years, we believe that if the person who is rebelling can do an internal rebellion, and the partner can look at his own survivor parts, there is a good chance the relationship can survive.

How long can the partner stay in this relationship while the other person is doing external rebellion? There are few rewards, warm fuzzies, or good feelings in a relationship with a person in external rebellion. You have to continually put up boundaries in order to avoid being blamed for the rebellion with its contradictions and inconsistencies, and in order to care for yourself. You'll continually have to ask, "What do I want?" "What do I need to do for myself?" "How can I meet my needs?" "How long can I remain strong?" The ultimate question will be "How do you know when to end a painful relationship?" The answer is, "When you have had quite enough of the pain, and things are not getting better."

The person in rebellion typically has a third-party relationship. What is the chance of its lasting and becoming long term? The third-party relationship does *not* have a good foundation to become a long-lasting relationship. It will probably be in trouble before very long if the person tries to make it something more than a healing, growing relationship.

We realize how important this third-party relationship can be for the person in rebellion. We have found that the person in external rebellion will usually continue the relationship with the third party until she is able to grow into internal rebellion.

We encourage the person in rebellion to find a safe and neutral person such as a therapist to provide support and affirmation. Having what looks like a love relationship adds considerable stress to the process. Unfortunately very few people read this recommendation before they start their rebellion process. Very often they are already involved with another person.

Will we have to go through this again sometime in the future? It has been a painful experience. It is appropriate to ask if you have to experience this hurt again. For the person who is rebelling, the better you understand the process, the better you will do at finding your identity. If you abort the process before finding your identity, you probably will have to do some more searching for identity in the future. People who don't complete the process often will have the internal pressures build up again. If you both experienced your process well and have embraced and accepted your Adaptive-Survivor behaviors, you probably will not have to do it again.

You want to keep your old room when you leave for college! "My partner in rebellion decided to move out and separate in order to find enough 'emotional space.' This person took very few belongings and appears to continue to want to call this home. I feel confused as to whether she has left or not."

We think the answer to your confusion is to point out that the person leaving home is like a teenager leaving for college who wants a room at home even though he has left. He wants to have a safe place to come home to. It is often a scary journey to do a search for identity. It feels good to have some security at home. It feels pretty insecure to travel out into the "real world."

When will she want to come home? The person in rebellion doesn't want to come home to yesterday's newspaper. She will observe the partner's behavior rather than listen to empty words. She will want a person who has made peace with his Adaptive-Survivor parts instead of still being controlling.

Should you file for divorce? "My partner has moved out but says he doesn't want a divorce. All of my support friends and my therapist are telling me to forget the relationship and start divorce proceedings. I've got to protect myself. The first person to hire an attorney has an advantage. Should I listen to my friends and therapist?"

Your friends are there to support you. They don't want to see you get hurt more than you already have been. You have to keep going back to what you really want. Can you stay in the relationship and still do your self-care?

If you force the other person to make a decision about whether he wants to continue the relationship when he is early in the process, he will probably say, "NO!" Is that the answer you want? It takes patience and inner security on your part not to demand a decision immediately. It takes courage to stand up to your friends, and possibly your therapist, who are pushing you to end the relationship. Remember, you have plenty of growing to do yourself. Why not take this opportunity to grow? The seeking-identity relationships we have worked with that have not ended have all had a partner who could be patient and allow the other person enough time to go through the growth process. Why not wait to file for divorce until both of you are further along with the process? Let the decision whether or not to divorce be a Loving Choice instead of a decision made of desperation and frustration.

Is this a "male mid-life crisis"? How can a male mid-life crisis happen to both males and females at any age? Rebellion is more likely to start during a passage or bottleneck in your life. Many males do it while in their forties. Many females go into rebellion around their thirtieth birthday. Other people start rebelling after their parents die. We have found that either gender can do a mid-life correction at any age.

It is common for males in their forties to try and do all the living they feel they have missed out on before they are "too old to do it." This process is similar to the seeking-identity process but it may not result in the male finding a better and stronger identity. Hopefully these males will look at the survivor parts that have kept them from doing the living they are seeking.

You make it sound desirable to be in the love stage. Is it okay for me to be in the Shell stage if I am happy being there? If you're in the Shell stage, you can't simply choose to be in the Rebel or Love stages. If you *evolve* to the love stage, you can choose to go back to either the Shell or Rebel stage if it's appropriate. For example: if you have suffered a great loss, you may choose to go back to the Shell stage. You might move back to your parents' home and withdraw while you grieve and recover from your loss. A second example: you may have a situation at work or elsewhere where you want to bring about some changes in your environment. You may choose to be in rebellion because that will allow you to make changes. You may want to change some things about yourself. Rebellion may help you to do that.

In the Love stage, you have choices available that you don't have in the other stages. But on the other hand, we believe everybody is in all three stages all of the time. We don't believe we ever evolve to being completely in the Love stage.

Can Rebellion be healing? Rebellion can be a time of growth and changing old patterns. It is a process that can be used to heal many different kinds of pain and trauma. If you were abused in your childhood and continued to carry your pain in the Shell stage, rebellion might be useful to work through your pain. If you are in a battering relationship, some positive rebellion might give you the strength and courage to leave the relationship. If you are not satisfied with your relationship with God and are still living up to other peoples' expectations, rebellion might be an avenue for choosing what kind of spiritual relationship you want.

The process of finding an identity of your own will make a difference in many areas of your life.

What does Internal Rebellion look like? How do I know if I am doing it? We have found very few who can go directly from the Shell stage into internal rebellion without doing some external rebellion. It is hard to stop living up to family of origin and societal expectations without rebelling against those expectations.

There are several indications you are doing internal rebellion. When you find the strength and courage to stop believing another person is responsible for your internal pressures, and start owning your own internal war. When you are facing the feelings underneath your Adaptive-Survivor behaviors. When you can make a Loving Choice whether to let your Inner Children out without your Adaptive-Survivor parts being in control. When you are making progress at creating internal peace, instead of continuing the old battle between your Inner Critic and Adaptive-Survivor parts. When you can say out loud that you are seeking an identity through rebellion, instead of blaming another for your unhappiness. When you are doing what you want and are being who you want to be, instead of needing to rebel so you don't feel controlled. When you can truly make Loving Choices in your life, instead of being controlled by the need to do the "shoulds" or by the need to rebel.

An Example of a Self-Encounter About Rebellion

My **topic** is: *My partner left me, stating she needed more space in order to find herself.*

Logical importance is a ten. **Emotional charge** is a ten. My **motivation** is a ten because I want to make this crisis into a creative experience.

My **facts** are:
My partner suddenly informed me of her need to find emotional space. She separated and moved out two months ago. She told me she didn't love me any more and possibly wanted a divorce.

My **thoughts** are:

1) I think I was more devastated when she moved out than I have ever been in my life.

2) I thought she was crazy for abandoning me and our children.

3) I think her moving out caused me to expand my awareness and to look at myself more than I ever have.

4) I think I realize after reading this chapter how powerful my over-responsible survivor part has been in our marriage.

5) I think it is time to take care of myself instead of taking care of her.

My **body sensations** are:
When she moved out, I experienced stomach pains. I felt as though I had been kicked in the stomach. I still experience tension in my neck and shoulders.

My **feelings** are:

1) When she announced she was moving out, I felt devastated, overwhelmed, sad, angry, confused, scared to death, lost and fearful of how I would handle the kids.

2) After reading this chapter, I still feel devastated, but challenged, less confused, aware of what I need to do, and angry at myself for doing so much for her and so little for myself. I'm determined to deal with my survivor parts.

My **old Inner Critic** says:
"You sure were stupid to not see the problems that had been building in your relationship with her for several years. You deserve to be left for being so unaware and insensitive."

My **tamed Inner Critic** says:
"I suggest you make some commitments to improve your relationship with yourself. It is time to forget and forgive the past hurts and pain and get on with your life."

My **Inner Children** say:
"I enjoy spending more time with you. I am getting more attention from you than when she was living here. I don't want her to come back because she may demand all of your attention again. I feel sad, I feel confused. I hurt."

My **Wise Nurturer** says:
"This crisis has been one of the most important experiences in your life. The courage you have shown to rise to the occasion has been commendable. You have been able to nurture and parent your children while in the depths of pain. How do you feel about the strengths you have found in yourself?"

My **intentions** are:

1. I intend to invest in the relationship with myself. I want to remain open to any future there is in my relationship with her. I don't want to sacrifice myself for her anymore. It doesn't feel good to me and doesn't help her to find her identity.

2. I want to support her in finding her identity but not at the expense of diminishing the process of healing myself.

My **commitments** are:

1. I am committed to doing Self-Encounters and Internal Family Dialogues daily or as needed.

2. I am committed to doing a Self-Encounter and sharing it with her. I am open to listening to her response.

3. I will continue my therapy relationship as part of my process of letting go and transforming my survivor parts.

4. I will share some of the information I learned in this Chapter with her without expectations that she will respond as I want her to.

5. I will respect her seeking her identity process instead of judging and criticizing her.

6. I will take this opportunity to grow and develop a stronger identity myself.

An Example of an Initiator Encounter by Leslie: "Seeking My Identity."

Here is another example of a Self-Encounter that a woman participant shared with her husband in the Loving Choices Seminar. Leslie gives a good example of a person who has become tired of being controlled and overwhelmed by some Adaptive-Survivor parts, especially the people-pleaser and over-responsible parts. Leslie "hits the wall" emotionally when it becomes necessary to make some changes because she can't continue on the path that has become overwhelming to her.

Females often identify with this encounter more than males — for perhaps obvious reasons. It describes the identity process that many women find it necessary to go through when they start letting go of the Adaptive-Survivor parts that kept them from having an identity of their own. Here's Leslie:

My concern or topic for this encounter:
How my "Hitting the Wall" emotionally a year ago has affected us as individuals, our relationship and our children.

1. I **think** that the importance of this topic is a 10 because of the major changes this year has brought along with the pain, confusion, and joys.

2. The emotional charge I **feel** for this topic is an 8 or 9 although it has been a 10. I feel it is less emotional now than it has been.

3. My **motivation** for doing this Encounter is a 10 because I believe that the Self- and Healing Encounters were the tools we were missing.

My facts or observations:
I observed myself become extremely depressed last spring. I became numb, confused, and very dysfunctional. When I started counseling, I asked that you be there to help and support me. When asked by counselors what I needed or wanted, I had no idea—I wanted

someone to tell me. I became more depressed, angry, bitter, and confused. I withdrew from you completely without much communication or explanation, as I had no grasp or understanding of what was happening.

I could not get enough space. I was unable to communicate with you or to accept your love and caring. We continued living together, but our lifestyle changed. I insisted that we not work together as we had for 5 years. I spent more time with myself than with you. I observed that you became depressed, confused, and dysfunctional. You also began individual counseling. I heard you say that you were afraid our relationship was over, and that divorce was a good possibility.

My thoughts or perceptions:
I think my depression this last year was due to my disconnection, my loss of myself. I had not allowed myself the time to do what I needed for my own balance. I spent too much time worrying about what others were doing, what they needed. I had learned through my life to act secure and strong on the outside, while feeling scared to death on the inside. I found myself hollow and empty, unable to give to others or to myself.

My fear was being confused by my anger. I knew I was not as angry at you as the extreme anger I was feeling, so my pattern of withdrawing took over. I was afraid to communicate because my emotions were so overwhelming. I was afraid of not being good enough, of you criticizing me, telling me what I should do, trying to fix me to make things better for me. I perceived that your love was true and that you were genuinely wanting to help, but it distanced me further. I was feeling smothered, choking, unable to breathe, I wanted to run. I really didn't think this was about you, but I couldn't sort it out.

I perceive that this is changing for me, that I'm more able to see the growth process, to separate my fears and to be more balanced. I wish the process could have been less painful, less traumatic, less confusing, but I am so happy to be where I am today. I believe that taking the time I need for myself to fill my own cup will allow it to overflow. I think that life is full of mysteries and miracles, and I am looking forward to slowing down to explore and enjoy them with myself and with you and our children. I think I'm beginning to believe I deserve it.

My body sensations:
My body is tense as I write this, my stomach's queasy and tears are flowing. My body feels cold and shaky. My neck is stiff and hurts.

My feelings:
I still feel very guilty about how my pain and confusion hurt you and the kids. I feel sad thinking about it. I feel frightened thinking back to past hurt and pain and fearful about falling back into it. I feel angry at myself realizing how much precious time I've lost in letting fear overwhelm me. I feel mad as hell, and I'm not going to let it happen anymore. I feel less pressured, less anxious, more confidant, and more connected to you than ever. I feel motivated, excited, energized, hopeful. I feel honored that you love me and that you didn't leave when I was pushing you away. I feel sorry for all the times I hurt you and didn't let you know how special you are to me. I was unable to compliment you because I couldn't accept compliments and didn't believe them. I feel grateful for realizing that it wasn't you I was so angry with, that it was the dysfunctional patterns we were living in.

My survivors:

- My **perfectionist** part says, *"I may never be a perfect wife, person or mother so why even try."*

- My **under responsible** part says, *"I wish someone would just take me in their arms, make everything right, so I wouldn't have to do anything, because I can't do it myself."*

- My **work-a-holic** part says, *"The busier I keep myself, the less time I have to focus on the pain."*

- My **loner** part says, *"If I could just be alone, if everyone would leave me alone, I could be happy."*

- My **procrastinator** says, *"As soon as I get time, I'll work on this. There is always tomorrow."*

- My **pessimist** part says, *"Things will never work out!"*

- My **people-pleaser** says, *"I really want to do what makes you happy. You are more important than me. I will try to do what makes you happy."*

- My **rebel** says, *"I don't give a damn about anybody. Nobody's ever been there when I <u>really</u> needed them. Life is up to me and*

I'll do whatever I want, whenever I want, I really don't care. I will act tough so no one can hurt me."

- My **victim** says, *"Why am I always a failure? Why does my life have to be so difficult?"*

My Inner Critic:
"You're taking way too long to write this; hurry up! There are other things you should be doing. You think you're so smart. Well, you're not. You think you can do things but you can't. You can't stay focused, you can't accomplish anything right. You have big plans, but you never succeed. You should just give it up and accept that you're a failure."

My wounded Inner Child:
"I hate it when you talk to me like that. I want to leave and never come back. I hate you. You never listen to me!"

My playful Inner Child:
"Why can't we all just be happy and go out and play? I know we'll feel better if we all play and laugh. If we let ourselves have fun, I know we can all do what we want."

My Wise Nurturer:
"Boy, it's been a big year for you. You have really grown a lot, and I know it's been painful. I know things didn't go perfectly, but they went. You can be proud of where you are now. I know you're angry about not realizing and starting on all this sooner. It's O.K. to be angry and to use that energy to push on and do what you need to do.

"Listen to what your survivor parts are saying. Your loner knows you need time for yourself, so do it. Your people-pleaser knows you want to make people happy and feel important: do that for yourself. Also, work with your pessimist to say "Things will work out." Your perfectionist says why even try to be perfect? Good point, you don't need to be perfect. Be easier on yourself. You are trying and doing the best you can. You'll make more mistakes, suffer more pain, but you will also grow and experience the joys, the freedoms, the miracles of life.

"I know you're afraid—take it one day at a time. When you feel unbalanced, think about what you can do to get back in balance. You are worthy of it, you're a wonderful person, you have a wonderful husband and together you have a wonderful life and children."

My intentions:

1. I want to do more Self-Encounters to get more in touch with my inner voices.
2. I want to do more Healing Encounters with my partner to improve our communication.
3. I want to prioritize my needs and schedule them to fit into my daily life.
4. I want to continue experiences like this book and classes to continue learning.
5. I want to do more inner child work and do some regression work through hypnosis to better deal with my fears and childhood trauma.

Commitments:

1. I commit to continuing to do Self-Encounters regularly.
2. I commit to doing a Healing Encounter with you at least once a week.
3. I commit to continuing to use Tuesday (or another) night as a time for you and me to grow and share.
4. I commit to finding out prices and setting up an appointment for hypnosis therapy.

I will carry through with the commitments listed above. I have completed the above Self-Encounter to my satisfaction.

Comments on This Initiator Encounter

Leslie's partner did a profound Respondent Encounter. They stated this Healing Encounter was an important part of their healing process. The participants in the Loving Choices Seminar were blown away emotionally and gave a round of applause to the couple upon completion of the Healing Encounter.

Notice how authentic each of Leslie's parts were. Even reading it you can hear the difference in her voice as she shared each part. There were no weak or missing parts in her Encounter.

Notice the many Adaptive-Survivor parts she shared, and how she nurtured these survivor parts with her Wise Nurturer. None of these survivor parts will have as much power and control as they had before she did this Encounter.

This Encounter is a good example of a person evolving to internal rebellion. Her partner shared a Respondent Encounter, letting go of the parental, over-responsible and controlling Adaptive-Survivor parts. This couple is making their crisis into a creative and growing experience.

What topics emerged for you in this chapter? Did you find any new concepts that were intriguing or fascinating? Do you disagree with any ideas or concepts in this chapter? Your learning and your disagreements would make good topics for your own Self-Encounters. Why not schedule yourself a Self-Encounter on any topics that were important to you in this chapter?

How Are You Doing?

The following statements are designed to help you internalize and integrate the material in this chapter. Mark those statements that you have completed.

1. *The number of Self-Encounters I am committed to do about understanding the search for identity process____ .*

2. *The number of Internal Family Conversations I am committed to do to heal my Inner Children ____.*

3. *The number of Healing Encounters I am committed to do with my partner in order to help make this crisis a creative experience for us ____.*

4. *I have identified which stage of the seeking identity process I am in.*

5. *I have the strength and courage to be able to do internal rebellion.*

6. *I understand the process of seeking my identity separate from the expectations of my family of origin and society.*

7. *I understand which stage of growth and development my partner is in.*

8. *I understand which stage of growth and development my parents are in.*

Check list for the person seeking identity

1. *I am working towards the stage of love and forgiveness.*

2. *I have identified which of the seven behaviors typical in external rebellion are relevant to me.*

3. *I have identified which survivor part(s) were controlling me in my Shell stage.*

4. *I am able to detach and look objectively at my relationship with another person.*

5. *I am committed to talk to my partner about my process.*

6. *I own that my process has very little to do with my partner.*

7. *I am open to ask for help, to be less independent, and to be open to new ideas that may help me reach the love and forgiveness stage.*

Check list for the partner

1. *I have examined my controlling survivor parts.*

2. *I am doing an adequate job of self care.*

3. *I am not taking my partner's process personally but am remaining detached.*

4. *I have made the decision whether I want to leave the relationship or to remain.*

5. *I am able to listen objectively to my partner even though sometimes I don't like what I am hearing.*

6. *I am clear how I feel about my partner's other relationship and what my limits and boundaries are.*

CHAPTER TEN

Your Inner Children

IT'S NEVER TOO LATE
TO HAVE A HAPPY CHILDHOOD

*The **challenge** is to connect with and build healthy
relationships with your many Inner Children.*

*The **loving choice** is to listen to and accept all of your
Inner Children.*

*I*n this chapter, we're going to learn more about those inner
children who've been with us all our lives. The Wise Nurturer,
whose job it is to care for the Inner Children, will take us on a
"tour" through the World of the Inner Children. If you've been
wondering how to connect with the child(ren) inside you, here's
your chance to find out!

World of the Inner Children: The Tour

I am the **Wise Nurturer** and your designated tour guide. I invite
you to come along with me to visit an inner sanctuary — a beautiful
place inside you — that I call The World of the Inner Children. I
invite you to relax and come along with me as I guide you into the
wonderful, magical, and sacred world of the children within you.
There is much for me to share and teach you about yourself and
this world.

Look! We're coming to a gate leading into a beautiful garden.
The name of the guard standing there is **Protector.** His job is to take

care of the Inner Children; he won't let them talk to strangers or anyone who might be dangerous. Let me point out that there are all kinds of protectors. Some of the Inner Children have a big, strong, mean protector who won't ever let the children out. These Inner Children live within people who were abused and wounded as they were growing up, and are really hurting because they don't get enough love and attention.

All of the Inner Children have a protector guard at the gate. That teenager over there has a guard that says things like, "I met this therapist, and I told her that I don't talk to therapists." Over there is a sad little child who feels as if she doesn't have a friend in the world. Most people won't have much to do with her. Her protector tells her things like, "Never trust anyone — you'll just get hurt!" There's a lonely and hurt group of children who live with a super-logical protector who never even acknowledges that he has feelings. These children are very rarely allowed out because, when they do come out, all they do is cry.

Usually when I acknowledge and say nurturing things to the protectors, they will let me talk to the Inner Children they're protecting. If you want to get to know your Inner Children, you can do the same. Make friends with the protector. These guys are really sharp, and not easily fooled; they take their jobs very seriously. If you don't really care about your Inner Children, they will know it, and not let you in.

Often, after friends have been made with the protector guards, more questions arise. What do you say? How do you contact your Inner Children and tell them you want to get to know them better? Here's a suggestion: Find some pictures of yourself as a baby. Spend some time looking at them. Try to imagine what the baby in the pictures was feeling. Ask the baby directly and honestly, and then listen with your heart. Did you feel wanted? Did you trust others? How much confidence did you have? Was the world a safe place for you? Did you feel loved? Now do the same with a pre-school-age picture. Were you closer to your father, mother, or another adult? Did you find the world a fun place to be? Did you feel secure? You may want to repeat this exploration with pictures of yourself in early elementary school.

Before we proceed, I want to point out — over there, beneath that arch — another guard: **Caretaker-Survivor.** He came on the scene a long time ago, and actually helped the children develop some important survivor skills; he's a real caretaker. Most everybody likes Caretaker because he nurtures them. Since he gets so much attention for taking care of everybody, he's decided to hang around. He keeps doing so many nice things for you that you'll rarely notice the lonely Inner Children hiding in his backpack.

Ready to move on? Rather than talk "about" the Inner Children, I want to allow them to speak for themselves. Let's go farther into the sanctuary and meet some of these children.

Hi! Would you tell us who you are?

"I call myself the **playful child.** I'm just naturally creative, spontaneous, playful, and fun-loving. I enjoy the present; I don't care about what happened yesterday, and I never worry about tomorrow. The person I live within doesn't let me come out very often. I'd like to bring more joy into his life because he is so serious most of the time. I love it when we fly a kite, play Frisbee with his dog, dance in the rain, or play in mud puddles."

On the other side of the trees is a child with a camera who has been watching us. Let's go meet her…

"Hello. I am known as the **creative child.** I feel so joyful and happy! I love to draw and paint wonderful pictures, write words about new ideas, and think of a challenging new game to play. Life really is a big game to play, you know. One of my favorite things to do is to make puppets and put on a show. Lots of people say that I'm fun to be around because I am so unusual. I am having fun taking pictures right now."

And, standing over there in the corner…

"They call me the **spoiled child.** I've always gotten anything I wanted. I think the whole world revolves around me and what I want. Lots of people say that I have never been frustrated in my entire life, but that's not true. I get really, really mad when I don't get what I want, and I throw temper tantrums until I get my way."

Over there is a child that looks unhappy.

"I'm the **neglected child.** I was always left alone and had to learn to get along without much nurturing and love. I don't believe anyone in the world could love me. How could they? I don't even know how to love myself. I need someone to spend some time with me. I want someone to see me and to know that I am here. I am hurting a lot. I don't think that I am lovable. I feel so sad. I want to cry and cry. I wish you would take care of me."

See those children with the sad look on their faces?
    "We're the **abandoned children.** Some of us have been adopted, and some of us were just left alone while our parents were busy making money or becoming famous. Some of our parents were just trying to survive —just like we are. We are always fearful about who's going to abandon us next. We all need someone to really listen to us talk about our pain. We are starving for some extra attention and reassurance that we are okay. We need to feel safe and to know that we won't be left alone. We are so lonely."

Over by the river a child is hiding in the shadows.
    "I'm the **fearful child.** I was always criticized when I was little. Now I feel anxious all the time. I don't believe I can do anything right, so I never try any new games. I need lots of encouragement and positive affirmations. I am really scared. That's why I hide."

Right behind the fearful child is a group sitting on the ground.
    "We are the **vulnerable children.** We all huddle together because it feels safer when we are in a group. We all feel very exposed and open. We talk to each other about what it is like to feel naked, because we are!"

And there is a child alone in the field.
    "I am the **unbonded child.** I never learned to be close to anyone. I feel totally alone and isolated, and am afraid of being intimate with anyone. Some times I do take the risk of getting close, but then I become afraid and I figure out clever ways to keep from experiencing intimacy. I live an isolated life, and even a small flame of intimacy feels hot to me. I need lots of attention to gradually trust other people."

Even farther in the distance:
    "I am the **discounted child.** I'm ignored and treated as if I don't even exist. I feel invisible, as though I don't matter at all. I wonder all the time if I am really okay. I need to love and be loved. I don't believe in myself; no one else does, either. I wish I knew why."

On the other side of the hill are children peeking their heads over the top.

"We're the **traumatized children.** We feel as if we've been in the war zone, with bombs going off all around us. Some of us just sit around and stare because we are so frightened. Some of us were traumatized by alcoholic parents. Most of us were abused in one way or another. We never knew what was going to happen, so we learned not to talk about our feelings. We still don't know what is safe. We all are so hurt and scared, and wish that someone would come and help us. Will you?"

There is another group sitting together in the woods.

"We are the **wounded children**. Some of us were physically and sexually abused by adults; all of us have scars on our chests, near our hearts. Some of us were verbally abused by angry parents, and we're still very afraid to be around anyone who is angry, because they might hurt us even more. We are very shy and passive. We have a lot of angry feelings inside, but we are afraid to let our anger out. We have lots of fears. We all wish that someone would come along with a first-aid kit and heal our pain; it is so great."

Our last group of Inner Children are playing on the highest hill in the sanctuary. Their laughter can be heard like a silver bell, ringing in the distance.

"Hi. I'm called the **wise child.** I am here on this beautiful hill with my two best friends. We love being together. We were talking about dreams, and we decided that a dream is a thought with a mind of its own. Dreaming and believing is what I do best. So many of the other Inner Children here in the sanctuary feel so much pain and hurt, and we want to share our wisdom and love with them. I hope that they are listening. Now I want you to meet one of my best friends…"

"Hello. I'm the **spiritual child** — the child who believes in angels. When I look at the sun and the moon and the stars, I remember who I really am. I love being alive and love living on this beautiful Earth. I love to remind everyone that we are all children. And speaking of children, our other friend wants to meet you, too."

"Hi! I'm over here! I love flying through the air, hanging onto an umbrella. Do you remember the movie *Mary Poppins?* When I saw it, I knew that I could fly just like Mary. I really can! They call me the **magical child**. I also love Peter Pan, Tinker Bell, and fairy dust. I like to think that we're all magicians. I'm really happy that I got to be the last child in the sanctuary to speak, because I want to remind you again: '*It's never too late to have a happy childhood.*'"

Connecting with Your Inner Children

Thanks for letting me be your tour guide. It was a great pleasure to introduce you to some of the children in the sanctuary. Now I hope you'll allow me to share with you some of what I've learned as the Nurturer of the Inner Children.

Before I begin, take a moment and close your eyes. I invite you to gently and lovingly go inside and ask yourself, "What is my inner sanctuary like? How do I want to act with my Inner Children? What can I learn from my Inner Children? How many of the Inner Children that spoke in the preceding pages am I aware of within me? How do I assist all of these Inner Children to feel loved and accepted?"

One of the most important concepts to remember is that *you have all of the Inner Children that we've just met within you*, and more, and they're all ages. Most people are aware of *some* of their Inner Children; we invite you to begin to recognize *all* of your various Inner Children. This process of opening to The World of the Inner Children can enhance your life in miraculous ways!

There are dozens of ways you can connect with your Inner Children to help them heal, feel loved, and be happy. Children have a way of connecting with other children that many adults don't understand or know about. Sometimes just a glance or making eye contact can express what might take a thousand words to communicate.

In the earlier chapters of *Loving Choices* you learned how to do Self-Encounters and Internal Family Conversations. It is amazing to see how your Inner Children respond to these encounters. Many people share that the Inner Children finally feel listened to. The Self-Encounter provides a chance to write what those children inside you have to say. Spending time to do the encounters will assist you in slowing down long enough to hear the children's voices cautiously begin to speak.

It is amazing how excited the Inner Children become when you do the Internal Family Conversation. At that time the Wise Nurturer can say all the things that the Inner Children have been longing to hear, allowing them to blossom like flowers. It is very important to allow your adult Wise Nurturer to nurture your Inner Children.

One of the special ways of conversing with your Inner Children that many have found rewarding is to write a question to one or more of the children *with your dominant (writing) hand.* Sit back quietly and listen for the answer, then write the answer *with the other hand.* (Don't worry about penmanship!) Sometimes the answer will come in picture form, rather than words. It is fun to watch the Inner Children use this technique to say the things they have wanted to say for a long time. The wise child speaks up and points out that as long as you stay in your left brain, logical mode, the Inner Children cannot penetrate the cold, unfeeling thoughts. When you start using your right brain — which isn't used to writing — the child jumps in and expresses what it wants to say. The logical part of your brain is temporarily distracted, allowing another kind of thought pattern to emerge. (You're probably aware that research has shown that the non-dominant hand is directed by the creative, non-logical, half of the brain.)

When you start talking to the Inner Children, ask what they would like to eat tonight, what would make them feel loved, what special gift they might like. Ask what gift they would like to give you. Your goal is to get to know your Inner Children and to make an emotional connection with them. For instance, we all like to be called by our names. Ask the Inner Children what they would like to be called.

It's very important to begin taming the Inner Critic. That voice from the past keeps beating up the Inner Children, and can perpetuate trauma and pain from childhood. When you use the Internal Family Conversation, I — your humble servant and Wise Nurturer — can stand nose-to-nose with the Inner Critic, and provide affirmation and support. I also protect the Inner Children in a loving way against the Inner Critic, who has not yet been tamed, and may not yet know what love is.

When I nurture the Inner Critic, the children often heave a big sigh of relief. The children know that when the Inner Critic is nurtured enough it relaxes, and they will not have to worry about being hurt by it anymore.

This is often when the rebellion starts. For years the Inner Critic has kept the Inner Children suppressed — in the closet, so to speak.

When the children are let out of the closet and start having fun, they may lose control and play havoc with your life, causing rebellion. Hopefully this book will help you transform the Inner Critic into a good internal parent. Inner Children need to have fun and be heard, but in order to keep balance in your life, the Inner Children also must have some emotional and psychological limits.

My hope is that this tour has assisted you to better know your Inner Children, who have been longing to know *you* better for a long time. The Loving Choice to connect with this precious part of yourself will assist in profound healing, and result in a healthy relationship with your Inner Children. As we end the tour, and return you to the teaching mode, I invite you to remember the *magical child,* as she joyfully repeated Claudia Black's advice: "It's never too late to have a happy childhood!"

Gary's Inner Child Self-Encounter

Gary was a 33-year-old participant in the Loving Choices Seminar who gained a great deal from touring the World of his Inner Children. We'd like to share his Self-Encounter following the tour. This encounter was a deeply buried memory that emerged from Gary's newly-found "teenage Inner Child." He had great fun expressing this memory and sharing it with us.

The **topic** is: *Going out on my first date to a high school dance with Ginger.*

- The **importance** is a 10
- The **emotional charge** is a 10
- The **motivation** is a 10, because I don't want to blow this golden opportunity to be with Ginger — the most beautiful girl in the whole world.

My **facts** are:

- It is Sadie Hawkins day at my high school, where the girls ask the boys for a date.
- Right after math class, Ginger asked me to go to the dance on Friday night.
- I have never been on a date with a girl.
- Ginger is a cheerleader and is very popular with the other kids.

My **thoughts** are:

- I can't believe this beautiful and popular girl has asked me out!
- I think I will be uncomfortable being on a date.
- I think I would never ask a girl out for a date, and the only reason I am going is because I didn't want to hurt her feelings by saying "no."
- I think this will be an important experience for me.

My **body sensations** are:

- My stomach is upset and I feel like I am going to throw up.

My **feelings** are:

- I feel afraid, anxious, excited, inadequate, immature, and fearful I will make a fool of myself.

My **Adaptive-Survivors** are:

- My "go-fishing" Adaptive-Survivor — the one that protects me by being gone — wants to go fishing with Tom and not tell anyone where I am.

My **Inner Critic** says:

- You're not old enough to go on a date with such a pretty girl. You are going to screw up this situation. You will probably throw up at her doorstep when you pick her up.

My **playful Inner Child** says:

- I'm scared to death. I'm afraid she won't like me. I hope she doesn't try to kiss me. I am going to practice what I will say to her. I have asked Tom to look out for me and make sure I'm doing okay. I am going to talk to my mother about how I feel. I'm sure Mom will give me some good pointers on how to act and be supportive of me. I am going to dress up so my date won't laugh at me. I wonder if I could take my dog along with me.

My **wise Inner Child** says:

- I'll always remember this first date for the rest of my life. I'll never be quite the same again.

My **magical Inner Child** says:

- Pick her up in a limousine and have the chauffeur serve us chocolate chip cookie dough and ice cream all evening.

My **fearful Inner Child** says:

- I'm afraid she will find out what I am really like and reject me. I'll hide my inner secrets from her and not let her get to know me.

My **wounded Inner Child** says:

- Don't let her hurt me. I feel very vulnerable around a new person that I don't know very well. A girl that is so pretty and popular will not be interested in hearing about how much I hurt deep down inside. I'm afraid I will let down my guard and talk to her about my sad and painful feelings from when I was abused.

My **Wise Nurturer** says:

- Good job. Keep talking out your feelings from all of your Inner Children and you will be okay. This is an important night for you and you will have a good time. You have a healthy playful child who enjoys life. This child will help you have fun on a date with Ginger. I suggest you leave your dog home; you'll do just fine on your date without Rover.

My **intentions, wants and needs** are:

- I want to have a good time on this date. I want to get to know Ginger better. I want to grow up and learn how to be comfortable with girls and not be so afraid.

My **commitments** are:

- I am committed to going out on this date. I am committed to listening to Ginger. I am committed to asking her how she feels about going out on a date. I am committed to going out on another date in the future.

When Gary presented his Self-Encounter to the seminar, the participants cheered him on. His wife, Valerie, cheered the loudest!

We encourage you to stretch, and enter the wondrous world of your Inner Children. You will never be the same!

HOW ARE YOU DOING?

1. *The number of Self-Encounters I am committed to doing this next week with a topic related to my Inner Children ___.*

2. *The number of Internal Family Conversations I am committed to having this next week related to my Inner Children ___.*

3. *The number of Healing Encounters I am committed to doing with another person related to my Inner Children ___.*

4. *I can describe what some of my protector parts look like.*

5. *I know and can identify some of my healthy Inner Children.*

6. *I know which of my healthy Inner Children I want to access and become more connected with.*

7. *I know which of my wounded Inner Children need more love and attention.*

8. *I believe I can assist in healing my wounded Inner Children by using the Internal Family Conversation.*

9. *I have transformed my Inner Critic so it does not beat up my Inner Children anymore.*

10. *I am committed to creating a better emotional connection with my many Inner Children.*

11. *I am committed to opening The World Of My Inner Children: playful child, creative child, spoiled child, neglected child, abandoned child, fearful child, vulnerable child, unbonded child, discounted child, traumatized child, wounded child, wise child, spiritual child, and magical child.*

12. *I am committed to inviting all of my Inner Children into my life.*

CHAPTER ELEVEN

Power Struggles

WHAT AM I GROWING THROUGH?

*The **challenge** is to discover that the Power Struggles you
are having with others are really your
internal conflicts projected out upon your
relationships with others.*

*The **loving choice** is to use Awareness, Commitment, and
Communication to take responsibility for
your contributions to the disharmony in your
relationships with others.*

ou really need to read this book. You have so many problems. You are always arguing with me over such
insignificant things. No matter how hard I try to get along
with you, you keep finding something wrong with me."

"You think *I* need to read this book? Your denial is amazing. I
don't know how you could have lived for forty years and still not
know anything about yourself."

When two people were engaged in a power struggle, an
exchange such as this could go on for three minutes — or maybe
three hours; it might be an example of how they spend most of
their time talking to each other.

No doubt you can relate to this scenario. Power struggles can
happen in any relationship — with your love partner, your parents,
your teenage children, a co-worker, a business associate, or almost
anyone. The power struggles that last the longest most often are
with your primary love partner or a family member.

This chapter will help you understand your contribution to the
disharmony in your relationships. It is so easy to look at how the

other person needs to change, but so hard to see what *your* contribution is. It is truly a Loving Choice to face the Challenge of changing a power struggle relationship into asking, "What am I *growing* through?"

Let's look at some characteristics of two people in a power struggle relationship.

• There is a continual struggle over power and control. "I don't feel *I* have any power or control, so *you* must have it all."

• Arguments erupt over small and ridiculous issues, such as how to squeeze the toothpaste tube. "Everyone knows it's supposed to be squeezed from the bottom. What's wrong with you?"

• Issues don't get resolved. The things that you were fighting over ten years ago are still being fought over. Even when you think you have an issue resolved, it will come up again and again. "I thought we decided last week that the bathroom tissue was to roll from the outside."

• Both parties feel desperate and hopeless. "Nothing is ever going to change. We have been fighting for years. I have become emotionally drained. All we do is slice and dice each other until we are both hurt, angry and feeling defeated."

• Usually the only part of the Self-Encounter used is thoughts and interpretations. The communication consists of "you-messages", with no one sharing or talking about feelings. The belief is that sharing a feeling would make you vulnerable and more easily hurt during the verbal exchange.

• The feeling of intimacy with each other is indirect, and a result of fighting. At least when you are fighting, you are no longer being ignored. We had a coup[le of sayings in graduate school that illustrated this idea: "It is better to be wanted for murder, than to not be wanted at all." And, "If you are shouting at me, I feel better than when you are ignoring me."

• If an outside party interferes, the two people will frequently turn on them as the common enemy. Police know how hard it is to handle a domestic dispute when they are called. Both parties blame the outsider who has interfered. "We don't need a law officer to settle this dispute. This is between us; leave us alone."

• The name of the game is to fight. If a therapist or a friend succeeds in helping the two people resolve an issue, they then find another issue in order to continue the fight. "I won't give up until you've admitted you are wrong."

• The power struggle can be either a hot war or a cold war. The hot war has lots of shouting, fighting, and loud arguments. The cold war power struggle consists of controlling through silence, by withdrawing and walking away. Refusing to talk may be a controlling, passive-aggressive act.

• A power struggle does not feel good. There are few "warm fuzzies" and affirmations. It's simply about hurting each other as best you can. "Every time I try to talk to you, I end up feeling hurt and angry."

• You can't let go of trying to change the other person long enough to look at yourself. "It's time for some changes. Why don't you change first?" is typical power struggle vocabulary.

A relationship has stages of growth and development, just as we physically grow and develop. By understanding these stages, you can more clearly understand the roots of the power struggle. (Thanks to Dr. Susan Campbell's books, *The Couple's Journey* and *Beyond the Power Struggle*, for many of the ideas in this chapter.)

Let's look at the first stage of a committed relationship.

Honeymoon Period

You want to be alone with each other when you first start the relationship. The honeymoon period is full of romance and passion. You look at life through rose- colored glasses. A friend shared that she thought being in love was not only blind, but it was also deaf. Advice or suggestions from others seem to fall on deaf ears. Many individuals are *emotionally blind and deaf* when they start a love relationship.

Perhaps you grew up believing the myth that all you had to do was find a partner and you would live happily ever after. If you weren't completely happy as a single person, you believed your relationship partner would make you happy. You may have been a half-person looking for another half-person, believing that the two of you would become one and whole. Making your partner responsible for your happiness is the beginning of a co-dependent relationship. It's a burden that many people place upon their partner.

Buried underneath the honeymoon enthusiasm are lots of unresolved issues. Eventually you have to dig down to these issues, and enter into the phase in your relationship that we call the *power struggle*.

Understanding the Power Struggle

There is an old adage, "When a couple starts trying to decide who is the boss, the honeymoon is over." Issues over power and control, and who is going to make the big decisions and who is going to make the little decisions can bring the honeymoon to a screeching halt. Instead of the honeymoon feelings of romance and passion, all of the unresolved issues begin emerging.

A common theme when couples come for counseling is that one person feels no power or control, therefore, this *must* mean the other person has it all. The partner stares back in amazement because he believed *she* had all the power and control. This is an important point in growth when the couple begins to expand their awareness. Who *does* have the power and control? Where did it go?

If we believe the common fairy tale theme — that all we have to do is to be in a relationship in order to live happily ever after — we've given the responsibility for our happiness to someone else. What a burden to start a relationship with, by asking the other person to be responsible for our happiness. Unfortunately, when you start working through the power struggle issues in a relationship, you often feel unhappy. At this point, *the person who was responsible for your happiness is now responsible for your unhappiness.* No wonder we slice and dice each other; no one wants to admit your beliefs are an illusion.

The resolution of the power struggle is easy to talk about and is a Challenge to accomplish. It is a matter of taking ownership and responsibility for your own happiness or unhappiness. No one else can make you happy or unhappy; your long-term happiness is a result of the way you live your life, the way you make decisions, the attitudes you adopt, and the way you resolve issues. When you take responsibility for your happiness — or unhappiness — then you are beginning to resolve the power struggle.

The Boiling Pot of Stew

A power struggle is like a pot of stew, boiling over on the stove. The belief that someone else is responsible for your happiness is the heat that keeps the pot boiling. There are numerous ingredients in the stew. These are the beliefs that you started cultivating in your childhood, many years ago. Each ingredient is an issue that you failed to work through and resolve. Eventually it got thrown into the power struggle stew. The more unresolved issues you have, the more the pot boils over. Resolving a power struggle is like picking out each ingredient from the boiling stew, being careful not to get burned, and then dealing with that issue by yourself. You thought the power struggle would not end until the person you are doing battle with changed. A big ingredient in the stew, however, is your projection of your own unfinished issues onto the relationship. *The power struggle diminishes when you begin resolving your own internal conflicts.*

Here are some of the ingredients; your unresolved issues:

The *ghosts of your ancestors* add a special flavor to the stew. In chapter 8 we shared that Bruce comes from a family of domineering males, and Nina comes from a family of powerful women. Our ancestor ghosts got thrown into the boiling pot. We had to overcome the power and influence of our family of origin in order to avoid becoming puppets, allowing them to have a power struggle through us. How many ghosts are in your pot of power struggle stew?

Any *stockpiled anger* that has been unexpressed is like a stick of dynamite, just waiting to be ignited. If you are frustrated with what feels like a lack of power and control, that might be the fuse that ignites the anger. It adds some beet-red coloring to the stew.

Rebellion can really stir up the stew and keep it boiling over. If you are trying to find an identity by rebelling, it is easy for you to believe your partner is the one responsible for your lack of identity. "If only you would change, I could be happy" is common vocabulary used by a person in rebellion.

If the pot's not boiling enough, mix in some *alcohol or drugs.* Pain and frustration can be overwhelming in a power struggle; it is easy to attempt to deaden the pain with drugs. Drugs keep you from recognizing underlying problems, and can postpone — or terminate — the healing of these issues.

For a little bit of extra flavoring in this boiling pot, add some *loneliness*. "You were supposed to love me the way that my parents didn't love me. I'm trying to feel intimate and close with you, and all I get is shouting and arguing."

Add some *gender role behaviors* to the pot. Stereotypic beliefs of who fulfills what role may become a factor in the power struggle. "What do you want anyway?" may be a common question. The response might be a passive expectation of, "If you really loved me, you'd know what I want without having to ask me." Both of these behaviors can turn the stew sour.

A *projector* is a person who believes that someone, or something else, is responsible for his pain. An *introjector* is a person who believes she is responsible for someone else's pain, and internalizes that pain. The two often end up in a relationship together. What often happens in the power struggle is that the introjector reaches a saturation point, and starts dumping back all the pain she has been internalizing. If the projector continues projecting, the pot of stew can really boil over.

The stew begins to thicken and become firm when the righteous person attempts to *turn thoughts and feelings into absolute fact*. This is a potent ingredient for a power struggle stew, because the righteous person has to prove the other person wrong in order to perpetuate her beliefs.

If one or both of the people *cannot access and talk about feelings*, those feelings keep growing inside like bacteria, eventually contaminating the stew.

It's easy to find an *escape* from the power struggle by becoming a work-a-holic, busy-holic, or alcoholic. Any escape will often feel better than the stress and pain of the continual fighting in a power struggle.

Maybe you learned a childhood pattern of *shouting and yelling* for what you wanted or needed. It worked as a child, and it may be another ingredient in the power struggle stew. "This stew is mine and you can't have any!"

Polarization

What is polarization? This is an important ingredient in the stew. It is an issue about which you disagree, or argue about, with another person. You take a rigid position, and become stubborn about your belief. Your partner does the same thing, and thus, you become polarized about the issue.

Your Adaptive-Survivor parts are usually compulsive and rigid because they act as protection for underlying unmet needs. (Review chapter 3.) You might choose a partner who has an Adaptive-Survivor part that is the opposite of yours. Adaptive-Survivor parts that you are not aware of, and that are still in control, will almost always add some polarization to the power struggle stew.

The relationship bridge is a good example of polarization. Over- and under-responsible polarization is seen as one person sweeping the bridge, while the other person fishes contentedly from the bridge. Over-responsible says, "If you want it done, and want it done right, you've got to do it yourself." Over-responsible sweeps the whole bridge, and resentment builds up because under-responsible is doing nothing but enjoying the fishing.

The fishing person, however, resents the bridge sweeper for continually sweeping the bridge and disturbing the fish. "I'm not catching any fish because you keep making so much noise with your broom." Adaptive-Survivor polarization can cause the stew to become too thick and firm because Adaptive-Survivor parts don't like to compromise, and have the illusion, "My Adaptive-Survivor is better and healthier than yours."

Let's discuss how polarization happens. Jerry learned not to express feelings because his environment was so emotional and undependable. He grew up to be a very rational and logical engineer-scientist. He married Janet because she could express the feelings that he had not learned to access. It worked in the beginning stages of the relationship, but as time went on, Jerry became more rational and logical, while Janet became more emotional. When she sensed that something was missing in the relationship and tried to ask him about what he was feeling, it was very threatening to him. He thought that if he talked about feelings in his growth and developmental years, he would be criticized, rejected, and would feel guilty. He had learned not to show feelings as a way of protecting himself from becoming hurt.

When Janet asked him to share his feelings, Jerry became even more rational and logical, and didn't allow any feelings to come out. They began to polarize; the more emotional she was, the more rational he became. They had a somewhat traditional male-female polarization, and unfortunately, Jerry ended up cold and lonely on the logical north pole, and Janet found herself on the emotional south pole.

If one person is ready to grow and change, and the other person isn't, polarization may result. It often seems the more one person wants to grow, the more "stuck" the other person stays. Visualize a relationship bridge where the growing end of the bridge keeps getting higher and higher, and the other end of the bridge shows no change. Pretty soon the bridge is at a steep angle and under stress. One says, "We need to change," and the other says, "I'm happy just the way I am." The analogy is meaningful when you think about the two people trying to connect on a bridge with a steep slant.

Let's look at polarization over guilt and rejection. Many couples consist of one partner who feels more guilt and another partner who feels more rejection. As a child, if you don't get your needs met, you developed an Adaptive-Survivor part. If you thought you were a bad person, you felt guilty; if you were ignored and discounted, you feel rejected. This polarization can also manifest itself in families, and a power struggle may be the result. Members of the same family often take the two opposite positions because of unresolved pain and wounds.

What about parenting? Jim's stereotypical position is that his children need strong discipline, more rules, and appropriate consequences for their behavior. His love is conditional: "I'll love you if you behave in appropriate ways." Joanne takes the position of listening. She believes that until somebody listens to her children's feelings, they will continue to misbehave. She believes rigid rules will result in their feeling "not OK." "They need warm, unconditional love and acceptance from us." Jim and Joanne are extremely rigid about their individual parenting beliefs, and their two very different positions result in polarizing power struggle arguments. Another ingredient in the power struggle stew.

Here is a variation of that polarization. George believes the man is supposed to earn the income, while the wife stays home and takes care of the family. He becomes more and more preoccupied with his work. Karen finds her only solution to the loneliness she feels in the relationship is to become the perfect housekeeper. The lonelier she feels, and the more her husband is unavailable, the cleaner the house. "At least if I can't be emotionally close to him, I will show him how much I love him by keeping the house really clean." His response is, "It doesn't feel good to come home when she is always cleaning the house. I think I'll work overtime tonight and show her how much I love her by providing money more 'things.'" It is easy for males and females to polarize in gender-role behaviors, and then contribute to the power struggle by blaming the other person.

A common belief today seems to be that relationship problems are the result of changing stereotypical gender roles. "Women who are becoming independent cause relationships to end." When we looked at the various polarizations in relationships, we discovered that many of them are an expression of the old-fashioned sex roles. It is interesting to speculate that polarization may diminish in relationships as people grow beyond the old gender-role expectations. Maybe the changing roles are an attempt to create more healthy relationships.

Consequences of Polarization

There are some serious consequences of polarizing. Of the people who participated in the Rebuilding divorce recovery seminars, over 80% identified themselves as over-responsible. It is an important factor, and may partially explain why the relationship ended. Not only does polarization contribute to a power struggle, it can also contribute to the relationship coming to an end.

It is interesting to speculate why the over-responsible person took the class, while the under-responsible person seldom did. A partial answer may be that the over-responsible person always wants to do things "right." "I am going to do everything I can to make things work." Secondly, the over-responsible person tends to give himself away and become emotionally drained. He would come into class hurting a great deal. The warm, supportive atmosphere of the class helped fill up the emptiness that came from a lifetime of giving. (Please note: Attending a class does not automatically make one over-responsible, just as not attending a class does not make one under-responsible!)

The over-responsible partner was nurturing and took care of the other person who hadn't been nurtured. Her little child inside did not feel loved and cared for. She gave to others because it tended to make her Inner Children feel good. It didn't work, however, because she continued to give more than she received. She was good at giving, but poor at receiving.

The over-responsible person often becomes emotionally drained and resentful of always giving. The last gasp of the over-responsible person is anger at the other person for never giving back. The anger is the last stage before the relationship ends, and attorneys become wealthy from the power struggle that continues into the divorce courts.

Underlying the power struggle in a relationship is an unmet need to be nurtured. It is as if the two Inner Children of the people involved were saying, "I can't make myself happy. You will have to do it for me." This is truly a difficult part of the journey toward healthy relationships. We have found that many people are not able to resolve their power struggle until they have competed working through the underlying issues —the ingredients in the power struggle stew.

Changing Power Struggles into Growing Pains

One way to resolve the power struggle is to ask yourself, "What am I *growing* through?" This implies ownership and minimizes blaming the other person. It dissipates your belief that your partner will have to change in order for you to be happy. You are taking responsibility for your own growth and happiness.

Words do make a difference. Can you hear more hope in the phrase "growing pains" than in "power struggle"? Not only does it sound more hopeful, but it is also more descriptive. Here are some suggestions to help you find out what you are growing through:

• The fire under the stew pot is a form of *projection* and *lack of ownership*. Making the other person responsible for your happiness is the main force that keeps you from resolving the power struggle. Taking ownership for your own happiness or unhappiness will diminish your power struggle more than any other thing you can do.

• The connection between projection and the *use of "you-messages"* is not a coincidence. When a couple involved in a power struggle uses "I feel," instead of "you should" messages, they will notice a change from the power struggle to growing pains.

• Related to this is using *communication skills*. Self-Encounters encourage ownership, which will lead to resolving the issues common to the power struggle. Keep working toward closure in your Healing Encounters. Realize it will take a strong commitment and motivation to reach closure around emotionally charged power struggle issues. Keep in mind what we like to say, "The Self-Encounter is the main course; the Healing Encounter is the dessert." *Two-way Healing Encounters will not work in a power struggle relationship if you haven't done the Self-Encounters first.*

• There is a *lack of boundaries* when you are in a power struggle. Making the other person responsible for your happiness is a boundary issue. Identify and become aware of boundaries so you can separate each other's issues and not become convoluted. (More about this in the next chapter.)

• Keep searching for the *unresolved issues* — the ingredients — that you are throwing into the boiling stew pot. Discovering and working though this list can be a life-long Challenge.

• *Self-Encounters* and *Healing Encounters* become very important in resolving power struggles. People in a power struggle, however, often use only the thoughts part. They typically make "I think you" statements, which are badly disguised "you-messages". If each person can learn to change the "I think *you*" statements to "I think I" statements, the power struggle diminishes.

Here is an exercise for you: Write out the Self-Encounter with as many "I think you" statements as possible. This allows you to express anger and blame with as much force as possible. It is a cleansing experience, allowing you to express as much of the anger in your system as possible.

Now the important part. Before you share the "you-message" encounter with another, go through and change all of the "you" statements to "I think I" statements. It is a way of owning your anger, and using your projections as a mirror back into yourself. This will help you find unresolved issues that you have been projecting out into the relationship.

• People in a power struggle avoid talking about feelings for a number of reasons. If the underlying issues are fuel for the power struggle, talking about feelings can bring those issues to the surface, making you feel vulnerable and like a target for the "you-messages" from your partner. By not expressing your feelings, you avoid dealing with the unresolved issues. We suggest you make a Loving Choice to talk about feelings as much as you can.

Try doing a Self-Encounter on the topic of *"My contribution to the disharmony in my relationships."* You may need to do a Repetitive Self-Encounter with such a powerful and important topic.

We also suggest that you make a Loving Choice to do an Internal Family Conversation and nurture your Inner Children. Take the time to heal yourself. See what you can learn from your Inner Children about their needs. If appropriate, do an initiator encounter to share with your partner about how you have learned to heal your Inner Children. If you have been boiling a power struggle stew, make a Loving Choice to attempt to change your behavior.

Conclusion

Ultimately you will progress far enough to realize that the *external* power struggle is really an *internal* power struggle projected out upon your relationships. As you learn to access your many self-talk voices, you will become aware of how your various parts can have their own power struggles.

For example, your Inner Critic is telling you that you will need to understand all the concepts of this book the first time around. Another part of you feels inadequate and unable to comprehend this task. The battle begins. You become angry at the individual you perceive to be pressuring you. Your *internal* battle ends up being fought *externally* with that person. If you can solve your internal war by improving your feelings of self-worth, the external war may become resolved also!

The roots of the problems in your relationships go back to why you entered into the relationship. You probably bought into the myth that if you were involved in a committed relationship, you would be happy. If you started the relationship with a foundation built upon unmet needs, it will take a lot of hard work to build a new foundation.

Be gentle with yourself. It will take a lot of work and effort to slay all the dragons emerging as you start making Loving Choices. Take it one day at a time. Study each chapter in this book and see how many issues you can resolve around each topic. Don't worry if you don't start resolving power struggles or finding closure as soon as you would like. We invite you to be patient and kind to yourself as you begin the transformation from power struggles to growing pains. What a gift this transformation will be to you and others!

Example of a Power Struggle Self-Encounter

Topic: *It's time for you to change.*

- My **importance** is a 3.
- My **emotional** charge is a 3.
- My **motivation** is a 10, *because I can easily tell you what you need to do to become happier.*

The only inner voice the person uses in a power struggle Self-Encounter is the thoughts and interpretations voice. *I think you need to go for therapy. You are always arguing and fighting. You don't know how to relate to another person. You are so unhappy all of the time. Why don't you ever laugh and smile? I think your parents spoiled you.* (Notice all of the "you-messages"?)

Example of a Growing Pains Self-Encounter.

Topic: *My contribution to the disharmony in our relationship.*

- My **importance** is a 10
- My **emotional charge** is a 10
- My **motivation** is a 10, *because I want our relationship to be different.*

Facts: *Yesterday we went to a therapy session. We started arguing like we have done for years. The therapist asked if we were paying money for therapy so we could continue to argue. She suggested we had "practiced" doing that long enough.*

Thoughts: *I thought it made a lot of sense when the therapist asked who I thought was responsible for my unhappiness. I quickly replied, "My partner." I had never thought about that question before. I agreed with the therapist when it was pointed out that believing another was responsible for my unhappiness was a sign of co-dependency. When I think about it, I am responsible for my unhappiness.*

Body Sensations: *I experienced my shoulders being very tense and tight when I began to take responsibility for my unhappiness.*

Feelings: *I felt chagrined when I realized my part in our co-dependency. I felt inadequate talking about my feelings. I felt stressed. I feel relieved that I can begin to heal myself.*

Adaptive-Survivors: *I definitely have a projector Adaptive-Survivor that finds it easy to blame others when I am feeling pain. I learned that* *from my mother who was an introjector, who always took responsibility when I was feeling unhappy. I also have an angry Adaptive-Survivor that protects my Inner Children by distancing others with my anger.*

Inner Critic: *I've been telling you for years that you needed to change. I'm glad you are finally waking up. You need to listen to those who are wiser than you.*

Inner Children: *I'm feeling really scared right now. I have been ignored for so long with nobody paying any attention to me. I feel sad — really, really sad. I feel hurt and lonely. I don't know what people will think of me. I am so afraid.*

Wise Nurturer: *I am so glad you are taking the time to listen. Now you won't have to hide behind all those mixed messages. I admire your courage when you take ownership for your unhappiness. That may be the beginning of finding more happiness than you have ever known. Keep up the good work!*

Intentions, wants and needs: *I want to learn as much as I can about the illusions that I believed for years. The illusion that someone else is responsible for my unhappiness is a good example. I want to learn to heal from the long years of feeling hurt. I want to learn how to do the Internal Family Conversation, instead of striking out at others when I am feeling hurt.*

Commitments: *I am committed to become responsible for my happiness and/or unhappiness. I am committed to find other ways that I can interact with my partner without getting into a power struggle. I am committed to work on answering the question, "What am I growing through?"*

Kids Can Resolve Internal Power Struggles Too!

Our son Rob often refers to his dogs, Shadow and Daytona, as his Wise Nurturer. We recall an incident a few years ago, when Rob had an internal power struggle with an apparent inner war going on between his little wounded, hurt, guilty children, and his big, mean Inner Critic. One particular morning, after lots of tears and hurt feelings, Rob came running in with a big smile on his face. When we asked him what happened, he grinned widely and exclaimed that he had "sicked the dogs on his Critic!"

HOW ARE YOU DOING?

The following statements are designed to help you internalize and integrate the material in this chapter.

1. *The number of Self-Encounters, Repetitive Self-Encounters, Internal Family Conversations, and Healing Encounters. I am committed to do on the topic of "What am I growing through?"*

   _____

2. *I can more easily recognize when I am entering into a power struggle relationship with another.*

3. *I am committed to understanding and owning my part in the disharmony I am experiencing in my relationships with others.*

4. *I am going to change my vocabulary from "It's time for some changes. Why don't you change first?" to, "It's time for some changes. Why don't I change first?"*

5. *I am committed to explore the various ingredients of things I am growing through, instead of dumping them into my power struggle stew.*

6. *I understand the concept of polarization. I am committed to take ownership for my end of the polarization issues in my relationships.*

7. *I am committed to work on Adaptive-Survivor parts that are contributing to my power struggle stew.*

8. *I am committed to change my power struggles into growing pains.*

CHAPTER TWELVE

Boundaries and Ownership

WHAT IS YOU AND WHAT IS NOT YOU

*The **challenge** is to become aware of Internal
and External Boundaries and to develop Ownership.*

*The **loving choice** is to create and practice appropriate
Internal and External Boundaries so you develop
Ownership and Self-Responsibility.*

*"No" is a complete sentence! What part of "No"
don't you understand?*

After teaching the Loving Choices Seminar for several years, it became apparent just how important it is to talk about the issue of *boundaries*. It is essential to understand the importance of healthy boundaries. It will be a Loving Choice for you to integrate this concept into your relationship with yourself and others.

People in the Rebuilding (divorce recovery) Seminar talk about losing their identities in their past relationships. They quite frequently blame their former love partner for this loss. In reality, maintaining an identity is the responsibility of each individual. With appropriate boundaries, a person can use a relationship to actually gain true identity rather than lose it.

Relationships without defined boundaries can become extremely complicated. It's hard to tell what issues are yours and what issues belong to your partner if the boundaries are not clear. This chapter outlines ways you can recognize your boundaries, and take ownership of your part of your relationships now or in the future.

Here are a couple of obvious examples: your *skin* is a boundary for your body. What is *inside* your skin is *you* and what is *outside* your skin is *not you*. But your skin is not a *barrier;* it also has openings that serve as passageways in and out of your body.

Your *home* is another form of boundary. Its floor, walls, and roof, form a boundary, while its doors and windows allow people and possessions to pass in and out as you wish.

Thus you may welcome family and friends but exclude others you don't care to have inside.

You also need *emotional, psychological* and *intellectual boundaries* in your life. Like the openings in your skin and the windows and doors in the walls of your home, these boundaries need permeability — openings. So, boundaries are different from walls and barriers. It is healthy to have boundaries that are flexible and permeable.

Do you think about boundaries as a way of keeping others from invading your space? We agree that is an important boundary. What about the boundary you develop to keep you from crossing over and invading another person's space? Quite frequently a lack of this boundary is part of being over-responsible, caretaking and rescuing.

It is helpful to have both internal and external boundaries. Let's take a look a visual picture of what a boundary may look like.

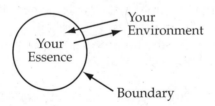

The essence of who you are is inside your boundary. What is outside your boundary is your environment—everyone and everything you are in contact with. There is two-way communication across the boundary — between you and your environment. You can be in control of the two-way communication, both outgoing and incoming.

The stronger your *identity,* the fewer boundaries you will need. And vice versa: the weaker your identity, the more boundaries you will need.

When you are with a loved one, your boundaries may be more flexible. In a healthy relationship you may choose to be more vulnerable. When you are around an angry or hostile person, it is appropriate to be more closed. When you are in a relationship with someone who has been a victim and feels helpless, it's easy to cross boundaries and become the caretaker. It is possible to support another person while maintaining your own boundaries.

Lack of boundaries contributes to disharmony in relationships. When you access and take ownership of your Adaptive-Survivor behaviors, you help to develop boundaries. Establishing boundaries and taking ownership increases your awareness of what you're doing to contribute to relationship problems. This assists in making the Loving Choice to change your behavior.

When you are able to describe what is happening in a relationship, you tend to feel less guilty and/or rejected. You tend to describe objectively what is happening instead of blaming. The mechanic looks at your car with care and concern, but is not emotionally hooked when it breaks down. This concept is what we call *detachment*. You feel and you care, but you can be objective and detached.

This concept of detachment is applicable in many other situations. If you have pain or disharmony in other areas of your life, do you blame another person for it? If you realize someone is hurting or in pain, do you take responsibility for their pain? The Challenge is to put up appropriate boundaries: to remain detached from what is happening instead of blaming or being over-responsible. The Loving Choice is to learn to stop crossing over your boundaries under the guise of helping others. We're not suggesting you avoid *empathy* — understanding and being with the other person — just that you not take her burdens and pain on as if they were your own.

The *active listening* exercise described in chapter 4 demonstrates another kind of boundary. If you are easily seduced into fixing or rescuing someone, active listening helps you stay inside your boundary by listening with detachment. Instead of thinking about how you can *help* the other person, you are *listening* to what she is saying. Practicing active listening skills gives her the space to be herself without you trying to fix or rescue her. Active listening acts like a mirror. You're listening to what the other person is saying and reflecting it back. This helps keep you from taking the other's comments personally, and from entering her space. It acts as a flexible boundary.

Let's talk about another boundary. What about your *reaction to the behavior* of other people? You can't do much to change the behavior of others, or whatever happens around you, but you do have a choice about *your reaction to external events.* Do you find yourself getting emotionally hooked, defensive, or rebellious? Are you able to put up boundaries and not react to others' behavior personally and emotionally? It is possible to learn how to detach, and if you can, it allows you to hear and observe someone's behavior while remaining objective. Becoming aware of the difference between external behaviors and events and your reaction to these influences is an important boundary.

Do you believe other people are responsible for your reaction to their behavior? Supposing their behavior has been intrusive, perhaps aggressive, critical, or projecting. It becomes more complicated when you are in a close intimate relationship. You would like to be as open to your partner as possible. How can you remain open and vulnerable and still put up boundaries? Again, detachment and awareness boundaries become options. With detachment you can observe intrusive behavior without becoming emotionally hooked. With an awareness boundary, such as becoming aware of the pain the person has behind "you-messages," you can understand their intrusive behavior and not let the behavior affect you personally.

We mentioned the need for flexibility so that boundaries don't become walls. The need for flexible boundaries is especially significant when you are in a personal growth process. As you expand your awareness, some boundaries may be inappropriate. This is especially true as you work at being open and getting in touch with your feelings. When you're going through a personal change, a new vulnerable part of you begins to grow, like a little plant coming through the ground. That fragile part of you, which feels vulnerable and needs safety, is easily damaged and harmed. Its needs may change from time to time. The flexibility of boundaries will meet this need.

Sometimes creating boundaries is like putting a protective fence around the plant. The boundary may protect the plant from powerful elements like the wind, storms, and hungry animals. On the other hand it allows the sunlight to nourish and feed the plant. As you can see, creating a flexible boundary that allows you to feel free and open, but still protects the new fragile part of you, is challenging.

When you are in the process of seeking identity, you may need to create emotional space. You need to have a space that will assist your growth. Boundaries will give you the emotional space you need to find your own identity. Frequently a person seeking identity will say things like, "I need to run away from home." "I need a room of my own in this house with a lock on the door." "I need to be free to go out one night a week and not be accountable to anyone." Part of the seeking-identity process is learning to create appropriate boundaries.

Have you thought about the connection between the boundaries you have in your adult relationships and the boundaries you learned from your parents in your formative years? You typically have boundaries similar to what you learned from the significant adults in your childhood. How did you learn to create boundaries in your family of origin? Are these boundaries appropriate for you now?

If you experienced some form of childhood abuse you probably did not develop strong boundaries. Part of the destruction from childhood abuse is not allowing the abused child to have a separate identity. If you were not allowed to develop and create boundaries while being abused, you may have difficulty believing that you have a right to them as an adult. It is difficult to know how to create and develop them in your adult relationships.

Some families do not have boundaries between parents and children. Without boundaries family issues become convoluted and it's difficult to differentiate the parents from the children. Consider, for example, the issue of how to handle money in the family. In a healthy family, the parents take responsibility for the finances. They are the wage earners, the spenders, the ones who make financial decisions. Although parents in a healthy family may ask the children for their opinions on financial issues, the ultimate responsibility for earning and spending money rests with the parents.

However, the issue becomes convoluted if the parents say things to the kids like, "You're always wanting toys. How are we ever going to make the payments for our house and for our food if we're spending money on you kids?" Such statements imply that the kids are responsible for the financial problems of the parents. The parents' lack of boundaries leaves the kids feeling guilty and confused. They feel responsible for something over which they have no control.

This leads to another problem with boundaries. Were you closer to your mother or to your father when you were growing up? You may have had fewer boundaries with the person you were emotionally closest to. If you had serious conflicts with one parent, you tended to have more boundaries with that person. Imagine boundaries with a father whom you had conflicts with. Now imagine boundaries with a mother you were close to. No doubt the boundary would be thicker in the relationship with your father. It might even be more like a wall. Think of someone in your adult life you perceive as a male authority figure. You may have thick boundaries with that person that are actually leftovers from your relationship with your father.

If you developed boundaries that were more like walls because of unmet needs in your childhood, you probably have an underdeveloped sense of your identity. This leads to a need for more walls because of the sensitive little child inside. The thicker the walls, the smaller your identity. The smaller your identity, the bigger the need for protective walls. This may lead to loneliness and isolation.

In chapter 3, we discussed the feelings that reside underneath Adaptive-Survivor behavior. It is important to understand that you may feel guilty, rejected, angry and fearful as you begin to establish boundaries. Using the Self-Encounter will help you identify these feelings. Making the Loving Choice to nurture yourself during this transition will be very healing when you start to establish boundaries.

Have you become aware of an important side benefit of the Self-Encounter? It is an excellent way for you to develop a stronger and more profound sense of your identity. Each time you access your voices and express them in a Self-Encounter, you need fewer external boundaries because your identity becomes stronger.

One of the activities we've done in the seminar is to ask for definitions of words, as an exercise in improving communication skills. Carolyn wrote the following definition for intimacy: "Intimacy is taking down the last barrier and finding out that I didn't need it." In healthy relationships with good communication, very few barriers and walls are needed. You can be open and vulnerable and be yourself.

A Self-Encounter can be a way of marking your territory. The Challenge is to establish boundaries by using "I-messages" about what you think, feel, want, or need. *This is me* and *this is not me* are by-products of the Self-Encounter. The Loving Choice is to state "this is me" in a healthy manner. Instead of being other-directed (focused outward), you have become more inner-directed (focused inward). It is hard to lose your identity if you continually do Self-Encounters.

Another benefit of the Self-Encounter is to help you develop *internal boundaries*. In this way you can identify your self-talk voices — Inner Critic, Inner Children, Adaptive-Survivors, Wise Nurturer — and keep them separate from your total identity. Each time you access one of your self-talk voices, you have created an internal boundary. As you access all of your parts, you learn that you are a composite of many different parts. *You* are the total picture puzzle, and all of your parts are just pieces in the puzzle. Becoming acquainted with your various parts allows you to develop clear internal boundaries — and greater awareness.

Here are two different ways of dealing with projected anger. Judy often accused John of being just like her father. It would be easy at this point for John to become defensive and start protesting how different he is from her father. Instead, he is willing to help Judy be able to discern that she may need to work through a longtime conflict she has had with her father. Judy's father criticized her and never took the time to listen. He never seemed to hear or discover who she was and what she thought or felt. John supported Judy to do some Self-Encounters around the issue with her father. Judy was amazed to learn that she had anger at her father that she was projecting out upon John. John was able to listen to her without becoming defensive when she shared her Self-Encounter with him.

On the other hand, Judy has realized that John does not express his anger very well. He denies expression of his anger for a long time, then explodes. He very often makes Judy the target when he does let go. She realizes his anger has very little to do with her. Instead of taking it personally, she encourages him to do a Self-Encounter around the way he "stuffs" his anger. He discovers he learned to stuff his anger in his childhood, and now believes he has been venting at Judy the anger he felt toward his mother.

Does hearing other people say certain things seem to make a strong impact upon you? For example. If you have a large and yet untamed Inner Critic, you will easily hear criticisms from others. In fact you may be creating relationships with critical people to reinforce the Inner Critic voice you hear inside your head. This criticism you think is directed at you may in fact be a form of *projection*.

The voice from the other person is like a puppet and you are the ventriloquist. You are actually speaking from one of your inner voices but the other person is mouthing the words. You attribute the comments to another and make that person responsible for what you think and feel when you are criticized. It does not occur to you to ask why some comments from others affect you so deeply. Maybe it is because they are echoing one of your self-talk voices?

The Self-Encounter minimizes this projection by helping you identify your self-talk voices. Recognizing the words the other person is saying as the same words you are writing in your Self-Encounter can lead to ownership instead of projection.

Assertiveness Is an Important Boundary

Assertiveness means verbalizing your intentions, wants and needs. *Passivity,* on the other hand, is indicative of weak boundaries. Yet a third behavioral style, being *aggressive,* is forcing yourself into another person's space. When you're assertive, you're honest about what you want and need while maintaining appropriate boundaries.

Karen grew up with domineering parents and she easily fell into a passive pattern. She allowed her parents to control her life by making most of her decisions for her. When she became involved in adult relationships, she found that she was tired of being told what to do. She always agreed when anybody suggested going out to eat or going to a movie. She went through a period of saying, "I'm going to suggest which movie we go to tonight," or "I'm going to tell people what restaurant I want to go to." She suffered the reaction of her friends, who watched her behavior and said, "Karen's really becoming gritchy isn't she?"

Karen was learning to be assertive and found the Intentions part of the Self-Encounter very helpful in this process. As often happens when the pendulum swings, she was sometimes aggressive in her attempt to find a happy medium. Also, friends who were used to the "passive" Karen found it troublesome to deal with the "new Karen," who spoke up and asked for what she wanted.

Although it's a challenge to keep growing when others disapprove, eventually the rewards are worth it. Using the Intentions part of the Self-Encounter is a practical and specific way of learning to be assertive. If you don't ask for what you want or need, you probably won't get it. Verbalizing your intentions is like keeping the boundary full of air. It is like a strong balloon that holds its shape. Not verbalizing your intentions is like slowly letting the air out of the balloon. The boundary becomes soft and is easily pushed out of shape. (*Your Perfect Right* is the best book on assertiveness if you want to dig deeper into this topic.)

"I-Messages"

We stated earlier that learning to use "I-messages" is one of the best ways to improve your communication skills. We believe there are at least two reasons why more people don't use "I-messages." First, it is hard to use "I-messages" when you're not sure what you think, feel, want, or are committed to. Secondly, "I-messages" tend to make you feel vulnerable and exposed. You may feel criticized and misunderstood and be easily hurt.

Here are some responses or ways you can react to "you-messages" from another person. You can emotionally distance them and put up walls to protect yourself. You can react by getting defensive. Some people choose to end the relationship. A more Loving Choice would be for you to continue using "I-messages" until eventually the other person becomes aware of your boundaries. The awareness boundary is understanding that the person using "I-messages" is more aware and operating at a higher level of communication. The boundary is a protection because you understand that the person using "you-messages" is actually covering up emotional pain, anger, fear, or a multitude of other emotions by using "you-messages." "You-messages" keep them from learning and getting to know themselves. Your boundaries allow you to understand this process. You understand that the criticism coming from the other person has more to do with them and their pain than it does with you.

It is hard to do a Self-Encounter without using "I-messages". What did you see or hear? What are you feeling? What do you want or intend to do? These questions are difficult to answer with a "you-message." It is easiest to misinterpret "you-messages" in the thoughts part of the Self-Encounter. "I think you _____" is a disguised "you-message." We suggest you write out your Self-Encounter and use "you-messages" in your thoughts if it makes you feel better. Then go back and change all of the "I think *you*" into "I think *I*" statements. Do this before you share it with your partner. This simple exercise will help you take more ownership and establish better boundaries.

Helpful Hints in Setting Boundaries

It's probably apparent by now that setting appropriate boundaries for all kinds of situations and relationships is a challenging process. Here are some general guidelines to help you learn how to set appropriate boundaries.

1. *Learn to say, "No."* "No" is a complete sentence. You don't have to say anything else. Learn to say no when people ask you to rescue them. If they ask for anything that would result in you sacrificing yourself, say "no." This is learning to be assertive. If it is an appropriate "no," it will help you develop a positive boundary that will protect your identity.

2. Whenever you feel your identity slipping away, dust off your communication skills and *do a Self-Encounter* on the topic, "I feel I'm losing my identity when ____." Another example: "How to develop an appropriate boundary in this situation so I don't lose my identity." Completing a Self-Encounter communication exercise is an effective way to develop boundaries.

3. *Develop your awareness* so you understand when your identity is eroding. Awareness of your boundaries helps you separate yourself from others. Boundaries prevent you from losing your identity either by becoming over-responsible and trying to "fix" someone or by playing the victim and expecting someone to "fix" you. Both over- and under-responsible are a form of crossing over.

4. *Practice asking for what you want and need.* Again, use the Self-Encounter communication exercise to develop the part of yourself that recognizes wants and needs. This is another way of setting a boundary. The opposite of stating what you want is to wait passively for someone to give you the things you want and need. This represents a lack of ownership and responsibility on your part. No one else can perceive and meet your unidentified and unspoken needs. "If you really loved me, you'd know what I want" is a common unspoken phrase many believe. This is expecting some one to read your mind — not very likely to get you what you need!

5. *Complete some self-help programs* for yourself. This could encompass a variety of activities. Perhaps you will go to the library and read books or take a college class. It might involve doing

something you've always wanted to do, like enrolling in a dance class. Maybe you simply need to invest time in yourself so you can become a human "being" instead of a human "doing." Do a variety of things and focus on ways you can invest in yourself that will strengthen your identity.

6. *Take responsibility for disciplining yourself.* Perhaps you need to say, "No" to *yourself.* Maybe you need to encourage yourself to do some physical exercise. Do you need to create a better balance between your little child part (which wants lots of different playthings) and your adult part (which says, "First you need to do something that will make you a better person!")? Exercise self-discipline, not by having rigid rules and carrying out "shoulds," but in a way that says, "I will be a better person if I engage in this particular behavior."

7. *Practice developing boundaries.* Every time you feel that your identity has been sacrificed or that your essence has been trampled, sit down and practice setting different kinds of boundaries. Practice saying "I feel hurt when you do that," or "I feel angry when you say that." And practice saying, "I'm going to do what I need to do, not necessarily what you want me to do. I want to build a better identity for myself."

8. *Explain to a friend that you are working on boundaries* when you tell him you can't help him. Give yourself some time each day for self care. After you have practiced on boundaries which are easy, take some bigger steps. Ask your boss for what you want or need. The most challenging boundary may be with your love partner. Can you tell her you need some alone time this week, even if she feels rejected or angry?

Learning to Develop Appropriate Boundaries: An Exercise

Here is an exercise designed to help you create better boundaries:

• Think of a situation where you have invaded someone's boundaries — sticking your nose into a private matter, for instance, when you knew it was none of your business. How did you feel later? How could you improve your boundaries? How would you behave differently? Could you check your nose at the door next time?

• Then recall an instance when you have allowed someone to come into your space — maybe your people pleaser survivor part was afraid to say "no" when a friend asked you an unreasonable favor. Inside, your thoughts and feelings said "NO" but, instead of expressing yourself, you said "Sure! No problem." How did you feel later in this case? How could you improve your boundaries? How would you behave differently? Could you practice saying "no" assertively enough so others will understand you mean it? How would it feel to assert yourself? Could you be assertive in other situations?

• Do a Self-Encounter on the topic, "Improving my boundaries." Write out a specific plan of how you will improve your boundary and when you will do it. Will you improve your boundary today, next week, or next month? It will help you to sign and date your written plan to increase your motivation and commitment to complete this task. When you have finished developing a specific boundary to your satisfaction, we encourage you to do another Self-Encounter on the topic, "My reaction to successfully completing an appropriate boundary."

Here is another exercise; this one designed to help you learn more about detachment and ownership.

• Think of a problem you have in a relationship with another person—something that's causing you pain or discomfort. Are you blaming the other person for your discomfort? Do you feel responsible for the other person's pain? Can you think of a way you can take more ownership for the problem instead of blaming yourself or the other person? We invite you to do a Self-Encounter.

Here's an example: Your love-partner tells you that she needs "more emotional space," that she wants to spend more time alone. Your first reaction is to attempt to take control and not agree to her boundary. Did you take it personally when she set up a boundary by asking for more space? Have you been over-responsible or parental with her? Do you believe you are responsible for her happiness? Is she responsible for your happiness?

The Challenge in such a case might be to do a Self-Encounter on the topic, "My reaction to my partner asking for more emotional space." The Loving Choice would be to take ownership of your feelings. You will become more aware of the dynamics of what is going on. You can be more detached and thus diminish the feelings of rejection.

As you establish clear boundaries — internal and external — and begin to take active ownership of your thoughts, feelings, needs, leftovers, and behavior, you will find your relationships with yourself and others growing and developing remarkably. You'll also have a much clearer sense of your own identity — who you are and what you need. Boundaries are a key part of defining yourself!

HOW ARE YOU DOING?

1. *The number of Self-Encounters and Repetitive Self-Encounters I am committed to do on the topic of boundaries and ownership* ___.

2. *The number of Internal Family Conversations I am committed to do on the topic of boundaries and ownership* ___.

3. *The number of Healing Encounters with my partner I am committed to do on the topic of boundaries and ownership* ___.

4. *I understand the connection between boundaries, responsibility for self, personal ownership and personal identity.*

5. *I understand the difference between boundaries and walls.*

6. *I understand I am developing boundaries when I stop blaming others and start taking responsibility for my happiness and/or unhappiness.*

7. *I am able to emotionally detach and still remain caring and loving.*

8. *I understand and am practicing inter-generation boundaries between my parents and my children.*

9. *I understand and am practicing internal boundaries between my inner voices.*

10. *I understand and am practicing developing awareness boundaries that allow me to stay centered and objective.*

11. *I understand how I can project my inner voices out upon another person and thus lose my boundaries.*

12. *I am able to be assertive by asking for what I want and need in the Self-Encounter.*

13. *I understand and am using "I-messages" as a way of building my essence so I won't need as many boundaries.*

14. *I understand the stronger my identity the less need I will have for boundaries.*

CHAPTER THIRTEEN

Relationships Are Your Teachers

WORKING TOGETHER AS A VEHICLE FOR GROWTH

*The **challenge** is to utilize the communication tools and awareness gained from reading* Loving Choices *and apply them to your relationships with yourself and others.*

*The **loving choice** is to learn your lessons from each of the relationships that you have created. This will assist you in becoming a more loving, whole and empowered human being.*

$\mathcal{B}$ruce has a story about growing up on a farm that makes a wonderful analogy for understanding the concept that "relationships are your teachers." The story goes back to the end of an era when farmers used horses for farm power to till and cultivate the soil. The family had both a tractor and a large farm truck. The truck had dual wheels on the back axle and single front axle. This story begins when the truck got stuck in the mud out in the field.

Because the field was so muddy the tractors were also disabled. No tractor could get close enough to the truck to pull it out of the mud. What to do? The hired man — memory suggests his name was Evan — had a wonderful team of gray mares. They had been in the Iowa State Fair wagon-pulling contest and had performed well. Evan suggested he harness his team of horses on the front of the truck and pull it out. The younger folks watched skeptically, wondering what a team of horses could do with such a big truck?

Evan proceeded to harness the team to the front bumper of the big truck. Then all he did was make a clicking noise with his mouth.

The horses started pulling together, each one straining in harmony with the other. That's right! It worked. By working together they were able to pull that big Ford truck out of the mud!

The secret, of course, was the way the horses pulled *together*. Some teams don't pull together; first one pulls and then the other. They haven't learned how to work together as a team. This team of horses had learned to pull together.

This chapter is about the Challenge of learning to pull together with your partner in any relationship. The Loving Choice is to pull your relationship out of the mud it may be stuck in.

When the Needs of Our Inner Children Are in Conflict

When you begin to heal your Inner Children, the unmet needs of your Inner Children may be in conflict with the unmet needs of one of your relationship teachers. Arnold and Louise illustrated this principle in their relationship.

Arnold had been raised by a guilt-producing "martyr mom." He developed a strong *caretaker* Adaptive-Survivor part, responding to his mother's unmet needs. (Caretakers do that, you know.) He carried many of the feelings she was unable to express because she was busy being the martyr — an extreme caretaker Adaptive-Survivor part. As a young adult, Arnold entered into a relationship with Louise, unaware that he was creating a relationship to learn an important lesson.

Louise had grown up with an alcoholic mother. Louise's needy Inner Children, with fears of rejection and abandonment, wanted Arnold to take care of her so she wouldn't feel rejected. Arnold got "hooked" into caring for someone again; he felt guilty if Louise felt rejected.

We suggested that Arnold and Louise each think of a "perfect weekend" for the two of them — one that would help them to heal and relax from the stressful power struggle going on in their relationship. Arnold immediately responded that he envisioned a weekend in the mountains *by himself*, with no one he had to take care of, would alleviate the tension that had been building between them. Louise thought of the mountains as well. Not surprisingly, however, her solution was for *the two of them* to spend a relaxing weekend at a romantic inn at a beautiful spot in the high country. She wanted to feel completely taken care of, not rejected or abandoned.

While you heal your Inner Children, your needs will often conflict with the needs of your relationship teacher. How can you heal your Inner Children under these circumstances? Arnold and Louise made a Loving Choice to use the three-legged stool of *communication, awareness,* and *commitment,* and were able to resolve the conflict.

They used the Internal Family Dialogue *communication* exercise to converse with their own Inner Children. Neither of them found it necessary to involve the other person for this step. They became *aware* of the conflicting needs of their Inner Children, and used this awareness to help become better relationship teachers for each other. Arnold learned to deal with guilt when his partner wanted him to heal her feelings of rejection. Louise learned to deal with the rejection she felt when Arnold refused to become her rescuer. They took ownership of their feelings and became *committed* to healing their own Inner Children, instead of expecting the other to heal it for them.

Healing Childhood Abuse While in Relationship

Far too many people have experienced childhood abuse: verbal, physical, sexual, or psychological. If you deny the abuse and fail to deal with it, it will continue to affect your relationships in subtle — and sometimes very adverse — ways. When you start accessing and healing the abuse, it may become a source of stress in your adult relationships.

Females are more likely than males to have been sexually abused in childhood. (This is not to say that males do not suffer sexual abuse — it just happens less often.) It is quite common, therefore, for a man to be in a relationship with a woman who is attempting to heal childhood abuse. We assume that many (most?) of the male readers of this book are warm, loving, sensitive males who are committed to helping their partner heal. Men who find it easy to take on the role of helping their partners to heal often find it difficult to remain centered, to continue to meet their own needs, and to do their self-care. For this very reason, some men's groups have the goal of helping each other stay focused on personal growth. As the saying goes, "If you don't take care of yourself, you won't have anything to give to taking care of another."

If you are working through childhood abuse while in a relationship, the stress will be expressed in many different ways. The person who abused you is more than likely of the opposite sex. It is easy to transfer your pain, hurt, and anger to your relationship partner as you access these feelings towards the abuser.

The obstacles in some relationships may be very challenging, depending upon which person was abused. In some cases both people have suffered some form of abuse. If you are the partner of the abused, it may seem that you are continually being tested. It is helpful to be aware of this test so you can avoid being drawn into your partner's process. Her behavior may be a strong test of your love and ability to stay centered.

In reality, if you are a *caretaker* (Adaptive-Survivor part), you may be contributing to the stress. Your survivor parts may include over-responsibility, people-pleasing, or being the nice person. You may have connected with an abused partner to live out your own Adaptive-Survivor parts. It's important for you to recognize and deal with your survivor parts in order to stay centered and not take on the role of rescuer.

The abused person has already suffered a great deal of pain. Unfortunately, the hurt, pain, and anger she experienced will tend to be experienced again as she heals the wounds. That emotional pain is likely to be played out in her primary relationship — with you. An abused person often distances from her partner while she attempts to heal the abuse. A very confusing situation for both parties!

If you are the abused, you carry a learned fear being abused again. Every time you feel close and intimate, this fear likely emerges. You don't mean to be giving the other person a test; you just need to feel and express your fear. You don't want to be hurt. Learning to trust that you won't be abused in some way is very difficult. You want to work on your own process — making your way *around* the other person — while you heal, but your strong feelings very easily erupt, and you may well process *at* him. Healing childhood abuse in a love relationship is challenging, stressful, and sometimes overwhelming.

The Challenge for the abused person is to be able to heal his childhood trauma within the relationship. He wants a safe place to heal and grow. The Challenge for the partner is to stay centered, detached and continue to be aware of her survivor behaviors. The Loving Choice is to use the three-legged stool of **communication, awareness,** and **commitment** to work through these challenges.

Self-Encounters are a wonderful tool to assist you in finding the many parts of yourself that were disowned in childhood. Commitment and motivation to heal will be helpful. Boundaries and ownership become very important. Healing Encounters with your partner as you heal could very well save your relationship. The communication tools will never be more important than when you are attempting to heal childhood abuse through your relationships with yourself and others.

Problem-Solving Men

Men easily fall into the role of solving problems. Women usually want to talk about something that is bothering them. Rather than listening, the male often feels he needs to come up with a solution.

Molly, a participant in the seminar, often had to deal with some very difficult customers at work. She would come home wanting to talk about what had happened, how she felt about it, and to consider ways to handle it in the future. She felt she could be more objective after discussing it with someone. Her partner, Adam, had a simple solution: resign from this stressful job and find one with less stress. He saw this as the obvious solution, the most appropriate answer to the problem. Molly was willing to learn from her relationship teachers at work. She felt discounted and not listened to when she tried to convey her concerns to Adam. She wanted to be *heard*, not to be presented with logical solutions that had very little to do with her needs.

The Challenge for the person who wants to talk through her feelings is to make this known to her partner. The Challenge for the problem-solver is to learn to actively listen instead of discounting the person's ability to work through her own issues. The Loving Choice is to become aware of your own process, whether it be talking through or problem solving. Use the communication tools to accomplish your goal. Be *committed* enough to change the pattern so that both of you can have your needs met in a positive manner.

Doing Shadow Work

This may be a new concept for you. Your *shadow* side is composed of the parts of yourself that you don't like, don't want to admit belong to you, and don't want to know about. These shadow parts have much more control over you than you may be aware.

Your shadow side may have started to emerge in your Self-Encounters. Your Wise Nurturer can be very accepting of your disowned shadow parts. By doing Self-Encounters the Wise Nurturer can gently coax parts of your shadow to reveal itself. It can be very healing to have a relationship that is safe and trusting enough to allow you to access your shadow parts. Your relationship teacher may be more accepting of your shadow side than you are. When another person understands and accepts your shadow side it makes it much easier for you to accept those parts.

John, for example, felt very uncomfortable about crying. He had been made fun of as a child for crying. He was called a "sissy" if he cried. John's partner, Ruth, was very comfortable with his tears. In fact, she felt tender and loving toward him when he cried. Gradually, he was able to internalize her acceptance of his tears. Her understanding and affirmation helped him feel more comfortable and self-accepting. He was able to integrate a part of his shadow side with the help of his partner. Their relationship contributed to a very profound healing for John.

With awareness, patience, and understanding, exploring your shadow side becomes an ongoing Challenge of self-discovery. The Loving Choice is to create warm and supportive relationships that enhance the process of accessing and accepting your shadow parts. We suggest that you remember that this is a *process* of discovery. As this process unfolds, the reward for making this Loving Choice will be the healing of some very deep wounds.

Wiping the Blackboard Clean

Relationships start with a clean slate. As the relationship progresses, marks begin to accumulate on the blackboard. These marks are usually about issues that you have failed to resolve. Some of the marks may be angry things you have said to each other. Some marks may represent hurts that one or both of you have suffered. Some marks may be a comment made in the heat of an argument. The temptation is for both of you to continually point out the marks that you perceive were made by the other person. These marks are probably affecting the interaction in the relationship with this person.

The Challenge is for both of you to wipe the blackboard clean. Agree to stop bringing up things from the past. You may need to resolve these old feelings in Self-Encounters or in a therapeutic relationship. You would like to believe the other person is responsible for them when in reality they may be your own unresolved issues.

The Loving Choice is to start from scratch and begin new ways of communicating. In this way you can remain detached and objective, instead of becoming defensive or emotionally hooked by the other person's comments. This is a wonderful opportunity to practice your active listening skills. A relationship is a schoolroom — a place to learn a variety of subjects.

Leftovers

A *leftover* is a conditioned response to a stimulus that's long-gone. The person with whom you are in relationship now provides a new trigger to bring up the old response. You've learned to react in a predictable way, even though the person providing the new stimulus may not be the person with whom you learned the response originally. Nevertheless, the roots of the learning are deep, and you're conditioned to respond the same way no matter who provides the reason. You need not be aware of what you're doing, which results in mixed messages and confusion in a relationship.

Elaine had carried a deep hurt and fear from her childhood. This affected her relationship with Paula, her best friend, in a destructive way. As a child, whenever Elaine allowed herself to be vulnerable and share intimately about herself, her sharing would be used as ammunition against her in the next family fight. She was afraid to share with her friend Paula for fear Paula would use her comments in the same way her family had. When she became aware of this pattern and was able to recognize it as a leftover, she had the opportunity to begin healing.

A healthy way to heal leftovers is through communication. Elaine prepared a Self-Encounter which resulted in an initiator encounter with Paula. As she began to recognize and own her wound from the past, Elaine discovered that she had the choice of changing how she would interact in her relationship with Paula. With time, she was able to be more vulnerable and share her feelings without the fear that she would be hurt. Their friendship was more open and healthy,

Leftovers can accumulate from a variety of relationships. They will ultimately affect current relationships. A helpful response when someone reacts with a leftover is to simply say, "That doesn't fit me; can we talk about it some more?" Helping another person to identify leftovers can be done by using "I-messages."

The Challenge here is to monitor your interactions. Learn to recognize and own your leftovers. Have you thought about how much energy it takes to carry around a bag full of leftovers? The conditioned responses you have learned keep you from having flexibility and spontaneity in your current relationships. Each time you can identify a leftover, it gives you more freedom and energy to be yourself and to make more Loving Choices.

Hidden Agendas

Hidden agendas are similar to leftovers in that they are brought from the past into current relationships. They are hidden in the sense that you are not aware that certain things are part of your belief system. Your hidden agendas can include a wide variety of issues but are often connected to your fears. Discovering your hidden agendas will help you to identify some of your fears.

Here are some examples of hidden agendas: Did you believe that another person is responsible for your happiness? Are you a woman trying to be emancipated and independent, but carrying a hidden agenda that says, "I am not a complete person unless I am in a relationship with a man"? Or, you are a man who believes, "I will not be happy until I have someone who will take care of me"? Perhaps you are fearful of being independent and responsible for your life.

Unless you become aware of hidden agendas in your relationships, they will very often result in anger, frustration, irritation, and disappointment. The Challenge is to discover the hidden agendas that are influencing your interactions. The Loving Choice would be to make a list of these agendas and do a Self-Encounter to help you recognize any fears under your hidden agendas. Discovering your hidden agendas and sharing them with another person will often take away their power, which allows you to make more Loving Choices.

Dreams: Another Relationship Teacher

The Self-Encounter is a wonderful way to understand how your dreams can be powerful teachers. (There are two pages in the *Loving Choices Workbook* devoted to dream interpretation using the Self-Encounter.) A dream journal or tape recorder can easily incorporate Self-Encounters. Your writing or taping of the dream become the facts of your Self-Encounter. After you record the dream, it is usually easy to identify the topic. Complete the Self-Encounter form with the thoughts, feelings, and other important things about the dream. When you use the Self-Encounter to interpret your dreams it helps make them another relationship teacher. Most people are unaware of the profound messages that our dreams offer. The Challenge may be taking the time and making the effort to record your dreams. The Loving Choice is to allow this information to assist in your healing and growth process.

Detachment

Some people perceive *detachment* as not caring or emotionally distancing yourself. We have found it to be just the opposite. We view detachment as profound caring without becoming emotionally hooked. In the early stages of your process, you are likely to be emotionally subjective and over-responsible in your thoughts and feelings. Your own unresolved issues may keep you from being more objective. If this is the case, you cannot see or hear the other person clearly. You may be looking through an "emotional windshield" which is clouded with your own "stuff". You become emotionally attached to the other person's comments and behavior. He is not free to talk about what is important to him because you immediately start talking about what is important to you. You are *attached* rather than being *detached* and objective.

If you find yourself reacting and becoming emotionally hooked in your interaction with another person, use that as an opportunity to take an inward journey. This is an opportunity where you can almost always learn something about yourself. The lack of detachment in your response usually indicates you have some unresolved issues of your own.

The Challenge is to be able to evolve to a place where you are centered, have an identity of your own, and can observe the people around you objectively. You will be able to actively listen to another person instead of continually processing your own thoughts and feelings. The Loving Choice is to appropriately detach in order to create a healthy and healing relationship. Recognizing detachment as a relationship teacher will be an empowering experience.

Changing the Form of Your Relationship with a Healing Separation

There are a number of people today who are in an important growth process. It may be they are seeking identity, healing childhood abuse, overcoming family of origin influences, or experiencing another form of growth and change. They need to put a top priority on their individual process and make a choice to physically separate from their love partner in order to have enough time and emotional space to work on their own process.

Some couples are at a place where their love relationship is not working. They don't want to divorce but are unable to make the changes necessary to heal while in relationship. An alternative for them is to physically separate so they can find freedom from the destructive patterns in their relationship which are inhibiting their individual and personal growth.

Bruce wrote about the concept of a Healing Separation in his book, *Rebuilding: When Your Relationship Ends.* It is an idea "come of age," because we have received many phone calls and letters from couples doing a Healing Separation. Many people want more information and help in doing this very challenging process. If you do, you'll find the material in Rebuilding — including a detailed description and a sample Healing Separation agreement — of great help.

We also suggest you use the communication tools you've learned in this book, along with the *Loving Choices Workbook,* to help you experience the personal growth necessary to complete the Healing Separation. It is difficult to carve out a new relationship while still in relationship. We have found the communication skills very helpful in doing this. A successful Healing Separation is making a Loving Choice about the future of your relationship with yourself and others.

HOW ARE YOU DOING?

The following statements are designed to help you internalize and integrate the material in this chapter.

1. *The number of Self-Encounters, Internal Family Conversations, and two-way Healing Encounters I am committed to do this next week with topics from this chapter ____.*

2. *I understand how relationships can be my teachers, instead of being a place to project my pain upon another or play the victim role.*

3. *I have identified some of the lessons I am learning in my present relationships.*

4. *I am ready to face some of the feelings and lessons that I have been avoiding in my relationships with self and others.*

5. *I understand how the needs of my Inner Children can conflict with those of another person's Inner Children. This may be a topic for a Self-Encounter for me.*

6. *I understand the potential problems caused by the healing of childhood abuse in my relationships.*

7. *I am able to access some of my shadow parts by either having my Wise Nurturer or my partner help me accept those parts.*

8. *I am committed to wiping my blackboard clean.*

9. *I am aware of some of my leftovers and am dealing with them appropriately.*

10. *I have identified and shared some of my hidden agendas with another person.*

11. *I am committed to recording some dreams and to processing them with Self-Encounters.*

12. *I am working on becoming detached and remaining more centered in my interactions with others.*

13. *I am committed to learning more about myself when I become emotionally hooked by another.*

CHAPTER FOURTEEN

Loving Choices

CHANGING CHALLENGES
INTO LOVING CHOICES

*The **challenge** is to recognize that you are a
unique individual. You are also a precious being similar
to all other human beings.*

*The **loving choice** is your commitment to invest
in yourself and your personal growth every day
for the rest of your life.*

*T*he diamond is a beautiful and precious jewel, just as your essence is beautiful and precious. As you look at the diamond that is you, you can see your many different facets with all their various brilliant colors. These facets represent your various parts, each with a different hue, a special color, a unique view into your essence.

Inside your diamond is a light, a glow that we call Self-Love. Unlike diamond gemstone, which requires an external light source to shine, you can shine through your various facets from your inner light. Each of your facets needs to be cleaned and polished so the light can shine through. If your facets are dirty, you won't shine as brightly.

Your homework — for the rest of your life — is to continue to clean and polish your many facets, using the three-legged stool of awareness, communication, and commitment we've described in this book.

We want to affirm you for taking this journey, for polishing your diamond, for becoming better connected with your source of love, and for having your light of Self-Love shine even more brightly.

Rob was only four years old when he asked us, "Where does my love go when I go to sleep?" We assured him that we felt his love for us whether he was awake or asleep, and that his love continues on while he is sleeping. That question led us to think about our own parents' love. Bruce still felt it strongly long after both of Bruce's parents passed away. And it is still there for Nina, whose father died when she was two years old. The love that glows through the facets of your diamond continues whether you are awake or asleep.

(Nina and Rob miss Bruce terribly, but they've known his love every day since his death in May 1998.)

Over the years we have asked each of our seminar participants to write a definition of love. Another question we have started asking ourselves is, "Where are the receptors in my body for receiving love?" We know we can feel it when we are loving ourselves. We can also feel it when others are loving us. How do we know that?

We both experienced the euphoria of falling in love. What a warm and bubbly time that is! Scientists are now able to measure the *endorphins* (literally, "endogenous morphine") our bodies produce when we experience emotional highs, like falling in love. Will scientists eventually find ways of finding our senders and receptors for sending and receiving love? Is the feeling of loving and being loved simply a certain chemical produced in our body? (Some amazing recent research in brain biochemistry and neuroanatomy make it seem that such knowledge may not be far off!)

Until science figures it out, however, these questions about love have led us to look beyond ourselves and our bodies into the world of the spirit. We've wondered, for instance, about defining the word "soul." What is a soul? Does my love come from my soul? Where in my body does my soul reside? Does it continue on after my body ceases to function? When did my soul and my body connect? Where did my soul come from? Has it been here on earth before me in another living body? Is it absolute and unchanging? Can I alter my soul? Can I heal my soul? Can I enhance its capability to love myself and others? Is the concept of soul confined to my religion? Do people of other faiths and religions have souls? Can a person who has *no* religion have a soul? Is soul the permanent, constant truth of my being and Self? We have asked these questions of ourselves for many years, as we searched for balance and clarity in our lives. It is profound deepening process, that continued even as we wrote this last chapter.

Our lives are about learning to love and be loved. If you were taught love as a child, you easily learned about love. If you were not taught to love yourself when you were a child, you have a greater Challenge in learning how to love yourself and others. *The good news is that you can relearn or reprogram what you've been taught. Now it's UP TO YOU to make that choice.*

Our life process has been about learning to love ourselves and to live our lives from that place of love. You are invited to join in our commitment to making each moment in life a balance between loving and being loved, both internally and externally.

We believe that everything is connected and interrelated. Everything is here now to teach and assist in our Self-discovery. We have found many parts inside that limit our ability to love and be loved.

Anger distances others until we accept that it is there to show us and teach us yet another lesson. Anger is there as a very human emotion. We need not deny or identify with anger. Rather, experience it as a teacher showing us a deeper truth. As we learn and understand each lesson we are empowered to love more deeply.

Fears keep us hiding from love because we are afraid of being hurt. As we utilize that fear as our teacher and begin to see the illusion behind our beliefs we will be able to heal past hurt with respect and compassion. Within this healing is the avenue to the truth. This finally is the path of freedom allowing us to see love and to be seen as love, which is what we already are.

Living up to the *expectations* of family and society keeps us doing what *they* think we should do. When we become aware of those expectations we have the chance to question what we really want in our lives. This results in making Loving Choices instead of doing what we are expected to do. For us, this has meant a commitment to cleansing out everything in us that does not support our capacity to give and receive love.

Writing this book has been our way of sharing our own personal process of learning to love and be loved. We have been honored to share with you the gift of our relationship journey, in the hope that it will enhance your life process of learning to love and be loved. Your Challenge is to discover your own process, and how you want to take your own journey. The most beautiful and precious diamond you can create is your own individuality and your own style of learning to love and be loved.

We began *Loving Choices* with the observation that "the longest foot in the world is the twelve inches from your head to your heart." Changing that foot into a superhighway takes on new importance. What is the connection between loving and being loved and your feelings? What is the connection between your feelings and your wounded Inner Children? Are you able to stay with yourself and your inner healing when your Inner Children are crying out for love? What is the connection between your thoughts and your commitment to love? Changing the longest foot into a super-highway opens up all kinds of questions and Challenges.

How are you doing? Can you say an "I feel" statement as easily as you can say an "I think" statement? Have you discovered how important your internal family parts are? Which of your inner voices enhances your ability to love? Which of your voices inhibit your ability to love? Have your Adaptive-Survivor parts been protecting your vulnerable Inner Children and obstructing the path to loving and being loved? Have you been able to make more Loving Choices after becoming friends with your survivor parts?

Summing Up

Let's review each of the elements we've discussed in *Loving Choices*.

The **Self-Encounter** is a specific tool to help you learn to love yourself and others in a deeper, clearer, more profound way. It connects you with, and helps you listen to, your internal voice of love—your Wise Nurturer. It assists you in taming your Inner Critic voice. The Self-Encounter assists you in finding all of your parts so you can choose to love yourself and others from a place of wholeness, maturity, and respect.

Repetitive Self-Encounters assist you in going deeper into yourself emotionally. They offer a wonderful opportunity for healing!

The **Internal Family Conversation** provides a specific avenue for healing all of your wounded parts. Your Adaptive-Survivor parts always need more love, and the Internal Family Conversation provides a self-care vehicle that is always available to you. Inner peace is your reward.

Healing Encounters with others is a profound avenue for deepening the inner peace. Honest, direct, open encountering with yourself is the main course of communication. Sharing this with others who have meaning in your life is the dessert.

If you can picture yourself as an arrow, your **Family of Origin** and society were the bow from which you were shot. The three-legged stool of awareness, communication and commitment assist you to sprout wings on your arrow. With your own wings you may now choose to direct and guide your life journey and destiny.

Finding your own **Identity** is a lifelong task. From the time you first begin to come out of the protective shell that surrounded you in childhood, through the rebellion of adolescence (or later!), you have been trying in one way or another to discover who you really are — and who you want to be. The Self-Encounter is a very powerful method to help you "redefine yourself" throughout your life, and to make healthy life-course corrections as you need and want to.

Your **Inner Children** probably have been hidden away, wanting desperately to be seen, heard, and acknowledged. Now you've visited the World of the Inner Children and have discovered the joy of getting to know all of the many children within you. What a magical discovery this is! The wounded and vulnerable children can be held and nurtured, The playful and creative children can play and laugh and dance and sing. All of your Inner Children are available to you.

That boiling "pot of stew" that symbolizes the **Power Struggles** in your relationships is heated by your belief that others are responsible for your happiness or unhappiness. The three- legged stool can help you rid yourself of the unwanted ingredients in the stew: projection, poor communication skills, lack of boundaries, unresolved issues, you-messages, and more. The good news is that you really are responsible for your own happiness and you deserve to love and be loved. Transforming your **Power Struggles** into growing pains is one of the most responsible and self-caring gifts you will ever give yourself — and the others you love.

Establishing clear **Boundaries and Ownership** in your life allows you to further define yourself and separate the *you* from the *not-you* in your relationships. It helps you know when you're sticking your nose in where it doesn't belong, and when you're not paying enough attention to yourself. Making Loving Choices about your internal and external boundaries, and being aware so you may access your boundaries, gives you a place to come home emotionally — a safe port in the storm. From home port you can choose to venture out, or to invite in who you want, when you want them.

Relationships are **Your Teachers** — a vehicle for growth. Have you experienced the joy of creating a growing relationship that is healing and healthy? Have you discovered how much you learn about loving and being loved in that relationship? Have you learned that probably the most exciting lessons about love are shared with another person? It is an acid test to see if you can make Loving Choices with regard to another person and still maintain boundaries, have minimal power struggles, use the relationship to grow through unresolved family of origin issues, and keep polishing the many facets of your diamond.

Challenges into Loving Choices — To Learn and to Love

Sometimes you may run from Challenges, become overwhelmed by what feels like too many Challenges, become discouraged because you are not able to love and be loved as much as you would like. Please be gentle with yourself during those times. The process is like peeling an onion, taking off layer after layer as you go deeper and deeper and deeper into your Self. Peeling the onion of Self-discovery may lead to tears. Once again the good news is that tears are the cleansing of the Soul. So keep polishing the many facets in your diamond essence even though sometimes you may feel washed away or may be temporarily blinded by your tears.

We invite you to join us in our vision: Remember every day that *we are on Earth to learn and to love.* Our lives are a process of surrendering to the truth of who and what we really are. We will continue to discover and love a new part of ourselves until the day we die. We are committed to pulling out the three-legged stool each time we feel discouraged in our journey of learning how to love and be loved. We are committed to our passion of changing each new Challenge into a Loving Choice with communication and awareness.

What is *your* vision? What do you want your journey to be like? Is learning about loving and being loved important in your journey? Whatever form it takes, we wish you Godspeed.

You may feel unimportant when you think about what a small grain of sand you are in this Universe. You may wonder what you can do to change the world. Always remember, every time you are more loving the whole world is different.

Out beyond ideas of right-doing and wrong-doing

There is a Field.

I'll meet you there.

When the soul lies down in that grass

The world is too full to talk about.

Ideas, language, even the phrase "each other"

Doesn't make any sense.

— Rumi

HOW ARE YOU DOING?

The following statements are designed to help you internalize and integrate the material in this chapter.

1. *I am committed to creating a vision of what my healthy, healing process will be.*

2. *I am committed to continue using the communication tools I learned in this book.*

3. *I am committed to learn to love myself and others to the best of my ability.*

4. *I am committed to cleanse out everything that is limiting my ability to love myself and others.*

5. *I am committed to speak "I think" and "I feel" messages equally well.*

6. *I am committed to identifying the chapters and concepts in this book that will assist me in my journey into self discovery.*

7. *I am committed to continue to learn more about how to make Loving Choices in my life.*

8. *I am committed to learn to accept the parts of myself that I don't like.*

9. *I am committed to continually examine and recognize whether or not I am going back to the old thought and behavior patterns of my past.*

10. *I am committed to continue the growth that I experienced in reading this book.*

♥

BREATHING AND CENTERING EXERCISE

THERE ARE TWO EXERCISES in this Appendix. The first is to be used immediately at the beginning of the book. The second is to be used after you read and understand the Self-Encounter and Internal Family Chapters. We suggest you make your own audio tape by recording with your voice the following written exercise.

First Breathing Exercise

There are two parts to this breathing exercise. The first may help you to be more awake, and the second may help you to relax and possibly go to sleep.

Here's the waking up one. It can be used when you are driving and become sleepy, or anytime when you want to stay awake. Sit in a comfortable position, preferably with your feet on the floor. Close your eyes if appropriate. Breathe deeply with some belly breaths resulting in your belly button going in and out as much as possible. Fill your lungs completely. Breathe in through your nose and exhale out your mouth. This helps cleanse your body of the toxins you may be carrying. Exhale loudly and rapidly. Make as much noise with your exhale breathe as is possible and appropriate.

On your next few inhale breaths try raising your shoulders until you feel them hitting the base of your skull. Hold your shoulders tightly against your skull for a few seconds before exhaling loudly. Let your shoulders collapse with the exhale breath.

Do this rapid and loud breathing until you feel invigorated and awake. Notice how much better your body feels.

Next is the relaxation and going to sleep breathing. You might like to know this breathing assists you in reaching an altered state with your brain operating in "Alpha Brain Waves." Normally in your waking state you are in a higher frequency brain wave pattern called "Beta Brain Waves."

Again, breathe deeply, filling your lungs completely. Instead of the rapid exhale, now try exhaling slowly, making your exhale last as long as possible. Pucker your lips as though you were going to whistle but let your breath escape as slowly and quietly as possible. It may help to focus your attention on your breath as you exhale. Do this slow breathing as long as is appropriate. Notice your entire body is feeling more relaxed and peaceful. This breathing exercise may help you to go to sleep at night.

Feel free to experiment with variations of these breathing exercises. Try opening your eyes instead of closing them. See what it feels like to do the exercises while lying flat on your back, especially if you are trying to go to sleep. See if it feels as helpful for you to exhale from your nose as your mouth. Try tensing up other muscles in your body instead of those in your neck and shoulders.

Do these breathing exercises daily or as needed for relieving stress and tension. Be creative in finding a place to do them.

There are some benefits from doing these exercises on a regular basis. Use them along with your prayer and meditation. It may help to make your prayers and meditation more effective. Think of it as being comparable to physical exercise. Instead of keeping your physical body in good condition, think of it as keeping the rest of your psyche in good condition.

Have fun doing your self care. You deserve plenty of freedom from stress and tension.

Second Breathing and Centering Exercise Using Self-Encounter and Internal Family Concepts

This is an expansion of the above exercise. Again, there is the part to keep you awake and the part to help you relax and sleep. In addition there is a third part to help you heal yourself using and applying some of the concepts from the Self-Encounter and the Internal Family to your breathing exercise.

Both Nina and Bruce have had childhood experiences that are some of our fondest memories. Both of us, having grown up in rural areas, found ourselves as children in nature soaking up the spring and summer sunshine. It was such a healing and comforting experience to feel the sun's rays penetrating our young bodies with their warmth.

Now, when we are doing the healing part of the following breathing exercise, we think about how that warm sun felt when we were children. When we ask for love from our Wise Nurturer, we imagine a small sun just above our head with golden sunshine warming and healing our bodies. Perhaps you can also use the same source of golden love in your breathing exercise.

Start this breathing exercise the same as we did the previous one. Sit in a comfortable position, preferably with your feet on the floor. Close your eyes if appropriate. Breathe deeply with some belly breaths resulting in your belly button going in and out as much as possible. Fill your lungs completely. Breathe in through your nose and exhale from your mouth in order to help cleanse your body of the toxins you may be carrying. Exhale loudly and rapidly. Make as much noise with your exhale breath as is possible and appropriate.

On your next few inhale breaths try raising your shoulders until you feel them hitting the base of your skull. Hold your shoulders tightly against your skull for a few seconds before exhaling loudly. Let your shoulders collapse with the exhale breath.

Do this rapid and loud breathing until you feel invigorated and awake. Notice how much better your body feels.

Next is the relaxation and going to sleep breathing. Breathe deeply, filling your lungs completely. Instead of the rapid exhale, now try exhaling slowly, making your exhale last as long as possible. Pucker your lips as though you were going to whistle, and let your breath escape as slowly and quietly as possible. It may help to focus your attention on your breath as you exhale. Do this slow breathing as long as is appropriate. Notice your entire body is feeling more relaxed and peaceful. This breathing exercise may help you to go to sleep at night.

Sometimes your mind won't stop and you find yourself thinking of all the things you need to be doing. Your Inner Critic may come along and say something like, "You can't even do this exercise right." Just listen to it and than say, "Thank you for sharing." Then start watching the show in your mind as though you were watching a movie. Notice the different pictures or thoughts with detachment. If you want, you can focus on your breath as you inhale and exhale. This usually allows you to let go of some of the pictures and thoughts going on in your mind.

Next check into any body sensations you are experiencing. Are there some places where you are feeling tense and uncomfortable? Are you experiencing tension anywhere in your body? Are there some places needing some love and attention? Focus on a particular area in your body that you would like to heal.

You know that your breath goes into your lungs. However, imagine when you inhale that you are breathing into the place of tension in your body. Breathe into the pain and tension no matter where it is in your body. Let the healing aspects of your breath go into and heal that place of tension.

While you are breathing into that spot, call upon your Wise Nurturer. Ask it to send some love and nurturing to that place in your body. See if you can imagine warm sunlight coming from a small sun just above your head. Allow yourself to just be while you are feeling the warm sunshine on the place of tension and stress in your body. Allow all of the cells in your body to soak up the warm sunlight.

Your Wise Nurturer may say some loving words like, "Thank you for asking for some love and attention. Your body sensation message was heard and received. We are sending you some love and attention. You can relax and let go of the thoughts, confusion, and painful feelings that you have been carrying."

Keep breathing deeply but gently with a slow exhale coming out of your puckered mouth. Make the exhale last as long as possible. Let your breathing cleanse and heal your body.

If your Inner Critic comes in with some disrupting messages, listen to it. Let it talk and be heard. It may say you aren't doing your breathing right. After it has spoken say, "Thank you for sharing." Check to see if your Wise Nurturer has anything to say and if there is still more warm sunlight coming from your imaginary sun.

Next, go to one of your Inner Children and ask what it has to say about the place of stress and tension in your body. Maybe it is feeling badly about what the Inner Critic has been saying to it. Maybe it is needing love and attention. When you are healing a place of tension in your body, you may in actuality be sending love and attention to your Inner Children.

Keep breathing deeply as you are doing this internal dialogue. Keep exhaling the toxins. Use your breathing and your love and nurturing from your Wise Nurturer as a healing team working together.

Next, imagine where your Inner Children might reside in your body. It may be in your stomach area. Breathe and send loving energy into the spot where your Inner Children reside. Let the golden sunlight warm your Inner Children. Give your Inner Children some Wise Nurturer affirmations like, "You are special. I want to get to know all of you, Thank you for being inside of me. It is okay for you to feel everything that you are presently feeling. I love you very much." Check again to see if your Inner Critic is trying to say anything. Listen to it and again say, "Thank you for sharing.

Notice what body sensations you are feeling. Often you will feel changes when you are doing the slow exhale breathing. You may feel a release of tension and stress when your Wise Nurturer is speaking. Acknowledge whatever you are experiencing in your body.

Find a place in your body that is tight and tense. Place one of your fingers directly on the tight muscle. Now inhale and exhale slowly from your mouth. Usually the tight muscles will relax underneath your finger as you exhale. You often can feel with your finger the results of your breathing exercise.

If you have time, find another tight place of tension in your body and breathe into it. Send love to it also. Heal as many places of stress and tension as you have time.

Gently and slowly begin coming back to the present. When you are ready, do some more breathing with fast and loud exhales. Wiggle your fingers and toes. Open your eyes when you are ready. Do one more check into body sensations. Are they different than they were when you started the breathing exercises? Take a minute or two to reflect on this experience.

What are your intentions? What are your commitments? When will you do this exercise again? Is it possible for breathing to become a healing and centering tool for you in your life?

BIBLIOGRAPHY

LOVING CHOICES ATTEMPTS TO cover many different topics. Each chapter is a "sampler," introducing a particular topic. There are many good books on most of these topics, and we have listed them in this Bibliography. If after reading a chapter you find you want more information, you should be able to find it in the following list.

Chapter One. An Overview of the Loving Choices Process

The following books have been found helpful in learning how to create healing and healthy relationships.

Covey, Stephen R. (1989) *The 7 Habits of Highly Effective People.* New York: Fireside (Simon & Schuster).

    Powerful lessons in bringing about personal change.

Fisher, Bruce & Alberti, Robert (2000) *Rebuilding When Your Relationship Ends* (third edition). Atascadero, CA: Impact Publishers.

    If you are adjusting to the ending of a love relationship, we suggest you read *Rebuilding* before reading *Loving Choices.*

Hendrix, Harville (1988) *Getting the Love You Want.* New York: HarperCollins

    Explores the unconscious factors shaping relationships and provides practical insights for transforming a damaging relationship into a healing one.

Hendrix, Harville (1992) *Keeping the Love You Find.* New York: Pocket Books (Simon & Schuster).

> This book will help you to start off your next relationship in a healthful manner and keep you loving for a lifetime.

Keyes, Ken Jr. (1983) *Your Heart's Desire.* Coos Bay, OR: Love Line.

> Tells how to create a loving relationship. Helps to gain insights which may change the way you think and feel about yourself and your relationship.

Paul, Jordan & Paul, Margaret (1983) *Do I Have to Give Up Me to Be Loved by You?* New York: Fine Communications.

> An in-depth program for creating loving relationships.

Progoff, Ira (1992/1975) At *A Journal Workshop.* New York: Jeremy P. Tarcher

> This book is probably the best known book on keeping a journal.

Satir, Virginia (1976) *Making Contact.* Berkeley, CA: Celestial Arts.

> Techniques to help you make intimate contacts with others.

Sky, Michael (1990) *Breathing: Expanding Your Power & Energy.* Santa Fe, NM: Bear & Company.

> How to utilize breathing as a way of healing.

Tessina, Tina & Smith, Riley (1987) *How To Be A Couple And Still Be Free.* San Bernardino, CA: Borgo Press.

> The title of this book really tells you what the book is about.

Smothermon, Ron (1980) *Winning Through Enlightenment.* Context Publications.

> You are already totally responsible for your life. The only question is "Will you acknowledge that?"

Welwood, John (1990) *Journey of the Heart.* New York: Harper Perennial.

> Based upon the belief that a committed relationship can be a process through which two individuals grow.

Chapter 2. Feelings

Here are some good books to help you learn to access and embrace your feelings.

Frankel, Lois (1992) *Women, Anger, and Depression.* Deerfield Beach, FL: Health Communications.

An excellent book of strategies for self-empowerment for women. It helps explain the connection between anger and depression.

Gray, John (1994) *What You Can Feel, You Can Heal.* Heart Publishing.

This book is helpful in overcoming fears of intimacy and enjoying more loving relationships.

Jampolsky, Gerald (1970) *Love Is Letting Go of Fear.* New York: Bantam.

To love you must be willing to let go of your obsession with the past and the future.

Jeffers, Susan (1987) *Feel the Fear and Do It Anyway.* New York: Fawcett.

Dynamic techniques for turning fear, indecision, and anger into power, action, and love.

Keen, Sam (1992) *Inward Bound: Exploring the Geography of Your Emotions.* New York: Bantam.

Authentic happiness is only possible when we allow ourselves to experience the full range of human emotions.

Lee, John (1993) *Facing the Fire: Experiencing and Expressing Anger Appropriately.* New York: Bantam.

If you were brought up to hide parts of yourself that were angry or sad, this book can help make you whole again.

Lee, John (1987) *The Flying Boy, Healing the Wounded Man.* Deerfield Beach FL: Health Communications, Inc.

This is a story about feelings—losing them, finding them, and finally expressing them.

Newman, Mildred & Berkowitz, Bernard (1971) *How to Be Your Own Best Friend.* New York: Ballantine.

Becoming your own best friend will help you deal with feelings more effectively.

Preston, John (1996) *You Can Beat Depression* (second edition). Atascadero, CA: Impact Publishers.

A succinct, comprehensive account of the causes, treatments, and manifestations of depression.

Viscott, David (1977) *Risking.* New York: Pocket Books (Simon & Schuster).

For those who have difficulty carrying out decisions because of fear.

Chapter 3. Inner Voices and Coping Strategies

The following books are helpful in gaining a better understanding of your inner voices.

Cameron, Julia (1992) *The Artist's Way, A Course in Discovering and Recovering Your Creative Self*. New York: Jeremy P. Tarcher.

> This book is about accessing your Wise Nurturing Part with free style writing on a daily basis.

Ferrucci, Piero (1982) *What We May Be*. New York: Jeremy P. Tarcher, Inc.

> Techniques for psychological and spiritual growth through psycho-synthesis of our many inner selves developed by the Italian Psychiatrist Roberto Assagioli.

Satir, Virginia (1978) *Your Many Faces. The First Step to Being Loved*. Berkeley, CA: Celestial Arts.

> A good book to help us accept our many faces and to recognize the potential in each one of our parts.

Stone, Hal & Stone, Sidra (1989) *Embracing Our Selves: The Voice Dialogue Method*. Carlsbad, CA: Hay House.

> "Voice Dialogue" is a conversation between your many inner messages or voices. The goal is to embrace all of your many selves.

Stone, Hal & Stone, Sidra (1989) *Embracing Each Other*. Novato, CA: New World Library.

> The authors take the "Voice Dialogue" concepts and apply them to your relationships with others.

Stone, Hal & Stone, Sidra (1993) *Embracing Your Inner Critic*. San Francisco: HarperSanFrancisco.

> The creators of "Voice Dialogue" show you how to recognize the inner critic and help it become an intelligent, perceptive, and supportive partner in your life.

Chapter 4. The Self-Encounter

Here is another widely used communication model.

Nunnaly, E., Miller, S., Wackman, D., & Miller, P (1988). *Connecting With Self and Others*. New York: New American Library.

> Describes the Awareness Wheel Communication Model developed by the Couples Communication Group.

Chapter 5. The Repetitive Self-Encounter

No books on this topic.

Chapter 6. Discovering Your Internal Family

Kramer, Sheldon Z. (1993) *Transforming the Inner and Outer Family.* Binghamton, NY: Haworth Press.

> Inner messages, internal family, breathing techniques, guided meditation, and healing in relationship with self and others are all described in this book.

Chapter 7. The Healing-Encounter

Here is a book which examines the different vocabulary that males and females often use. We believe this compliments the Healing Encounter communication model described in Loving Choices.

Glass, Lillian (1992) *He Says, She Says.* New York: G.P. Putnam's Sons.

> Learning about the different ways in which males and females talk helps the Healing Encounter be more effective.

Chapter 8. Family of Origin

Here are some good books to help you deal with the influences of your family of origin and childhood upon your adult relationships. You may have to look for some of the following books in libraries.

Bloomfield, Harold H. MD. (1983) *Making Peace With Your Parents.* New York: Ballantine.

> Explains how to make peace with your internalized parent.

Bradshaw, John (1988) *Healing the Shame That Binds You.* Deerfield Beach, FL: Health Communications.

> In an emotionally revealing way Bradshaw shows us how toxic shame is the core problem in our compulsions, co-dependencies, addictions and the drive to super achieve.

Davis, Laura (1991) *Allies in Healing.* New York: Harper Perennial.

> An excellent support book for partners if the person you love was sexually abused as a child.

Davis, Laura & Bass, Ellen (1994) *The Courage to Heal* (third edition). New York: Harper Perennial.

> A guide for women survivors of child sexual abuse. It is a groundbreaking book that will stand as a classic for many years to come.

Hansen, Paul (1991) *Survivors & Partners: Healing the Relationships of Sexual Abuse Survivors*. Heron Hill.

> An excellent book for adult survivors of abuse and their partners.

Karen, Robert (1990) "Becoming Attached." *Atlantic Monthly*, February, 1990.

> A discussion on the research concerning emotional bonding conducted by Dr. Mary Ainsworth. An excellent article!

Lee, John (1991) *At My Father's Wedding*. New York: Bantam.

> Men coming to terms with their fathers and themselves.

Lew, Mike (1990) *Victims No Longer*. New York: Harper Perennial.

> Not all sexually abused are females. This is a book for men recovering from incest and other sexual child abuse.

Liedloff, Jean (1996) *The Continuum Concept*. Reading, MA: Perseus Books.

> Describes the advantages children receive through emotionally bonding by continually being touched and held the first three years of life.

McGoldrick, Monica & Gerson, Randy (1985) *Genograms in Family Assessment*. New York: W.W. Norton & Co.

> Explains how to diagram three generations of your family by using a genogram. It has examples of some well-known people's Genograms, such as Sigmund Freud.

Newman, Margaret & Berkowitz, Bernard (1983) *How To Be Awake and Alive*. New York: Ballantine Books.

> Gives specific examples of ways to free yourself from some of the controlling aspects of your family of origin life script.

Woititz, Janet. (1990) *Adult Children of Alcoholics* (expanded edition). Deerfield Beach, FL: Health Communications Inc.

> Help for children that grew up in various kinds of dysfunctional families.

Chapter 9. Seeking Your Identity

There are very few books written about the search for identity through rebellion.

Bach, Richard (1970) *Jonathan Livingston Seagull*. New York: Avon.

> The seagull finds an identity by flying and soaring.

Berman, Morris (1990) *Coming to Our Senses*. New York: Bantam.

> The seeking identity theory is extended out to include society. We have an opportunity today on our planet to create integration between tradition (shell stage) and ascension (rebel stage) with the result of being in balance. (love stage)

Chapter 10. Your Inner Children

Here are some excellent books to help you create and build a loving and nurturing connection with your Inner Children.

Abrams, Jeremiah (ed.) (1990) *Reclaiming the Inner-Child*. New York: Jeremy P. Tarcher.

> A very comprehensive and informative reader on the various authors who have written about the inner child.

Bradshaw, John (1990) *Home Coming: Reclaiming and Championing Your Inner-Child*. NY: Bantam.

> The author presents the essence of the inner child workshop which he calls "the most powerful work I have ever done."

Capacchione, Lucia (1988) *The Power of Your Other Hand*. North Hollywood, CA: Newcastle Publishing.

> An important book that describes the process of accessing the inner child through the non-dominant hand doing writing and art work.

Capacchione, Lucia (1991) *Recovery of Your Inner Child*. New York: Fireside (Simon & Schuster).

> This book shows you how to have a first hand experience of your inner child by writing and drawing with your non-dominant hand.

Chopich, Erika & Paul, Margaret (1990) *Healing Your Aloneness. Finding Love and Wholeness Through Your Inner Child*. San Francisco: HarperSanFrancisco.

> This book outlines a self-healing process that can be used every day to restore a nurturing balance between your loving adult(Wise Nurturer) and loved Inner Child.

Davis, Bruce (1985) *The Magical Child Within You*. Berkeley, CA: Celestial Arts.

> Inside every adult is a child to love, and this delightful book helps you do it yourself.

Paul, Margaret (1992) *Inner Bonding: Becoming a Loving Adult to Your Inner Child.* New York: HarperCollins.

Heal the conflicts within your personalities. Learn to give yourself the parenting you need.

Whitfield, Charles L. (1987) *Healing the Child Within.* Deerfield Beach, FL: Health Communications.

Discovery and recovery for adult children of dysfunctional families.

Whitfield, Charles L. (1990) *A Gift To Myself.* Deerfield Beach, FL: Health Communications.

A personal workbook and guide to the best-seller, *Healing The Child Within.*

Chapter 11. Power Struggles and Polarization

These books help us to better understand the stages of growth and development in relationships.

Campbell, Susan (1984) *Beyond the Power Struggle.* Atascadero CA: Impact Publishers.

A powerful book which lists many of the issues we polarize over, and helps us find ways of dealing with polarization issues. (Now out of print, but available in many libraries.)

Campbell, Susan (1980) *The Couple's Journey: Intimacy as a Path to Wholeness.* Atascadero, CA: Impact Publishers.

This book does an excellent job of describing the stages of a love relationship and helps us to put the power struggle into perspective as one of the stages of evolution and growth in a love relationship. (Now out of print, but available in many libraries.)

Chapter 12. Ownership and Boundaries

Here are a few excellent books on boundaries.

Alberti, Robert & Emmons Michael (1995) *Your Perfect Right: A Guide to Assertive Living* (seventh edition). Atascadero, CA: Impact Publishers.

Learn to express your needs assertively to help yourself create appropriate boundaries.

Beattie, Melody (1987) *Codependent No More.* New York: Harper-Hazelden.

How to stop controlling others and start caring for yourself with appropriate boundaries.

Katherine, Anne (1998) *Boundaries: Where You End And I Begin*. New York: Fine Communications.

> How to recognize and set healthy boundaries.

Mellody, Pia & Miller, J. Keith (1969) *Facing Codependence*. San Francisco: HarperSanFrancisco.

> Excellent book on boundaries.

Mellody, Pia & Miller, J. Keith (1989) *Breaking Free*. San Francisco: HarperSanFrancisco.

> A workbook to be used with *Facing Codependence*.

Phelps, Stanlee & Austin, Nancy (1997) *The Assertive Woman* (third edition). Atascadero. CA: Impact Publishers.

> Answers to the most-asked questions about being assertive. A self-help program for women with tips on how to express yourself, stories of "hardy spirits," and more.

Powell, John (1969) *Why Am I Afraid to Tell You Who I Am?* Allen TX: Tabor/RCL.

> "But if I tell you who I am, you may not like who I am, and it is all that I have."

Whitfield, Charles L. (1993) *Boundaries and Relationships. Deerfield Beach FL:* Health Communications.

> Knowing, protecting, and enjoying the Self.

Chapter 13. Relationships Are Your Teachers

Some of the following books can open your eyes to the many kinds of healing available today.

Abrams, Jeremiah Editor (1994) *The Shadow in America: Reclaiming the soul of a nation*. Springfield, VA: Nataraj Books.

> A powerful book. A stark look into the eyes of our own blindness.

Bethards, Betty (1990) *The Dream Book: Symbols for Self-Understanding*. New Brunswick, NJ: Inner Light Foundation.

> Over one thousand dream symbols to assist you in your own interpretations of your dreams.

Borysenko, Joan (1988) *Minding the Body, Mending the Mind*. New York: Bantam.

The author is one of the pioneers of the new healing synthesis called psycho-neuroimmunology.

Bridges, William (1980) *Transitions*. Reading, MA: Perseus Books.

Strategies for coping with the difficult, painful, and confusing times in your life.

"Consumer Reports" (February 1993) *Can Your Mind Heal Your Body?*

Research indicates support groups help people become more physically healthy.

Gawain, Shakti (1983) *Creative Visualization*. New York: Bantam.

Why not learn how to visualize what you would like to have happen in your life?

Gawain, Shakti (1998) *Living in the Light*. Novato, CA: New World Library.

This book will help you learn to access and trust your intuition.

Hay, Louise (1984) *You Can Heal Your Life*. Carlsbad, CA: Hay House, Inc.

How physical pain can lead you to better understand what you are trying to heal emotionally and psychologically.

Hedva, Beth (1992) *Journey from Betrayal to Trust*. Berkeley, CA: Celestial Arts.

Making a Loving Choice to use betrayal as a gateway to personal and spiritual growth.

Johnson, Robert (1986) *Inner Work*. New York: HarperCollins.

A practical four step approach to using dreams in the process of personal transformation.

Johnson, Robert (1991) *Owning Your Own Shadow*. San Francisco: HarperSanFrancisco.

A powerful work from Jungian analyst Johnson. A guide through an exploration of the shadow, the dark side of the psyche.

Jung, C. J. (1933) *Modern Man in Search of a Soul*. Orlando, FL: Harcourt.

Jung examines some of the most contested and crucial areas in the field of analytical psychology, dream analysis, primitive unconscious, and the relationship between psychology and religion.

Kabat-Zinn, Jon (1995) *Wherever You Go, There You Are.* New York: Hyperion

> This book is a remarkably clear and practical guide to mindfulness meditation.

Moseley, Douglas & Naomi (1994) *Dancing in the Dark.* St. Cloud, MN: North Star Publications.

> At last a whole book explaining one of the main causes of problems in relationship, that of parent-child relationships.

O'Connor, Peter (1986) *Dreams and the Search for Meaning.* Mahwah, NJ: Paulist Press.

> Understanding and respecting our dreams can help us recognize parts of ourselves and help us in our journey toward self-knowledge and completion.

Powell, John (1976) *Fully Human, Fully Alive.* Allen, TX: Tabor Publishing/RCL.

> The author introduces his theory of vision therapy, a simple yet effective system for successful personal growth.

Sanford, John (1980) *Invisible Partners: How the Male and Female in Each of Us Affects Our Relationships.* Mahwah, NJ: Paulist Press.

> Demonstrates how the feminine part of a man and the masculine part of a woman are the invisible partners in any male-female relationship.

Tanner, Wilda (1978) *Follow Your Dreamzzz.* Cincinnati, Ohio: Dream Lady.

> This is a classic book with symbols but also a great deal of information about dreams.

Chapter 14. Loving Choices and Intimacy

Here are books about how to make Loving Choices. Some of these are "oldies" but "goodies."

Brennan, Barbara Ann (1987) *Hands of Light.* New York: Bantam Books.

> Healing with Bioenergetics, which is the study of the energetic field around our bodies.

Casey, Karen (1985) *Love Book.* Center City, MN: Hazelden Meditation Series.

> Daily meditations to help you learn more about the meaning of love.

Fisher, Robert (1990). *The Knight in Rusty Armor*. Los Angeles: Wilshire.

It is a lighthearted tale of a desperate knight in search of his own true self.

Fromm, Erich (1989/1956) *The Art of Loving*. New York: HarperCollins.

A classic written decades ago but still relevant.

Gibran, Kahil (1955/1923) *The Prophet*. New York: Alfred A. Knopf.

We suggest every home library have a copy of this classic.

Grof, Stanislaus & Grof, Christina (eds.) (1989) *Spiritual Emergency*. New York: Jeremy P. Tarcher, Inc.

Excellent for helping understand several different kinds of spiritual emergence.

Hendricks, Gay (1982) *Learning To Love Yourself*. New York: Simon & Schuster.

An excellent book about learning to love yourself.

Hendricks, Gay (1990) *Learning To Love Yourself Workbook*. New York: Simon & Schuster.

Companion to the *Learning To Love Yourself* book.

Keyes, Ken Jr. (1990) *Handbook to Higher Consciousness*. Coos Bay, OR: Love Line.

A classic on transforming into a higher consciousness with your mind.

Powell, John (1982) *Why Am I Afraid to Love?* Allen, TX: Tabor Publishing/RCL.

This book teaches how to tear down our walls and accept ourselves as we are.

Redfield, James (1993) *The Celestine Prophecy: An Adventure*. New York: Warner Books.

Beginning in the rain forests of Peru, this book takes you on a journey that explores nine key insights into human spiritual awakening. The story, the insights, and the creativity will hold your attention and expand your awareness.

Rodegast, Pat (1989) *Emmanuel's Book II: The Choice for Love*. New York: Bantam.

Fear tells you, "I want to make you safe." Love says, "You are safe."

Welwood, John, Editor (1985) *Challenge of the Heart: Love, Sex and Intimacy in Changing Times.* Boston: Shambhala Publications.

    This book discusses the challenges of love between men and women, addressing the questions and difficulties arising for people in relationships today.

Williams, Margery, (1983) *TheVelveteen Rabbit.* New York: Alfred A. Knopf.

    "It takes a heap of loving to become real."

Zukav, Gary. (1989) *The Seat of the Soul.* New York: Fireside (Simon & Schuster).

    A readable, thought provoking book on how our perceptions must change dramatically if we are to survive.

INDEX

Abandoned child, 160
Active listening, 187
Adaptive-Survivor Parts, 50
Adult rebellion process, 134-139
Ancestors, 122-123, 173
Anger, 24-27, 33-34, 173, 191, 213
Assagioli, Roberto, 41
Assertiveness, 37, 192-193
Attachment, 121-122

Beyond the Power Struggle, 171
Black, Claudia, 19, 164
Breathing, 36-37
"Busy-holic," 84-88

Campbell, Dr. Susan, 171
Caretaker survivor, 158-159
Childhood abuse, 201-203
Christ, 139
Closure, 103-104
Cole, Nat King, 2
Conflict, 115-116
Coping strategies, 14
Couple's Journey The, 171
Creative child, 159

Deadlock, 105
Depression, 32
Detachment, 207-208
Discounted child, 160-161
Divorce, 144-145
Domino effect, 117-118
Dreams, 207

Embracing Yourselves, 41
Emotional blocks, 30-31
Emotional bonding, 121-122
Emotional buttons, 35
External rebellion, 130-131

Fear, 27, 213
Fearful child, 160
Feeling Words, 69
Fisher Rebuilding Seminar, 129
Flowers for Algernon, 42
Forgiveness, 132
Freud, Sigmund, 41

God, 127, 146
Grief, 27-28
Growing pains, 178-180
Guilt, 29

Healing separation, 208
Healthy traits, 45
Hidden agendas, 206
Honeymoon period, 171-172
Humor, 28

"Identity crisis," 127-128
"I-messages," 13-14, 43, 44, 190, 193
Initiator encounter, 95, 100-105
Inner voices, 14
Internal rebellion, 131, 146
Introjector, 174
It's Never Too Late to Have a Happy
    Childhood, 19, 164

Joy, 27

Lamaze, 1
Leftovers, 116-117, 205-206
Loneliness, 174
Love, 29-30
Loving Choices Workbook, 208

Magical child, 162
"Male mid-life crisis," 145
Mary Poppins, 161
"Mirroring," 33-34
"Myth of the Cave," 139-140

"Nature Boy," 2
Neglected child, 159-160

Pain, 119-120
Parents, 132-133
Peanuts, 47
Peter Pan, 162
"Pet rock," 53
"Pig Pen," 47
Plato, 139
Playful child, 159
Polarization, 175-178
Problem-solving men, 203
Projector, 174
Protector, 157-158
"Psychosynthesis," 41

Rebuilding: When Your Relationship Ends,
    1, 2, 208
Rebuilding Divorce Seminar, 2, 47, 185
Rejection, 28-29
Respondent encounter, 95, 100-105
Rumi, 217

Schulz, Charles, 47
Self-Encounter (exercise), 14-16, 63-73
Self-Encounter Form, The, 74-75
Shadow work, 203-204
"shoulds," 127-129
Spiritual child, 161
Spoiled child, 159
Stone, Hal, 41
Stone, Sidra, 41

Ten-Week Relationship Seminar, 15
Three-legged stool, 11-12
Tinker Bell, 162
Traumatized child, 161

Unbonded child, 160

"Voice dialogue," 41
Vulnerable child, 160

William Penn Colony, 1
Wise child, 161
Wounded child, 161

Your Perfect Right, 193

RebuildingBooks
Relationships – Divorce – and Beyond

Time for a Better Marriage
Training in Marriage Enrichment
Jon Carlson, Psy.D. and Don Dinkmeyer, Sr., Ph.D.
Softcover: $15.95   144 pages   ISBN: 978-1-886230-46-0
Provides invaluable tools to help make marriages more rewarding, effective, and satisfying by showing couples how to encourage each other, resolve conflict, communicate effectively, and maintain equality in the relationship.

Crazy Love
Dealing With Your Partner's Problem Personality
W. Brad Johnson, Ph.D. and Kelly Murray, Ph.D.
Softcover: $17.95   248 pages   ISBN: 978-1-886230-80-4
Enlightening guide to the odd but common disorders of personality and why so many of us are attracted to personality disordered partners. Provides strategies for detecting and avoiding such potential disasters and help for those in committed relationships to make the union more livable.

Jigsaw Puzzle Family
The Stepkids' Guide to Fitting It Together
Cynthia MacGregor
Softcover: $12.95   120 pages   ISBN: 978-1-886230-63-7
For kids wondering how the jigsaw puzzle pieces of their blended family will fit together. Engaging stories and gentle reassurance. Helpful suggestions for dealing with a new stepparent, new stepsiblings, new house, and more.

Your Child's Divorce
What to Expect -- What You Can Do
Marsha Temlock, M.A.
Softcover: $17.95   272 pages   ISBN: 978-1-886230-66-8
A friendly guidebook packed with helpful information and suggestions for parents of divorcing adults. Helps readers stay grounded through the emotional upheavals they'll share with their children and grandchildren.

Impact Publishers®
POST OFFICE BOX 6016 • ATASCADERO, CALIFORNIA 93423-6016
Ask your local or online bookseller, or call 1-800-246-7228 to order direct.
Prices effective November 2008, and subject to change without notice.
Free catalog of self-help and professional resources: visit **www.impactpublishers.com**

Please see the following page for more books.